GAME OF MY LIFE

TEXAS A&M

AGGIES

MEMORABLE STORIES OF AGGIE FOOTBALL

BRENT ZWERNEMAN

SPORTS
PUBLISHING

Sports Publishing books may be purchased in bulk at special discounts for sales promotion, corporate gifts, fund-raising, or educational purposes. Special editions can also be created to specifications. For details, contact the Special Sales Department, Sports Publishing, 307 West 36th Street, 11th Floor, New York, NY 10018 or sportspubbooks@skyhorsepublishing.com.

Sports Publishing® is a registered trademark of Skyhorse Publishing, Inc.®, a Delaware corporation.

Visit our website at www.sportspubbooks.com.

10 9 8 7 6 5 4 3 2 1

Library of Congress Cataloging-in-Publication Data is available on file.

ISBN: 978-1-61321-335-3

Printed in the United States of America

To the Loves of my life: Crystal, Will and Zoe.
Thank you, thank you for the daily inspiration.

Contents

Acknowledgments

Thank you to Rusty Burson, associate editor of the *12th Man Magazine*, for his admirable work on the Kevin Murray chapter. Also thanks to Brad Marquardt, Alan Cannon and Jackie Thornton with the Texas A&M sports news office, and to Cathy Capps with the Texas A&M Lettermen's Association.

Thank you to Steve French, for providing this fellow Oak Ridge boy a little shelter in Bryan-College Station, and thanks to Burt Henry and Doug Pils for their unfailing understanding on this project.

Thank you to Robert Cessna and Larry Bowen and the many sports writers—or, as I prefer, daily historians—through the years whose hard work provided so much of the background and accuracy for this project.

Thank you to Bob Deegan and John Skeeters, my coaches at Oak Ridge and Sam Houston State, for the life lessons they taught me through sports.

Thank you to the late Sam Sutton, my grandpa and an old Texas oilman, for his love of the written word, and for those countless hours of storytelling about a wild, untamed Lone Star State.

And a special thank you to the lovely and talented Crystal Galny Zwerneman—here's to your many late nights of transcribing tapes and offering wonderful advice.

Introduction

Inquisitive Aaron Glenn, Pro Bowler for the Houston Texans and true-maroon Texas Aggie, raised his eyebrows a bit and wondered, "So, how'd you come up with the list for this book?" I felt a bit like Texas quarterback Peter Gardere, whose errant pass Glenn once returned 95 yards for a touchdown (ch. 20, if you're wondering).

Good question, Aaron, glad you asked. First, for the original edition of this book, the fine folks at Sports Publishing L.L.C. requested a first-person narration as part of each chapter. A natural first chapter, then, seemed the team captain of the 1939 national champions, Mr. John Kimbrough (who, sadly, passed away in 2006). From the "Haskell Hurricane" on, I chronologically developed a list, through plain ol' no-brainers (John David Crow, Johnny Holland, Dat Nguyen, and the like) and by picking the brains of every Aggie punched into my cell phone (lots). A hugely unscientific poll on texags.com produced about 150 responses in a day's time, as well, offering much impassioned reasoning on which to chew.

One thing I quickly realized: Many worthy candidates, even some two-time All-Americans, wouldn't make the list of 25 chapters. The book, you see, is as much about defining moments in Texas A&M football history as it is a straight biography. When Dave Elmendorf, for instance, presented a game ball to the first African American to ever start for the Aggies, Hugh McElroy, following the 1970 game at LSU, that compassionate act struck me like a Jacob Green sack.

Hence, suddenly I had two chapters—Elmendorf and McElroy—from a woebegone 2-9 season. Doggone it, I stuck with 'em. On the flip side of such sentiment, only one player strictly from the 1960s, Edd Hargett, is on the list from that decade's lone winning season for A&M (1967). The book also is heavy on players from the late 1980s and early 1990s—with six conference titles in that span the primary reason why.

In any case, I had a blast writing this anecdotal, plentiful history of Aggies football, through the recollections of some of the best and most intriguing Texas A&M players in history. And, Aaron, you're one of 'em.

Brent Zwerneman

CHAPTER 1

JOHN KIMBROUGH

Name: John Aleck Kimbrough
Born: June 14, 1918
Deceased: May 8, 2006
Hometown: Haskell, Texas
Final Occupation: Retired farmer
Position: Running Back
Height: 6'2"
Playing Weight: 210 pounds
Years lettered: 1938-40
Accomplishments: Two-time All-American and two-time All-Conference (1939-40); placed second in the 1940 Heisman Trophy race to Michigan's Tom Harmon; finished A&M career with 1,357 rushing yards and 21 touchdowns; member of the National Football Foundation and Texas Sports Halls of Fame; first-round draft pick of the Chicago Cardinals in 1941, played nine years professionally.
Nicknames: Jarrin' John, Big John, and the Haskell Hurricane
The Game: Texas A&M vs. Tulane, Sugar Bowl, Jan. 1, 1940

John Kimbrough. *Photo courtesy of Texas A&M Athletic Media Relations*

THE LIFE OF YOUNG JOHN KIMBROUGH

The occasional sharp pitch of a cracking bone on the gridiron hardly stirred John Kimbrough's innards. Shoot, it mostly reminded him of home, sweet home back in West Texas.

"My father would slam an axe across the back of a possum's neck and you'd just hear it crack," Kimbrough said, recalling the good ol' days of his youth in Haskell. "We'd scrape the possum down with a butcher knife, and my mother cooked it. Some folks said, 'Oh, no, we're not gonna eat that greasy thing,' and others wrinkled their noses and said, 'Why, it looks like a big ol' rat!' But, my mother, she'd cook it with sweet potatoes. And my father, he just loved it."

But the idea of playing football creased the nostrils of one William Augustus Kimbrough, Haskell's first doctor, who moved there from Alabama in 1907. Chop a possum's neck? No problem—that set grub on the table. Scamper around a trodden field handling an inflated piece of cowhide, beating one another into oblivion? William Augustus figured that a waste of manpower at best and plain barbaric at worst.

But John Kimbrough's father passed away when the boy was only in the seventh grade, and John—the youngest of seven children—began playing football with the hopes of earning a scholarship as his means to college. He did, and the fledgling legend of the "Haskell Hurricane" began to take hold.

"The ones around here who don't know of Big John Kimbrough," says Joe Cortez, a gas attendant in Haskell, "are the ones who moved in yesterday."

Tulane offered the burly back a scholarship in 1937, which is ironic since Kimbrough eventually played the game of his life against the school. But in New Orleans, the Green Wave coaches tried turning "The Hurricane" into an offensive lineman—which certainly seemed a waste of a good nickname.

"They told me I'd make a good tackle," Kimbrough said, smiling at the seeming absurdity of it all. "Everybody wanted to make me a tackle."

Kimbrough refused to adjust to the shift and lost his scholarship to Tulane. He transferred to Texas A&M, where he joined the squad as an afterthought to what Coach Homer Norton figured to be an already fine class of '37. In the 1938 SWC season opener against No. 1 Texas Christian University, the Horned Frogs were whipping the Aggies so badly that Norton threw in his last-string players. He didn't want all of his No. 1s and No. 2s on the depth chart to get hurt against mighty TCU.

That group of benchwarmers included an unknown lad from Haskell. But once John Kimbrough earned a few carries—no one else wanted the ball against a brutal Horned Frogs defense—and left a couple of TCU players writhing on the ground in his wake, a short man in a coat and tie stormed the field.

The game's intruder then grabbed the unfamiliar A&M player whom he thought was playing dirty. But the six-foot, two-inch Aggie grabbed back and lifted the diminutive man by his tie to Kimbrough's eye level.

"He was yanking on my jersey and calling me all kinds of names," Kimbrough said of famed TCU coach Dutch Meyer. "I told him, 'Look, Coach, you're too little to jazz with me. You better get back over there on the sidelines where you belong.' I'd already hurt a couple of his players."

Kimbrough started every game of his A&M calling from that movie-like moment on, in a college career that even propelled the handsome running back into a couple of screenplays after graduation. Kimbrough, who later signed with 20th Century Fox to star in *Lone Star Ranger* and *Sundown Jim,* finished his A&M career with 1,357 yards and 21 touchdowns.

"He's a legend," says Bucky Richardson, who quarterbacked the Aggies in the late 1980s and early 1990s. "And the thing you hear most about him is that he was tough as an old boot."

Kimbrough certainly was on that memorable day in New Orleans, an afternoon that A&M fans will always fondly remember about "Big John" Kimbrough, a man with nearly as many fine nicknames as touchdown runs.

"John Kimbrough [was] 'Mr. Football' as far as Texas A&M is concerned," says John David Crow, Texas A&M's lone Heisman Trophy winner (in 1957). "He was a great player who played on a national championship team. He deserves to be the legend of Texas A&M football, because the ultimate goal of any player is to play on a national championship team."

THE SCENE

Texas A&M College fans, coach Homer Norton figured with an "aw-shucks" grin, are never satisfied. Still, Norton had plenty of reason for smiling two days before New Year's Day 1940, with his unbeaten team bound for the Sugar Bowl in New Orleans.

But the recently embattled and once deathly sick Aggies football coach nearly choked on his celebratory steak in Biloxi, Miss., at the pointed inquiry about his 10-0 squad. How might anyone question the Texas A&M offense, he wondered aloud, especially since a mere two days separated the boys of Aggieland from a shot at earning their first national title?

Especially after Norton had tried so hard the previous five seasons to match the novel flash (i.e., newfangled passing attacks) of several other

Southwest Conference coaches before finally reverting to a few old-school methods—blocking, tackling and a power running game—he'd learned as a young coach at Centenary College.

Why couldn't anyone ask him about Texas A&M's defense, which had allowed an incredible 76.3 yards per game? (Still an NCAA record, more than six decades later.) But, yet, here we go again about the offense, Norton thought, shaking his head and grinning.

"We haven't forgotten about the pass," the coach finally said, after swallowing hard on a particularly large chunk of meat. "We simply haven't had to throw the ball around. Our running game has been strong enough to win. We can pass and will when we have to."

But the 1939 Texas Aggies hardly had to, based on the bruising exploits of a certain 210-pound fullback from Haskell, Texas, dubbed "Jarrin'" John Kimbrough. The balding, weathered coach swallowed hard again upon hearing the name, this time for a happy reason.

"It's very seldom I praise any of my boys," Norton said. "But when I tell you he's the greatest player I ever coached, that's not enough."

Texas A&M hadn't finished first in the SWC in a dozen seasons until that mythical year in Aggies lore—1939—and the more well-heeled boosters had angled for Norton's firing headed into that season, following five years of mediocrity (including a 4-4-1 record in 1938). Rumors late in 1939 had linked Norton, in the final year of his contract, with Stanford University, and before the season Kimbrough & Co. figured that year to be the A&M swan song for their likeable leader.

"It wasn't any secret," Kimbrough said, "that they were trying to get rid of Coach Norton."

Ironically, the Aggies had little clue that an explosive season loomed ahead even after their starting quarterback, the irrepressible—but apparently quite flammable—Cotton Price, nearly blew himself up that summer of '39.

"He got burned bad," Kimbrough said. "He was putting gas in his truck and it backfired, and he got burned here, here and on his face."

"Here and here" signified just about everywhere on Price's body. Norton, 52, knew about how Price felt. A stinging, burning sensation in Norton's throat had carried on for 30 about months. Physicians diagnosed it as a severe case of streptococcus—but his condition had suddenly improved leading up to Texas A&M's season of all football seasons.

The precious memories of that season brought Kimbrough to release his grip from the arms of a wheelchair, proudly displaying a national championship ring the university awarded the team some 59 years later at a 1998 reunion in College Station.

"We're still the only football team to ever win a national championship at Texas A&M," Kimbrough said, smiling at the flamboyant bit of jewelry with his name inscribed on the side.

"I'd sure like to see 'em win another one. But they'd better do it pretty quick. I'm getting old, and time runs out on you."

The writing is on the wall at Kyle Field about Texas A&M's lone national football champions, and it's certainly not lost in the fine print of all of those conference titles earned through the years. Raised maroon letters across Kyle's middle deck practically yell, "National Champions 1939" amidst the smaller conference listings.

"These guys won a national championship," Texas A&M official Colin Killian reverently observed of the '39 team at the '98 reunion, "and then they went out and helped win a war."

And junior John Kimbrough, as handsome as Cary Grant and swift as the West Texas wind, led the charge on the gridiron that legendary season. Behind Kimbrough's hard and yet nimble running and an unflappable defense, Texas A&M surprisingly swept to an undefeated regular-season record in 1939 and a top ranking. The Aggies shut out Oklahoma A&M, Centenary, Baylor, Arkansas, Rice and even archrival Texas (allowing only three first downs to the Longhorns) along the way.

But in the Jan. 1, 1940, Sugar Bowl, fifth-ranked Tulane waited on its home turf, primed to pounce on that bunch of Texas farm and ranch boys who played football for that all-male agricultural and mechanical school in College Station.

*   *   *   *   *

On the same day Norton devoured a steak while defending his offense to reporters, German leader Adolf Hitler shrieked a New Year's speech from Berlin. The bloodthirsty dictator declared that the Third Reich was "fighting for the construction of a new Europe" and that "Germany and Europe must be liberated from the oppression and the constant threats which today, as in the past, originate in England."

But Norton and the Aggies paid little mind to the German tyrant, at least in that holiday week—there was football still to play. And in a more inculpable era before America entered The War, one in which many folks just felt fortunate to have continued weathering the Great Depression, college football offered a pleasant escape—if only for a few hours.

So the nation's ears—the Sugar Bowl wasn't televised, and besides, most folks didn't own a TV—suddenly honed in on that bushel-load of country boys from Aggieland contending for a national title.

"I give us," Norton said two days before the Sugar Bowl, choosing his words carefully so as not to stir the Green Wave, "a 50-50 chance of winning."

And, privately, Norton put 99 percent of the responsibility of half a chance to win on the broad shoulders of John Kimbrough.

THE SETTING

The top-ranked Aggies had outscored their opponents 198 to 18 through 10 games in 1939, so a true Lone Star state bravado reigned when about 10,000 Texans stormed New Orleans, many decked in big hats and cowboy boots, in the few days before Jan. 1, 1940.

The 210-piece Aggie Band even marched the streets of the Crescent City on New Year's Eve, and the "Aggie War Hymn" and "The Spirit of Aggieland" delighted the revelers—even the Tulane fans, who lined the streets to catch a glimpse of the famed unit. In addition, 1,500 members of A&M's Corps of Cadets wandered their way past the Atchafalaya Swamp to New Orleans.

The city's Association of Commerce estimated that 40,000 visitors spent an average of $20 per day while wandering Bourbon Street in the days surrounding the Sugar Bowl—a spending rate more than twice that of the typical Mardi Gras crowd of the time.

The largest crowd to ever see a college football game in the South to that point packed Tulane's on-campus stadium, called the Sugar Bowl, and the 73,000 fans certainly were in for a treat as 10-0 and No. 1 Texas A&M prepared to battle 8-0-1 and No. 5 Tulane.

"Other than having my baby," Tulane fan Edna Engert later said, "sitting in that packed stadium, listening to all of those people cheering, was the biggest thrill of my life."

Tulane had just increased the capacity of its stadium (later razed in 1974 to make room for student housing and a parking garage) by about 30,000. The Aggies hadn't played in a postseason game since toppling Centre College in the 1922 Dixie Classic, a match that gave birth to A&M's fabled 12th Man tradition. Then, a student, E. King Gill, hustled down from the stands and suited up for the Aggies, just in case he was needed because of injuries to the team members.

A&M, too, had big problems leading up to the 1940 Sugar Bowl, starting with quarterback Cotton Price's persistent charley horse (as if surviving all of those preseason burns wasn't enough).

"My quarterback spot is my biggest worry," Norton said. "Price has had that bad charley horse for three weeks now. It's better now, but if he gets hit hard, he'll have to come out. And Marion Pugh, my second-stringer, has been in the hospital a week with a stomach disorder ... so you can see what a danger spot this is for the Aggies."

Danger spots or not, Texas A&M prevailed 14-13 over Tulane, as

Kimbrough scored both touchdowns for the Aggies. The Haskell Hurricane carried the ball 25 times for 159 yards, which accounted for more than half of his team's offense. And a still smiling Norton knew whom he could point to as having helped save his job—and earned Texas A&M its first (and to date, only) national title.

"He's the greatest football player in the world," a triumphant Norton said of Kimbrough in the minutes following A&M's win. "And you can put my name on that with a picture."

THE GAME OF MY LIFE
By John Kimbrough

With those 70,000-something people all hollering and screaming in that place, it seemed a little tough to concentrate at first. That's about twice as many folks I'd ever seen in one place. Kyle Field only held about half as much at that time, so imagine how that glorious stadium must have looked to a bunch of wide-eyed kids from mostly small towns in Texas.

But we also knew we had to just focus on the game. And what a game!

We were pretty dinged up going into it. Cotton Price had those charley horses, and Marion Pugh was just plain sick to his stomach. But it'd have taken a freight train to keep either one of those fellows off the field.

I've heard people describe my running style as bullish, but I guess that all depended on how fast or big that defender was. If I saw a big one I'd try to go around him; if I saw one that wasn't so big, I might try and go through him.

But if I did run somebody over, I'd try to help the fellow up. The funny thing is, he'd usually just say, "Thank you." I didn't believe in all of that riling up the opposition. You don't throw wood on a fireplace—or gasoline on a fire—in those situations.

Bob "Jitterbug" Kellogg, he was an outstanding boy for Tulane, and he almost led 'em to a win. He returned a punt 76 yards for a touchdown in the third quarter that tied the game at seven. He also stopped me on several occasions, and after one I grabbed him and said, "You're the cleanest little tackler I've ever seen."

That's the way I tried to play the game—respect your opposition. After the win in the Sugar Bowl I tried to stay humble and give credit where due.

"Those 10 boys with me did the work," I told a cluster of reporters in the locker room late that afternoon. And then I patted halfback Jim

---

Running back John Kimbrough led the Aggies to their only national championship in 1939 and later served as a bomber pilot in World War II. *Photo courtesy of Texas A&M Athletic Media Relations*

Thomason on the knee. "And this boy did it especially—he's the best blocking back in the country."

And on that afternoon and during that year, we were the best team in the country.

To me, there wasn't any doubt whom all of those folks were hollering for on that day: The Aggies. I know, we played the game in New Orleans—home of Tulane—but that's the way I heard those folks hollering: for the Aggies. Maybe I just wanted to hear it that way.

GAME RESULTS

John Kimbrough's two-yard touchdown run gave A&M a 7-0 lead in the first quarter of the Sugar Bowl, but the Aggies trailed 13-7 in the fourth quarter, when Kimbrough endeared himself to Aggies forever. On a decisive, 69-yard drive, Kimbrough recorded the key play, slashing and rumbling 22 yards through a slew of Tulane defenders to the Green Wave 26-yard line.

"The thing that most of the fans and scribes went away marveling about was his agility and speed," penned John Sidney Smith of the *Bryan Daily Eagle*. "They had expected a pile-driving line plunger, but they had no idea the 210-pound back could skirt Tulane's widely heralded ends as he did."

Three plays after Kimbrough's 22-yard dash and from the Green Wave 22-yard line, Cotton Price passed to Herbie Smith in the right flat, who quickly ran into a wall of Tulane defenders. Smith then lateraled to Kimbrough, who dashed across the goal for the final touchdown on the day.

"Kimbrough stormed 18 yards on that last scoring run," Charles DuFour of the *New Orleans Tribune* wrote, "brushing off Green tacklers like Gulliver flicking Lilliputians off his coat lapel."

Price then kicked the decisive extra point. Moments earlier, Kimbrough had complimented Jitterbug Kellogg on his tackling. Kellogg, however, didn't respond.

"Any guy who tackles Kimbrough," Kellogg said afterward, "doesn't feel like talking for five or 10 minutes."

Penned Arch Ward of the *Chicago Tribune*, "Somewhere there may be a greater college football player than John Kimbrough, but you never will be able to convince the 70,000 spectators who Monday saw him almost single-handedly defeat a gallant team from Tulane, 14-13.

"And while Kimbrough dominated the Texans' play throughout, you couldn't escape the impression that you were watching one of football's greatest teams. It had sparkle and drive and spirit and eagerness. It tackled. It at times developed devastating blocking that seemed to spring up magically. Texas A&M was so smart against passes that Tulane, whose forward passes dazzled Southeastern Conference opponents in late season, was unable to complete a single aerial."

The Aggies discovered the Associated Press had crowned them national champions on a train ride home the next day, after celebrating all night in the French Quarter. Funny thing, A&M's season almost didn't end in New Orleans, although with as much revelry on Bourbon Street took place among the fellows, it might have been a while before the Aggies could don their leather helmets with any bit of effectiveness.

Idealists tried matching the Aggies and the University of Southern California, winners of the Rose Bowl (and some argued, the nation's true No. 1 team), in an extra game, with proceeds to benefit a Finland war relief fund. Even former President Herbert Hoover, overseeing America's Finnish assistance (this was a little less than two years before the Japanese attack on Pearl Harbor), discussed the matter and found the idea "interesting."

But alas, the game never transpired.

"I don't remember much about any Finnish relief fund," Kimbrough says, smiling. "But I do know that we'd just won the national championship."

WHAT BECAME OF JOHN KIMBROUGH?

"In the sweat of your face you shall eat bread till you return to the ground, for out of it you were taken; you are dust, and to dust you shall return."
— **Genesis 3:19**

John Kimbrough turned 85 on June 14, 2003. He lived in his beloved Haskell with his adorable wife of 62 years, Barbara. They built a house there shortly after World War II. John and Barbara had two children, also named John and Barbara, and two grandchildren. The couple had a splendid view of West Texas expanse out their back windows.

Kimbrough greeted visitors with, "John Kimbrough, from Haskell."

In Haskell, 370 miles from College Station by remote highway, the dust settles on pickup trucks as thick as brown sugar icing. Ironically, the clear fork of the Brazos River runs just south of here. Those same waters gather steam and sail swiftly past Bryan-College Station in Brazos County, much as Kimbrough did opponents like TCU, Arkansas, SMU and Texas six decades ago.

Kimbrough never cared much for the big city, although he met Barbara while in Houston.

"I was graduating from high school and there was a luncheon for me up on the Rice Hotel roof," Barbara said, smiling at the memory of her and John's beginning. "We were on an elevator together."

Kimbrough had elevated the Aggies to the national title only months earlier, and the next season (1940) Kimbrough finished second in the Heisman Trophy race to Michigan's Tom Harmon. At about the same time, the handsome Kimbrough became a poster boy for Chesterfield Cigarettes. He later served as a B-24 pilot in World War II in the Pacific and then as a pro football player before a heart attack slowed him at age 30.

John and Barbara last visited Aggieland on Nov. 26, 1999, when the Aggies beat Texas 20-16 in an emotional contest only days after the collapse of the Bonfire stack that killed 12 Aggies. John's ailing health—he had two heart attacks since the first 55 years ago—wouldn't allow any more visits to College Station.

"The good people of A&M were so nice to us," Barbara said of their final visit to Aggieland. "We sat in a luxury box, and instead of eating hot dogs they served us filet mignon. John David Crow was sitting in the luxury box next door, so we gave him a few high-fives through the glass."

While his body rested in a wheelchair during his final years, the undying spirit that led Texas A&M to its lone football national championship in 1939 continued to glow in "Jarrin'" John Kimbrough's blue eyes.

John Kimbrough passed away on May 8, 2006, in Haskell, Texas, from pneumonia.

CHAPTER 2

YALE
LARY

Name: Robert Yale Lary
Born: Nov. 24, 1930
Hometown: Fort Worth, Texas
Current Residence: Fort Worth, Texas
Occupation: Retired from the NFL, and multiple private businesses
Positions: Safety and punter
Height: 5'11"
Playing weight: 180 pounds
Years lettered: 1949-51
Accomplishments: The only Texas Aggie inducted into the NFL Hall of Fame; named All-Conference in 1951; hit .366 as a freshman outfielder on the A&M baseball team; school leader in career punt return average (18.1 yards); named as one of *Sports Illustrated's* 50 Greatest Sports Figures from Texas in 1999; third-round pick in the 1952 NFL draft; played in nine Pro Bowls as a defensive back and punter with the Detroit Lions and ranks among the NFL's all-time leaders in career punting average (44.2 yards); tallied 50 interceptions in the NFL and played for three league title teams (1952, 1953, and 1957).
The Game: Texas at Texas A&M, Nov. 29, 1951

Yale Lary. *Cushing Memorial Library*

THE LIFE OF YOUNG YALE LARY

A house doctor delivered Robert Yale Lary in 1930 at 1111 Northwest 16th Street on Fort Worth's northwest side, and thus, a future NFL Hall of Famer—incredibly, the only one from Texas A&M—came to be.

"My mother didn't want to have me in a hospital," Lary says. "She was afraid they'd get me mixed up with another baby."

The only child of Yale Buster (Y. B.) and Kathryn Lary, however, was easy to pick out on the playgrounds of his elementary school—as his amazing athleticism already was apparent by the time he was six years old.

"We'd punt the ball a lot during recess, and after school we'd go punt in the street," Lary says. "If you punted the ball over the telephone poles, that was three points. We were always playing some sort of sport."

And young Yale, thin but strong-legged, almost always won.

During World War II, Yale and his friends often journeyed over to Farrington Field in Fort Worth to catch traveling football teams like the Randolph Field Ramblers in action. The Ramblers, from a famed San Antonio air base, once tied the University of Texas 7-7 in the 1944 Cotton Bowl.

"We didn't have any money to get in to the games at Farrington, so we'd climb up this tree just past the fence near the end zone and watch," Lary says. "One time this guy kicked an extra point and it sailed over that wall, and we grabbed that ol' yellow ball—I'll never forget it—and that's the ball we kicked with in the streets.

"We wore that nose out hitting it on the pavement."

Yale—family legend has it his grandparents liked the college's name, and thus named his father as such—starred in two sports at North Side High: baseball and basketball.

"I attended A&M on a football scholarship, but I always loved baseball," Lary says. "That was my first love, really. Football was a lot of dern hard work. At A&M we worked out there on a practice field right beside the shower and dressing room, and the coaches would just run you up and down that field until you fell. One time this ol' guard from Houston, he just quit right in the middle of sprints.

"The coaches had yelled, 'You're not through!' to the team after a tough session, and he said, 'I am,' and just walked off the field. The windows on the dressing room were open and he was just in the shower a-singin', and we could hear him in there, just singing a song because he was so happy he was through with football."

Yale couldn't be happier in Aggieland, however, as a former Aggie football star—and war hero—had influenced him to attend Texas A&M.

"Marion Pugh had also attended North Side High, and we lived about four blocks from the Pugh Grocery Store," Lary says. "As a little boy, I'd ride my bicycle down there to get groceries, and Marion would always kid with me and mess around with me about one day going to A&M.

"In 1939 I was eight years old, and that's when John Kimbrough and Marion and that bunch won the national championship. I'd already started keeping a scrapbook of their exploits—an old spiral notebook deal that I'd cut and paste together with white glue. Marion, he was an exceptional player, and then he went on to fight in World War II."

Texas coach Blair Cherry, who'd coached Lary's father at North Side High in the 1920s, met with Y. B. and Yale in the parking lot of North Side one day during Yale's senior year.

"Son, I'd like to have you play at the university," said Cherry, who later became the first Texas coach to take the Longhorns to three different Jan. 1 bowls. "You're kind of slow, though, so I'd like you to play linebacker."

Lary still grins at the memory.

"Hell, I didn't weigh but 165 pounds," he says. "I told him, 'Well, Mr. Cherry, I 'ppreciate it.' We said 'adios,' and that was the last time I saw him. There wasn't any way I was gonna go down to Austin and play linebacker."

When he visited College Station, Lary fell in love with the place—especially those fine uniforms that new Aggies coach Harry Stiteler's staff showed him upon his recruitment.

"Back then everybody was still wearing the leather helmets and hightop shoes and khaki pants," Lary says. "But I went into the A&M equipment room and one of the coaches said, 'Look here, boy, look at these plastic helmets like Doc Blanchard and Glenn Davis [the 1945 and '46 Heisman Trophy winners, respectively] are wearing at Army. And look at these fine, silky-smooth pants. And these lowtops, boy, these are classy.'

"That, combined with the whole Marion Pugh connection, helped get me to A&M. So, my freshman year, of course, they give me those old hightop shoes, leather helmets and khaki pants.

"I finally got to wear that fine equipment my sophomore year."

THE SCENE

The University of Texas might have figured things wouldn't go its way on this day when Texas A&M's collie mascot, Reveille, barked furiously at the Longhorns' steer mascot, Bevo, during halftime festivities of the 1951 Thanksgiving showdown between the state's two biggest rivals.

"The dog raised merry Ned with him … and drew a big hand from the large crowd," one Kyle Field observer noted.

Even Reveille, so named in 1931 because the first collie mascot barked at the sound of the trumpet call, seemed fed up that the Aggies hadn't defeated Texas in a dozen years, or since the 1939 Aggies won the national championship. Things had gotten so disheartening around Aggieland that the *Bryan Daily Eagle* cited A&M as "the most jinxed team in the United States."

"In recent years it appears that all an opposing team has to do is holler 'jinx' and the Cadet eleven roll over and play dead," an article read on the day that A&M (4-3-2 record) and UT (7-2) met at Kyle Field.

Texas had even won the five previous meetings on A&M's hallowed grounds of Kyle, including a 42-14 whipping in 1949. Many Aggies blamed such gridiron shortcomings on the "lean" post-World War II years for the Cadets, as the war had drained much of the school's muscle and talent.

But tales of A&M jinxes and rolling over and such—even from the locals—couldn't fire up one Yale Lary, a versatile A&M senior from Fort Worth, any more than rivals had the year prior. That's when someone had messed with his baby—a black-on-black 1949 Chevrolet convertible—the night before the 1950 A&M-UT game in Austin.

Mary Jane Boothe, a Texas student and Lary's girlfriend (and later his wife), had driven the car back to Austin from College Station after attending a banquet with Yale, in the few days before the Aggies-Longhorns game. During the night prior to the contest, vandals spray-painted Lary's black beauty orange—inside and out—knowing that it belonged to Mary Jane's boyfriend.

So Mary Jane, along with several of her Scottish Rite dorm mates, furiously scrubbed the car clean. Fortunately, the culprits had used a water-based paint. She waited until after the game—a 17-0 A&M loss—to tell her boyfriend about the vandalism.

"I didn't want him to worry about it," she says, smiling now at the memory. "I was worried enough. But he was a good sport about it—he was able to not let things like that consume him."

The defacing, however, served as a piercing motivation for Yale Lary—a full year later.

"I was paying $60 a month on that car, and that was a lot then," he says, shaking his head. "While most of Texas's students were nice, it always seemed like we were running into something like that in Austin. As Aggies, we were the underdogs and Texas figured it was the hotshot college. There were quite a few Aggies who dated girls at Texas—and when they'd go to pick up their dates some of the Texas students would gang up on these guys who wore their senior boots, and they'd pull their boots off and mess 'em up.

"Real high-class stuff, I tell you. But things like that also gave us incentive."

*   *   *   *   *

Elsewhere around the country at about the same time A&M and Texas were donning their new plastic helmets in an annual renewal of strong incentives and extreme dislike, a debate stirred surrounding television broadcasting rights of college athletics—a new phenomenon that needed addressing.

"If they [colleges favoring unlimited TV broadcasting] really want to do an honest job in collegiate athletics, then let's take the dollar out of sports," said one proponent of restricting broadcasting because of unbalanced financial gains among schools. "Let's play the games for charity. TV receipts make bowl games receipts look like peanuts. So let's donate the TV receipts to taking care of foreign scholarships or displaced persons."

As farfetched as that idea seemed—then and now—President Harry Truman found even more disbelief in the notion that some members of the press might have penned fake ceasefire stories about the ongoing Korean War—"out of hot competition for news."

An Associated Press story out of Seoul, Korea, the day before the Thanksgiving game had reported that orders—possibly from the White House—had stopped ground fighting in Korea. That simply wasn't true, a mad Truman voiced from Key West, Fla., on the same day that A&M and Texas clashed for the 58th time.

As America grew more heavily involved in another war halfway across the world, collegians nationwide cast a wary eye toward the conflict while going about their business on the homeland.

"The Korean War was certainly on our minds," says Lary, who later served as a first lieutenant in the U.S. Army for two years, although the conflict had ended before he was called to combat. "It was very important that you passed your grades and very important that you stayed in the Corps of Cadets, because if you didn't, you'd be drafted."

But at least for a Thanksgiving day, the Aggies and Longhorns and all of their fans set aside their wartime concerns and duked it out at Kyle Field. Literally. The annual grudge match ended in a near brawl, with both teams' players hoisted off of Kyle on the shoulders of Corps of Cadets members.

THE SETTING

Old Aggie Louie Hamilton, considered one of the great drop-kickers in Southwest Conference history, settled into his seat at Kyle Field on Thanksgiving Day 1951 and spun a few tales of what it was like to play for Texas A&M from 1906-09.

"Today's athletes don't get enough practice," Hamilton preached before the '51 UT-A&M game. "We had to practice at least two hours a day and then run five miles back to the showers."

Hamilton, who once scored all 12 of A&M's points in a 28-12 loss to Texas in 1908, even lamented the loss of what he called the "onside kick" as part an offense's arsenal.

"Ol' end 'Doggie' Ward would race down and grab the ball, giving us a nice gain," Hamilton said, hearkening to the good ol' days. "We used the 'onside kick' more than the forward pass."

But the hard-to-please Hamilton was in for a real treat on this day in 1951, more than four decades after he'd last suited up for the Aggies. And even Hamilton (and his tales of a more rugged yesteryear) could appreciate the all-out toughness of Yale Lary, who substituted for injured teammate Bob Smith (an All-American in 1950) on the first play of the game against UT and played every down from there out.

A&M figured to have an excellent team in 1951, as it finally recovered from the drain on its students and athletes from World War II—but things hadn't gone as planned under first-year coach Ray George. After opening the season with four wins over UCLA, Texas Tech, Oklahoma and Trinity, the Aggies had failed to win a Southwest Conference game (Texas Tech didn't join the conference for another five years), although A&M had managed two league ties, against Baylor and SMU.

But there was plenty of reason for optimism headed into the annual Texas clash, because the UT offense featured the same Split T that the Aggies had handled against the Red Raiders and Sooners. Plus, A&M's players (and Reveille) seemed at a boiling point about not having defeated their rival since 1939.

A&M had played Texas to a 14-14 tie in 1948, when Lary and his fellow freshmen weren't eligible to play (the NCAA scrapped that rule in 1972). So Lary was one of 18 A&M seniors angling for one last shot at the Longhorns in the final game of their college careers.

"The boys realize that by winning this one they can make a success out of a disappointing season," George said.

The entire state, too, seemed very curious to see if the Aggies might make amends for years of losing to the Longhorns. The game officially sold out on June 21, and fans had booked all of the hotels and tourist courts ahead of time.

On the night before the Thanksgiving game, a crowd of about 10,000 soaked in what many of the old-timers considered possibly the largest and most glorious Bonfire to that date. A weekend of bad weather had set Bonfire's construction back, but workers toiled all Tuesday night by the aid of automobile headlights to finish the stack.

Following Yell Practice on the drill field, many of the students and alumni moved the party to Sbisa Hall for a post-Bonfire dance, with music provided by the Aggieland Orchestra. Such an event was about as cultured as all-male Texas A&M got in the post-World War II years leading to the Dwight Eisenhower presidency.

"My freshman year in 1948 there were about 8,500 students at A&M, and at least a couple of thousand of those were veterans who'd come back from World War II," Lary says. "College Station was just a small community. You had the Northgate district and a drugstore and a pool hall above the drugstore, a post office and ol' Loupot's book store.

"There weren't hardly any girls around, so on the weekend we'd try and get out of town. We were 90 miles from everywhere, it seemed like, and we'd burn up that road to try and go see our girls."

But on Thanksgiving Day 1951, folks from all over burned up the roads heading into College Station and thus witnessed one of the more thrilling A&M victories over archrival Texas, 22-21, in the series' fabled history.

THE GAME OF MY LIFE
By Yale Lary

We just seemed to plug along all of my years at Texas A&M, although we possessed some good talent. Halfback Bob Smith had earned All-America honors in 1950 and even rushed for 297 yards (a school record) in a game against SMU. But our senior year had been a frustrating one, because we'd started so strong but faltered in league play.

Ray George was in his first year as head coach and still trying to get ahold of the reins. We figured we could make amends for that year by beating Texas—that would be our bowl game—but things didn't look too good when ol' Smith got hurt on that first play. So I charged into the game, and at first I played the left half, and later the right half, in the T formation.

The third quarter was big for us, and I scored on a 68-yard run and a 38-yard reception. On the 68-yarder, I lined up at right halfback and quarterback Dick Gardemal handed off the ball to me, and I sprinted between the left tackle and left end. Suddenly I saw a little hole there, so I cut sharply to the right—against the grain—and the field just opened up, pretty as could be.

Future NFL Hall of Famer Yale Lary filled in for star halfback Bob Smith en route to scoring two touchdowns in the Aggies' 22-21 victory over Texas in 1951. *Cushing Memorial Library*

The 38-yarder for a touchdown took place on an odd play, but I liked the results. I had switched back to left halfback, and Gardemal threw a little hook pass to receiver Darrow Hooper, but Texas's Tom Stolhandske hit the ball, and it just kind of popped up and ricocheted right into my hands. I raced from about the 25-yard line for the touchdown.

Texas still had a chance to beat us there at the end. June Davis was their field-goal kicker, and I was standing just underneath the crossbars of the goalpost, right there on the goal line. It really wasn't that far of a kick—33 yards. He kicked it down the middle, but the ball fell short by about a foot, and we won 22-21.

There was a lot of pushing and shoving going on at that point, and I distinctly remember that's the only time I've ever been carried off of a field after a football game, thanks to the Corps of Cadets.

GAME RESULTS

While Yale Lary scored two touchdowns in the third quarter of A&M's first victory over Texas in 12 years, A&M running back Glenn Lippman also gained 173 yards on 19 carries from the fullback slot. In the locker room a jubilant Aggies squad presented George, 1-0 against Texas, with the game ball.

"I couldn't ask for anything more," a grinning George said repeatedly, before adding, "If we had played like that all season, we wouldn't have lost a game. But I'm thankful that fourth quarter ran out."

First-year Longhorns coach Ed Price, 0-1 against A&M, said his team was "keyed too high" in battling its archrival.

"We suffered from the jitters," Price said. "Then we lost our poise, and that hurt."

Lots of folks lost their poise by the end of the game, broadcast nationally on radio by Humble Oil. Following Davis's failed kick with two seconds remaining, A&M students rushed onto Kyle Field in celebration. But with seconds still on the clock, officials cleared the grass, and Dick Gardemal finally dropped to the ground on the A&M 20-yard line, killing the ball and running out the last of the time.

"The final seconds were clouded as a fight developed between the opposing teams, but the Aggie cheering section settled it by grabbing both elevens and hoisting them to their shoulders," one newspaper noted. "Then M. T. Harrington, A&M president, made the day complete by announcing a Monday holiday."

In his most memorable college game, Lary scored two decisive touchdowns and averaged 41 yards on five punts.

"There was a mob of people out on that field right after the game, and then some Cadets hoisted me up and carried me to the tunnel," Lary says. "I didn't get involved in all of that pushing and shoving. But I sure remember how happy all of us Aggies were."

Wrote Dick Peebles of the *San Antonio Express*: "Bedlam broke loose in historic Kyle Field much like it did at the Polo Grounds when [the New York Giants'] Bobby Thomson socked his historic home run [to clinch the National League pennant against the Brooklyn Dodgers in 1951]. The Kyle Field stands erupted and it looked for a few seconds that there would be an old-fashioned donnybrook, but hot tempers quickly cooled and the deliriously happy Aggie students carried their conquering heroes and the defeated Longhorns off the field on their shoulders."

Aggies, too, might have enjoyed the moment a little more had they known what the next couple of years held in store. George wouldn't beat Texas again in his brief stint in Aggieland, and by 1954 the college had replaced him with Paul "Bear" Bryant.

WHAT BECAME OF YALE LARY?

Yale Lary and his Aggie buddies got a kick out of all of those applications from pro football teams while they were seniors at Texas A&M—such a kick they'd often have a little fun at the pro scouts' expense.

"We'd get inquiries from the New York Giants and all of those other pro teams, but you've got to understand, pro football just wasn't that popular down here in Texas then," Lary says. "They'd ask your height, weight and speed in the 100-yard dash, and we'd put things like six-foot-four, 225 pounds and 9.9 seconds."

As much fun as the fellows had with the inquiries, Lary took it extremely seriously when the Detroit Lions selected him in the third-round of the 1952 NFL draft—the team's first pick that year.

"I didn't have much choice," Lary says, grinning about whether he even desired to play in the NFL—with baseball being his first love. "I'd just gotten married and everything, so I went ahead and signed with 'em. One of the best choices I ever made."

Certainly. Lary is the only Texas Aggie inducted into the NFL Hall of Fame, an honor he received in 1979 after earning nine Pro Bowl trips over an NFL career as a defensive back and punter spanning from 1952-64. Lary even missed a couple of seasons with the Lions while he served in the U.S. Army in 1954 and '55.

The NFL Hall of Fame began in 1963, and about seven years later, former Lions stars Bobby Layne and Doak Walker, along with Lary and their coach, Buddy Parker, gathered with their wives in Detroit's Sheraton Cadillac Hotel.

"We were up there just shooting the bull like we always did, and we start to walk out of the room and I tell Buddy how much I enjoyed playing for him," Lary says.

That's when Parker grabbed Lary by the arm and caught the nine-time Pro Bowl defensive back on his heels for one of the few times in his life.

"Yale, you'll be in the Hall of Fame," Parker said, right out of the Detroit blue.

"That was the first time I'd ever thought about it," Lary says. "When they called me at the house in 1979 to tell me about it, it took my breath away."

Lary was inducted into the Hall of Fame that year along with quarterback Johnny Unitas, linebacker Dick Butkus and offensive lineman Ron Mix—becoming only the fifth defensive back inducted. That July weekend in Canton, Ohio, Lary described his on-the-field attitude as a defensive back.

"I was scared to death all the time," Lary said, "that I was going to get beat."

He rarely did, however, and following his hugely successful pro career, Lary also enjoyed considerable achievement in the automobile and banking industries in North Texas. He celebrated 50 years of marriage with Mary Jane in 2002, and the adoring couple has two children, Yale Jr. and Nancy Jane, and four grandchildren.

These days Lary spends much of his time playing golf and simply relaxing with Mary Jane back home in Fort Worth.

"These young flatbellies out on the golf course out-drive me by a 100 yards," Lary says, smiling.

But on a sweet November 1951 day in College Station, no one achieved more in a span of 100 yards of precious grass than Texas A&M's "Mr. Everything," Yale Lary.

CHAPTER 3

GENE STALLINGS

Name: Eugene Clifton Stallings Jr.
Born: March 2, 1935
Hometown: Paris, Texas
Current Residence: Powderly, Texas
Occupation: Retired from coaching
Position: End (Offense and Defense)
Height: 6'2"
Playing Weight: 170 pounds
Years lettered: 1954-56
Accomplishments: All-Conference end in 1955; team captain of the 1956 SWC champions; coached the Aggies from 1965-71 (27-45-1 record); member of the Texas Sports Hall of Fame; Dallas Cowboys assistant (secondary) from 1972-85; head coach of the Phoenix Cardinals from 1985-89 (22-34-1); head coach at Alabama from 1990-96 (70-16-1), coaching the Crimson Tide to national championship in 1992.
Nickname: Bebes
The Game: Texas A&M vs. Alabama, Cotton Bowl, Jan. 1, 1968

Gene Stallings. *Photo courtesy of Texas A&M Athletic Media Relations*

THE LIFE OF YOUNG GENE STALLINGS

His Texas A&M teammates in the 1950s, his Aggie players a decade later and the Alabama boys that he coached to a national championship in 1992 might have all giggled a bit at how gravelly Gene "Bebes" Stallings protected himself as a child on the gridiron. Bebes sewed sheepskin inside his pants for extra insulation on the playgrounds of East Paris Elementary School.

"And I kept doing it on into high school," Stallings says, smiling. "I just had old bony knees that I needed to protect. I couldn't run fast, anyway, so it's not like the sheepskin slowed me down."

Had Texas A&M hired Paul "Bear" Bryant a year earlier, Stallings likely wouldn't have been a Junction Boy, much less an Aggie. He hardly made it to College Station under the sheepskin-soft reign prior to Bryant's—that of Ray George, whose only winning season at A&M was his first (5-3-2 in 1951).

"[Assistant coach] Gil Steinke, who recruited me to A&M, asked me one time why I even bothered coming, since the Aggies barely recruited me," Stallings says. "I didn't want to tell him it was because my girlfriend had encouraged me to go there, but that's basically the reason I did."

Ruth Ann Jack, Stallings's high school girlfriend (and later wife), knew exactly why she wanted Bebes—a childhood nickname derived from "Baby Gene"—to attend Texas A&M: No Girls Allowed. (Women didn't begin attending A&M en masse until the early 1970s.)

"It was a military school with no coeds," Stallings says. "I'd always wanted to go to Baylor, and Baylor had recruited me hard, while A&M hardly did. But Ruth Ann talked me into going to A&M."

In place of cuddly coeds at A&M, there was one Bear Bryant and the Corps of Cadets. And Bryant stood boot to boot with the Corps Commandant from the beginning of spring 1954.

"The football players were in the Corps, and we'd drill in the afternoon," Stallings says. "Coach Bryant told the Commandant that we needed that time to practice, and the Commandant responded that they needed that time to drill."

A defiant Bryant greeted the team shortly after his meeting with the Corps command.

"I'll show that military a thing or two about who's going to practice and who's not," Bryant said, shaking his head, with fire on his breath. "We're going to practice at night!"

"So we did," Stallings says. "We'd drill with the Corps in the afternoon and practice football at night. Of course, the ROTC folks didn't care whether we practiced at night or not."

Late in the summer of 1954, Bryant, on the recommendation of assistant coach Willie Zapalac, also chose Junction, Texas, for a little training camp excursion for his players.

"He told us to get a pillow and a blanket and a couple of changes of clothes," Stallings says. "He wouldn't tell us where we were going. He even bought us some candy at a little rest stop along the way—we were all just havin' a good ol' time. Finally, we pulled into Junction, and it was a pretty place. It had these little Quonset huts for us to stay in, and even a river behind the back of the facilities. We thought it was going to be great."

It was, in terms of creating eternally legendary stories. Following an unbelievable day—considering what lay ahead—of canoe races on the river, Bryant greeted his players at practice the next morning—before sunrise.

"We were on the field about 5:30 a.m., in full uniform," Stallings says. "It was just dark, really, and suddenly Coach Bryant walked out of his cabin, and the sun kind of came up over the mountain."

Many of the athletes would soon wish the sun hadn't risen, as Bryant had hauled 111 players to Junction and only 35 returned to Aggieland as team members 10 days later. The Junction training camp included full-speed practices early in the morning, breakfast, meetings until lunch, a rest period, evening practice, dinner and more meetings.

"Everywhere you looked there'd be a drill going on," Stallings says of the practices. "And there were these big old goatheads—you know, sand burrs. And everywhere you put your hand down was one of those big blue stickers."

Even the supposed relaxation period served as a thorn in the players' sides in the suffocating 110-degree heat of late summer in scorched South Texas.

"I was a sophomore, so I had a top bunk," Stallings says. "The roof was tin, so it was just like being in an oven, with the sun beating down on those huts."

Stallings's synopsis of the whole diversion became the line most associated with Bryant's infamous Junction trip.

"We left College Station in two buses," Stallings said, "and came back in one … "

The rest of Stallings's summary is usually dropped in the retelling. However, it's equally as revealing: "… and that bus was half full."

THE SCENE

Gene Stallings, sophomore country boy from Paris, Texas, had just returned with his teammates from Junction, as part of Coach Bryant's infamous training camp. And, mister, this practice on Monday, Sept. 20, 1954, in College Station—following a loss to Texas Tech in Bryant's first game as coach—was no "Junction."

It was tougher.

"We're going to take up where we left off against Tech!" a furious Bryant said, clutching a football and placing it on the 20-yard line at Kyle Field in the burning, late summer sun. His wary and stripped-down team (whittled from the Junction excursion) surrounded him. A&M had lost to the Red Raiders by 32 points, and Bryant never again would lose a game in Aggieland so badly as his first one.

An angry Bryant—who'd just turned 41—first challenged his biggest linemen with blocking drills that he participated in, prompting a newspaper reporter to yell over to the coach and ask whether he needed pads.

"No, not any harder than this bunch is hitting," Bryant retorted. "There's no danger of being hurt."

Bryant then began a full-fledged scrimmage for his startled players.

"It wasn't any of that going through three or four drills and loosening up first," Stallings says. "Keep in mind, in those days you played both ways. And during that practice we'd break the huddle and go to the line with an assistant coach right behind us, and we'd drive the ball the length of the field and then turn around and put it on the 20, and start back.

"Then after a while we'd line up and play defense—never taking a break—with our coaches right behind us, urging us on. There wasn't any of that hitting a knee and taking a rest business."

The simulated game—minus even a single breather—rambled on for about an hour.

"You can go out and fiddle for three hours at practice, or you can go out there and work hard for 30 minutes," Stallings says. "It's what you do while you're out there that's important—and everybody was going full speed the whole time during that practice."

Stallings, however, could have lasted another two hours that hot afternoon in College Station. His legs may have felt as sturdy as spaghetti late in the nonstop tussle, but his heart couldn't have beat stronger. All based on a few words of praise from Bryant (which was akin to a eulogy for anyone else, as one reporter noted), in front of the team immediately before the coach's toughest practice at Texas A&M.

"One of the mistakes I made against Texas Tech," Bryant said, pointing at an unsuspecting Stallings as the team prepared to scrimmage, "is not playing that skinny little end over there more. He was one of the few fellows out there trying to win the game."

The Aggies won a lone game that 1954 season, but didn't suffer a loss by any more than 13 points the rest of the year. Amazingly, over Bryant's final 40 games (following the humbling 41-9 loss at Tech in the '54 opener) in Aggieland, no opponent scored even 30 points on the Aggies, much less 40.

Stallings—recruited to A&M in 1953 by Ray George, who was fired the winter of his freshman year—hadn't even heard of Paul Bryant when A&M hired him from Kentucky. Bryant was simply known as "The Man."

"The only conference we knew in this part of the country was the Southwest Conference," Stallings says. "We didn't know anything about Kentucky and Alabama and Tennessee and those places, and we sure didn't know anything about Coach Bryant—his record, reputation or anything."

The Aggies soon would learn.

A&M's fabled run under Bryant—including their first Southwest Conference title in 15 years in '56—didn't begin on that legendary, 10-day trip to Junction in August 1954. It began the prior spring, when Bryant (hired in February '54) quickly asserted himself with what his players warily called The List.

"Coach Bryant would write out in longhand a list of who he wanted to report for practice," Stallings says. "And every day after class we'd go down there and check The List posted on a bulletin board, and if your name wasn't on it, you couldn't come out for practice."

The coaches mercifully didn't yank the deposed players off of scholarship, but an absent name on The List signified something worse: You weren't good enough to play for Texas A&M under the fiery new coach from the foreign Southeastern Conference.

"My name was always around the bottom of The List," Stalling says, "but I made it through the spring."

Had Bryant cut the skinny kid from Northeast Texas in the spring of 1954, he might've deprived college football of the man who'd grow most into The Bear's likeness as a tough, mightily respected coach—and even one day defeat him in the 1968 Cotton Bowl.

THE SETTING

Paul Bryant's young protégé busily soaked in mental notes on the art of coaching on Oct. 8, 1955, as a result of a punishment that hardly seemed fair. After all, the Aggies were beating Nebraska 20-0 at halftime when Bryant heatedly called out his best players in an until-then jubilant locker room.

"If we weren't playing against a sorry football team," Bryant said, slowly glancing around at his boys who'd built a nearly three-touchdown lead over the game's first two quarters, "we'd be behind by 40 points. Bobby Marks! You're gonna play, but I'm gonna have that camera right on you. Crow, you're not gonna play; Pardee, you're not gonna play; and Stallings, you're not gonna play. You're all just playin' awful!"

Sure enough, Stallings, John David Crow (a future Heisman Trophy winner) and Jack Pardee (a future NFL All-Pro) didn't play in the second half of a 27-0 win over the Cornhuskers, and on the following Monday Bryant listed the threesome as second team.

"We were playing TCU that week, and TCU was a great team," Stallings says. "They were favored to beat us by three touchdowns in Fort Worth. We worked like the devil in practice that week, and he finally put us back on the first team. That Saturday, we went up to Fort Worth and won 19-16."

Later, Stallings figured out that Bryant already was planning ahead to the TCU game at halftime of the blowout Nebraska contest.

"I'll always believe that Coach Bryant won the TCU game for us the week before at halftime of the Nebraska game," Stallings says. "It just shows that he was always a step ahead of most of us."

*   *   *   *   *

Across the Metroplex in Dallas a dozen years following that memorable win in Fort Worth, Stallings and Bryant met as opposing head coaches—Bryant at Alabama and Stallings at Texas A&M—in the pupil's most cherished Aggies game. And the underdog understudy, remarkably, finished a step ahead of the master, in a thrilling 20-16 A&M win over 'Bama in the 1968 Cotton Bowl.

THE GAME OF MY LIFE
By Gene Stallings

Coach Bryant called me into his office in late 1957, when I was an assistant on his staff, having finished up my playing days at Texas A&M the year before.

"Now, Bebes, I'm fixin' to go to Alabama, and I'm going to offer you a job on my staff," he said. "But if I read about it in the papers before I'm ready to announce it, you don't have a job."

My wife is the only one I told. We had to plan for our move—but I

Gene Stallings, who later led Alabama to a national championship following the 1992 season, guided Texas A&M to a 20-16 upset of the Crimson Tide and legendary coach Paul "Bear" Bryant in the 1968 Cotton Bowl. Stallings, pictured here with his arm around Bryant at the Cotton Bowl, coached the Aggies from 1965-71. *Photo courtesy of Texas A&M Athletic Media Relations*

didn't whisper a word to anyone else. I spent seven years on Coach Bryant's staff at Alabama, and I suppose the folks at Texas A&M thought that was important, because they hired me as a 29-year-old head coach going into the 1965 season.

At age 29, I didn't feel like I had a lot to prove as the nation's youngest head coach—although it was known all over as a tough coaching job and a hard place to recruit to because there weren't any women yet on campus. Plus, the Vietnam War had started and A&M had such strong military ties that it made the school harder to recruit to as the war grew increasingly unpopular.

In any case, it was good to be back in Aggieland, and I couldn't have been more excited to be A&M's head coach, even with tough times ahead in trying to whip the program back into shape. We finished 3-7 in my first year in 1965 and followed that up with a 4-5-1 record a season later. Then came 1967, when we started the year 0-4. But I was still optimistic, because we'd lost three out of four of those games by a combined eight points.

Finally, we had a huge breakthrough win (28-24) at Texas Tech, when quarterback Edd Hargett scored on the game's final play. We won our next five regular-season games—including 10-7 over Texas—in earning A&M's first conference championship since my senior year of 1956 under Coach Bryant.

And suddenly, we were matched up with Coach Bryant and Alabama in the Cotton Bowl, and I can't tell you how thrilled I was. My players had heard me talk so much about Coach Bryant that I wanted them to have the opportunity to be around him a little bit.

* * * * *

Wendell Housley, our fullback, had just an outstanding game that day against Alabama. He ran over 'em and around 'em in the second half and broke all kinds of tackles on a 20-yard touchdown run in the third quarter that put us up 20-10. In fact, (Texas coach) Darrell Royal will tell you that's really where he got the idea for the Wishbone, based on what we did against Alabama. We put the fullback right up there close to the quarterback, because Alabama's linebackers could really run. And by hitting Wendell up through the middle real quick, we hoped it would slow their linebackers down a little bit if we pulled the ball out and ran some plays wide.

It worked, and our defense also intercepted three of quarterback Kenny Stabler's passes and recovered two fumbles. Curley Hallman, one of our defensive backs, intercepted a pass late in the game to cap the 20-16 win.

When the contest ended I was numb, because it was so close and anything can happen in that situation. I headed across the field to shake hands with Coach Bryant, and he suddenly grabbed me at midfield and hoisted me up, saying, "I'm gonna carry you off this field, boy!" I had absolutely no idea he was going to lift me up like that.

A few minutes later our press conference was taking place just outside the dressing room when a manager came running over, yelling that Coach Bryant was headed our way. I thought he was coming to see me, so I stopped the press conference.

"Coach, are you looking for me?" I asked him when he walked in the dressing room.

"No," he said, smiling and shaking his head. "I've seen enough of you. I want to talk to your players."

And so he visited with our team for a few minutes, then wished the players well and offered congratulations. How many coaches visit an opposing team's locker room and offer congratulations? Not many, I'll tell you that.

GAME RESULTS

A Texas A&M fan yelled at the Aggies' 32-year-old head coach, "Stallings for President!" shortly after unranked A&M upset No. 8 Alabama in the 1968 Cotton Bowl in Dallas.

Gene Stallings stopped and waved to the supporter just outside the Aggies' dressing room and replied, "I believe I'd rather have my job than his."

Four years later, Stallings wasn't so sure. The Aggies figured the 1967 Southwest Conference title and the 1968 Cotton Bowl victory to be the first of many such victories under Stallings, but in the next four seasons his teams finished a combined 13-29. He was fired at the end of the 1971 season—as the Aggies wound up 5-6 that year, their best record since the '67 team finished 7-4.

"I felt like we had gotten the program headed in the right direction," Stallings says of his final year in Aggieland. "In fact, if we had beaten Texas, we'd have gone to a bowl game, and have the chance to finish 7-5. Instead, we lost [34-14], and later on that evening when the Board of Directors called me, the furthest thing from my mind was getting fired. I thought they were going to give me a raise, to be honest. I thought we were doing a good job with what we had."

Gene Stallings, who later won a national championship with Alabama, would never again coach in Aggieland after the 1971 season.

"Had I gotten an invitation to come back somewhere along the way, I certainly would've given it some thought," Stallings says. "I loved Texas A&M."

WHAT BECAME OF GENE STALLINGS?

B ear Bryant's trainer at Texas A&M, Smokey Harper, once forgot
the team's mouthpieces on a road trip to Baylor in 1956.

"Of all the places," Stallings recalls, laughing. "Baylor was *tough*.
When you got through playing Baylor in those days, you were beat up,
so that wasn't the place to leave the mouth guards at home. But we just
played without 'em."

The Aggies, by then a couple of years tough under Bryant, won that
teeth-clenching game 19-13 en route to the SWC title. And Stallings,
tough as an ivory tooth, has continued conquering obstacles in a storied
coaching career.

"Gene's a straight shooter, as clean as they come," childhood friend
Gerald Jack once said. "Even when he was a teenager, he thought everyone
should work hard and not stray. The man is tough, tough as a piece of
rawhide when he has to be. But he also can be as soft as a feather pillow."

Stallings served as Tom Landry's secondary coach for 14 years (1972-
85) with the Dallas Cowboys, as the NFL Cardinals' head coach from
1985-89 (22-34-1 record) and then as Alabama's head coach from 1990-96
(70-16-1). The Crimson Tide won the national title following the 1992
season, and Stallings retired four years later.

Gene and the love of his life, Ruth Ann, live on about 600 acres near
Powderly, Texas, and retirement hasn't gone quite as Bebes envisioned.

"I figured I'd be playing golf a whole lot more and having much more
free time," says Gene, who spends a large chunk of his week at speaking
engagements. "I live on a ranch and raise cattle, and it's a full-time deal
here. My desk just looks awful. Sometimes I catch myself just moving
things from the right side to the left side while trying to clean it."

Gene married Ruth Ann on Dec. 1, 1956, just two days after the
Aggies' first win ever at Memorial Stadium in Austin—and two days
following Gene's final game as an A&M player.

"We were supposed to get married between my junior and senior year,
but during spring practice I was voted a team captain," Stallings says. "And
Coach Bryant had a rule that the captains had to live in the dorm. And so
we had to put the wedding off until the season was over."

He adds with a grin, "I'm still paying for that."

Hardly, it seems. The couple has four children: daughters Anna
Lee, Laura Nell and Jacklyn, and a son, John Mark, born with Down's
Syndrome. When a doctor gave Gene the news on June 11, 1962, that
the couple may have a "mongoloid" baby, Stallings rared back to hit the
physician, only to pass out before following through.

Now, however, Gene would not trade the opportunity to have raised

Johnny, whose love he describes as "unconditional." And Stallings enjoys sharing favorite stories about his son. For instance, Gene once coached his boy on how he'd greet Tom Landry, legendary leader of the Dallas Cowboys.

"Hi, Coach Landry," Johnny faithfully repeated after his dad.

Finally, Gene introduced his unassuming, dear youngster to the coach.

"Hi, Tom," Johnny said, smiling and extending his hand.

Another time, following an Alabama bowl game, the Crimson Tide buses were delayed from heading back to the hotel. Finally, an assistant coach filled in an impatient Stallings as to why: Johnny's signing autographs outside.

The revered coach smiled.

"We'll wait," Stallings said, nodding his head in appreciation of the moment's beauty, and his son's wonderful life in bloom.

CHAPTER 4

JACK
PARDEE

Name: John Perry "Jack" Pardee
Born: April 19, 1936 in Exira, Iowa
Deceased: April 1, 2013
Hometown: Christoval, Texas
Final Occupation: Retired from the NFL as a player and coach
Position: Fullback, Linebacker
Height: 6'2"
Playing Weight: 215 pounds
Years lettered: 1954-56
Accomplishments: Texas A&M's first academic All-American, also All-American and All-Conference in 1956; rushed for 463 yards and five touchdowns while intercepting three passes as a senior ('56); member of the National Football Foundation and Texas Sports Halls of Fame; 14th player selected in the 1957 NFL draft, by the Los Angeles Rams; an All-Pro linebacker in 1963 and '64, didn't play in '65 while recovering from cancer; NFC's Defensive Player of the Year in 1972 with the Redskins; coached the Chicago Bears, Washington Redskins and Houston Oilers for 11 seasons in the NFL (five playoff appearances); 22-11 in three seasons (1987-89) at the University of Houston.
The Game: Texas A&M at Texas, Nov. 29, 1956

Jack Pardee. *Photo courtesy of Texas A&M Athletic Media Relations*

THE LIFE OF YOUNG JACK PARDEE

Jack Pardee, six-man football hero at tiny Christoval High School, adamantly and quietly survived Bear Bryant's infamous trip to Junction, Texas, for training camp in the summer of 1954. What else was he to do?

"There really wasn't any other option," Pardee said. "I was in good shape because I'd worked in the oil fields all summer back in West Texas, and so I was used to the heat and the hard work. Was I gonna go back to Christoval and work on an oil rig? Why would you leave and go to something worse?

"Plus, my parents would have been harder on me than Coach Bryant ever was if I'd have quit and come home. Once you started something, you never quit at our place. That wasn't part of the deal. It never really crossed my mind to quit at Junction. Dying did, but never quitting."

The thought of dying had crossed the mind of Jack's father, Earl Pardee, plenty of times as well, for quite different reasons. Earl and LeMeda Pardee and their six kids, in trying to treat Earl's pronounced arthritis, had moved from Exira, Iowa, to Mesa, Ariz., and a more arid climate. The family then moved to San Antonio, San Angelo, and finally Christoval, Texas, habitat of precious mineral waters, in search of a little relief for Earl.

"We'd lived on a farm up there in Iowa and Dad was so crippled that he couldn't do any work," Pardee said. "But once we wound up in Christoval—after so many other stops—he got over the arthritis and lived another 30 years and even went back to work. Texas and Christoval was a Godsend for him—whether it was the mineral water or God's hand at work, or both, he got well."

Christoval may have been known worldwide for its mineral water, but it was still small enough that Pardee played six-man football all through high school—scoring more than 300 points his senior year as he towered over most of his competition at six feet two and more than 200 pounds.

Pardee's size and stats—even on a six-man team—were enough to attract the attention of A&M coach Ray George, who'd be fired the next year and replaced by Bryant. And, shoot, free college seemed like a bargain to a boy working in the oil fields.

"I'd be on this hot, nasty job and these guys would drive up in a fancy white car or pickup and kind of roll down their window a little bit and air-conditioning would come pouring out of there," Pardee said. "Then they'd point out a few things to my boss that needed to be done and be on their way. I started in the fields when I was about 14 years old, and I'd wonder, what kind of job do they have? Turns out they were mostly petroleum engineers.

"I got my motivation to attend college early on, because that seemed like a pretty good deal. I started out at A&M to be an engineer, but in the back of my mind, I always knew I was going to be a coach."

Pardee, too, clearly remembers his first visit to College Station.

"I liked the military, and the campus looked like West Point," Pardee said. "Everybody was always wearing their Corps of Cadets uniforms, and that was one of the reasons I chose A&M. They'd give me clothes, because I didn't really have enough money to buy clothes."

Upon his arrival at Texas A&M in the summer of 1953, Pardee quickly found out the difference between six-man football—which was a lot like playing basketball—and big-time college football.

"Willie Zapalac was our freshman coach and we were playing John Tarleton [State]—the freshmen, of course, weren't eligible and played their own schedule—and early in the game I got a handoff and ran for about 12 yards," Pardee said. "As I was getting tackled, I looked around and saw [offensive guard] Dennis Goehring coming up, and so I pitched him the ball.

"In six-man you do that—you don't really get tackled with the ball. Well, Zapalac quickly let me know I wasn't back in Christoval playing six-man ball anymore."

"Pardee," an impatient Zapalac yelled. "When you're going down, you put the ball away!"

Remembering as much may have been Pardee's biggest adjustment to playing for A&M, and he quickly showed his versatility the next year under Bryant, who'd arrived from Kentucky bent on whipping his inheritances into shape. Athletes played both ways at that time, and Bryant liked to pick his players by how they performed on defense.

"Coach Bryant got there in time for spring training my freshman year, and I was fifth on his first depth chart, because the team wasn't hurting for fullbacks and linebackers," Pardee said. "While we were in Junction over that 10-day period, I played eight different positions on offense and defense. At one point Coach Bryant even tried to make a center out of me, but it didn't take long to figure out that I couldn't play there.

"So I played guard, tackle and tight end as players quit and left Junction. I started our first game that year as a halfback and cornerback, and after the first game against Texas Tech [a 41-9 loss] Coach figured out that wasn't my position either."

Pardee then made what now seems like an unheard-of move—from cornerback to end.

"But by the last four games of the season or so, one of our fullbacks and linebackers got hurt, and that's where I played the rest of my time," he said.

The Aggies finished 1-9 in Bryant's first season in 1954, and no one figured this seemingly motley crew would ever earn a conference championship in only two more seasons—no one but the players and coaches.

"I think I learned more from that first season than any year in my life," Pardee said. "You learned what being a part of a team meant, and to keep the faith, even when you're not winning. We weren't good enough then. But we stuck together and learned to count on each other, and we didn't start pointing fingers and doing all of the things that guarantee you're going to be a loser. Learning all of that was one of the most valuable experiences in my life."

THE SCENE

Good thing those two Texas students who clumsily tried setting the 1956 Aggie Bonfire to a premature blaze with a homemade bomb were caught by A&M College officials, and not ol' "one-armed" Murray Trimble, as he was known in the papers.

"Murray played offensive guard and defensive tackle for us," said Jack Pardee, himself a standout fullback and linebacker on Paul "Bear" Bryant's first and only Southwest Conference champions in 1956. "Murray was from Alabama, and his family was in the logging business and had bulldozers and such. Murray lost his left arm—it was a stub, just below the elbow—in a logging accident when he was a kid. He was one tough dude, let me tell you.

"He was really bulked up with these big ol' arms, and he'd use that stub as a weapon. He'd make a tackle and get players down on the ground and get that stub inside their headgear and mash their eyes and nose. But what referee was going to penalize a one-armed guy?"

The NCAA had penalized the heavily armed Aggies that year, for sure, for recruiting violations under Bryant. That meant no bowl for Texas A&M in '56, at least in the historical sense. Instead, the Aggies had renamed their annual showdown with rival Texas the "Turkey Bowl," because it was their final game of the season.

But the contest certainly hadn't lost its meaning to the 8-0-1 Aggies, considering they had never won at Memorial Stadium, which opened in 1924. The Aggies had entered Austin as heavy favorites in 1936, '38 and '40, only to lose to the swollen underdogs. Former coach Homer Norton, the only man to lead A&M to a national championship, had even carried a mighty special invitation in his pocket during the '40 contest.

It was a bid to play in the Rose Bowl for the national championship, but UT answered the challenge and won 7-0 to end A&M's 19-game winning streak in a defeat some Old Aggies still find hard to talk about. Such losses—and a 14-14 tie in 1948—in Austin had even earned the designation of a "Memorial Stadium Jinx" among the A&M faithful.

"We were certainly aware that A&M had never won a game there—and we wanted to do something about it," Pardee said. "Now, Coach Bryant wasn't one to bring it up and play the mental game with us. He was more interested in what we were going to do, as opposed to any so-called jinxes."

In an atypical move for the fervent coach, Bryant had given his players a day off on both the Saturday and Sunday prior to the Thanksgiving game, so they could spend it with their families. Upon their return he'd immediately regretted his rash act of charity.

"We were flubbing signals and counts," Bryant growled following the Aggies' Monday practice. "We didn't have any poise, and in general, we didn't look good at all. It was probably a mistake to give 'em that time off."

At least the Aggie Bonfire went off without a hitch the following night at Duncan Drill Field, despite the best efforts of the two roguish Texas students, whom guards immediately caught while they were trying to ignite the bomb on the Bonfire in the hours before the event.

Instead, the Bonfire burned on time, lustily and at attention for two hours before collapsing, setting a new record as simultaneous yells of, "Poor T-sips! Poor T-sips!" roared through the night—along with a few catcalls for the NCAA, which had placed the Aggies on probation.

With the Korean War over and a humming economy, times were good for everyone, it seemed, but Texas, which was 1-8 and featured a lame-duck coach in Ed Price. The former Longhorns standout athlete had tendered his resignation on Halloween Day, effective at season's end. But A&M, despite its supposed advantage, still had to shake that Memorial Stadium jinx.

*   *   *   *   *

Despite the supposed hex, most Aggies were thinking big that year, much like German scientist Eugen Saenger, who in late November 1956 claimed to international delegates attending a German Society for Space Research convention that "publicly accessible interplanetary trips" likely would be common by the year 2000. Saenger apparently forgot to add, "on the big screen."

Meanwhile across America and in Aggieland and Austin, most everyone liked Ike—popular President Dwight Eisenhower—and everyone loved Elvis Presley. Everyone, that is, but Louis Balint. On the same day the Aggies played the Longhorns in Austin, Balint spent a night in a Toledo, Ohio, jail, for taking a swing at Elvis in a bar.

Balint argued that a Presley crony had paid him $200 to fake the fight, claiming it would "make good publicity." About the same time the Aggies, in a bid for their own bit of good publicity and behind a handsome fullback and return man named Jack Pardee, "shook up" the Longhorns—and wiped out a jinx.

THE SETTING

People who say Aggies aren't ahead of their time weren't on hand late on Thanksgiving Day, 1956, in Memorial Stadium. That's when jubilant A&M players tossed Bear Bryant and his staff, fully clothed, into the locker-room showers—an early version of the Gatorade bath—and delirious Aggie fans tried tearing down UT's goalposts (with no luck).

"That wasn't common back then," Jack Pardee said of the latter, "not at all."

A&M folks, it seemed, just knew how to have a good time—even at an all-male school where joining the Corps of Cadets then wasn't optional. Pardee and his teammates got a friendly reminder of as much on their way to Austin that Thanksgiving, as they passed through towns like Caldwell and Dime Box on their way to a little history.

"The squadrons, the companies you belonged to in the Corps of Cadets, were like a fraternity," Pardee said. "We'd head out to the VFW Hall on weekends, and there were two or three different dance halls around where we'd go out and have a beer or two and get a little crazy, and sometimes get in fights.

"All of those little towns like Dime Box had a dance hall and would have weekend dances. In a lot of ways, that hasn't changed much."

Neither had A&M's luck against Texas going into that '56 game, especially in Austin where the Aggies hadn't won since 1922—before Memorial Stadium had even opened. In 1955 A&M expected to whip the Longhorns in College Station to win their first SWC championship since 1941, but UT had prevailed 21-6.

Now, Texas was 1-8 and already searching for a coach to replace Ed

Price, who'd won a couple of conference championships in 1952 and '53, but had done little since.

"They haven't been impressive in most of their games," A&M assistant Willie Zapalac warned before the game, "but they weren't impressive last year and they beat us."

Texas had gained much of its success in the early 1950s with a Split-T arsenal that zeroed in on the ground game. But now the Longhorns featured a passing attack behind quarterback Joe Clements, whose aerial exploits a year earlier had even outdone the first-year showings of the likes of conference legends Sammy Baugh and Bobby Layne.

"Texas's cupboard wasn't completely bare, even if their record wasn't very good," Pardee said. "We knew we were favored, but we also knew we never had an easy time with those guys."

That held to form on a beautiful day in Austin before 61,000 fans, although the Aggies scored more points in a 34-21 victory than they ever had against the Longhorns. Meanwhile, Bear Bryant wound up soaking wet and smiling. But the UT goalposts stayed firmly rooted at Memorial Stadium despite some Corps members' best efforts.

THE GAME OF MY LIFE
By Jack Pardee

We were picked to win big, but only led 20-14 at halftime. I trotted onto the field in the second half still a little bit stiff from sitting in the locker room, and I really wasn't completely warmed up yet when I received the kickoff. I'll say this: I really wasn't ready to return it 100 yards, or I probably would've.

The kick to start the second half was relatively short, and it hit the ground in front of me. I had to jump up and field it around the goal line or it was going to bounce over my head. The way the ball bounced may have shifted the coverage, but the timing on the thing—which happens on all good kick returns—was perfect as I snared the ball and received some super blocks.

Once I got through that first line, there wasn't anyone there but Joe Clements, who served as their safety on the kickoff team, and he had a good angle on me and stopped me short of the goal line after an 85-yard return.

It was the longest run I'd had in college, and, truthfully, I didn't get winded, I just tightened up. This was an era before specialty players, so you didn't come off the field. Besides playing linebacker and fullback,

Jack Pardee led the Aggies to their first Southwest Conference title in 15 years in 1956, as he rushed for 463 yards and five touchdowns while intercepting three passes defensively. He's shown here standing next to Coach Paul Bryant following A&M's win at Texas in '56. *Aggieland Yearbook*

I could field kicks, so I returned them. That was the biggest criteria for determining your return men: who could catch 'em and run with 'em.

I was pretty disgusted with myself for not scoring on that kickoff return, and I didn't get many calls to carry the ball as our fullback, but I was hoping for another chance. Roddy Osborne was our quarterback, and we ran the Split T option, that and a belly series where the quarterback rode the fullback coming through and then optioned later on.

The only way I was going to get that ball was to take it away from Osborne when he was riding me, and so on a play following the 85-yard kick return I took the ball when he shoved it in my belly, and I didn't turn loose. I wanted to score, and we did, on an eight-yard blast up the middle.

GAME RESULTS

J ack Pardee's 85-yard return and eight-yard bull rush for a touchdown weren't his lone highlights on a brisk winter day in the Capital City. He also returned another kick 58 yards later in the first half. Pardee had felt extra pressure against Texas, as he'd served as A&M's captain during that week of preparation.

"There were 10 seniors that year, and we had 10 games," Pardee said. "Before the season started we drew 10 numbers out of a hat, and mine was No. 10. If you won that week, then you got the game ball. As captain, you had to make sure that everyone wasn't slacking off or goofing off and preparing the right way. Coaches can only do so much, and that's why they talk so much about senior leadership. Many times you can accomplish more with peer pressure than you can authority."

Future Heisman Trophy running back John David Crow must have listened. He scored A&M's first touchdown on a 28-yard sprint in the first quarter, and the Aggies never looked back. On that play Aggies everywhere—including watching back home in College Station on Houston's KPRC or Temple's KCEN—celebrated A&M's first touchdown ever in the south end zone of Memorial Stadium.

That erased another supposed jinx en route to the 13-point win. For Texas center Robert E. Lee, A&M's first win at Memorial cut to the bone.

"We all knew the tradition couldn't go on forever," Lee groaned, already realizing the razzing he'd take from family members over Thanksgiving turkey, "but why did it have to be us?"

The Longhorns' loss also signified the first time in history that UT failed to win a conference game, and also marked their worst season (1-9) in history. High above the playing field, the retiring D. X. Bible shook his head at his final football game as UT athletics director. For Bible, the loss was bittersweet, because of his love for A&M.

He'd coached the Aggies from 1917-28, winning six Southwest Conference titles along the way, before moving on to Nebraska and then Texas. He'd lost his first two games at Memorial Stadium as Aggies coach before taking the Cornhuskers job, so he knew all about the supposed jinx.

But now a new man ruled the day in College Station and the state, a man named Paul "Bear" Bryant. A man dripping wet and smiling profusely following his first—and what turned out to be only—win over Texas as A&M's coach.

"My limited vocabulary prevents me from telling you how proud I am of you," Bryant told his team in the victorious locker room. "It's a long way from Junction."

As a voice piped up from the back, "It sure is!" a roar emitted from the gang that had just won the program's first league title since the beginning of World War II.

"It was all hardship and no rewards and no victories coming out of Junction," Pardee explained of that galvanizing moment in the locker room, "and everything good was happening then."

Bryant, ever the leader of men, hushed his charges one last time before setting them loose for more victory celebration.

"Just act like champions," Bryant said, always in control. "We'll see you next week."

Maybe ol' "one-armed" Murray Trimble best summed up the Aggies' feelings in the locker room following their first win in Austin in 34 years.

"Great, feels great," he said, while offering and accepting congratulations from his teammates. "Texas? Good bunch of boys, but not rough enough. They weren't raised right."

WHAT BECAME OF JACK PARDEE?

Back in 1954 Jack Pardee, who had just turned 19, couldn't quite figure out why his new coach, Paul Bryant, talked endlessly about the fourth quarter. It made much more sense decades later.

"Coach Bryant compared the fourth quarter to getting ready for life," Pardee said. "He'd say, 'What are going to do when you're 35 years old, you get your pink slip at work, you go home, your kids are hungry and your wife has run off with the shoe salesman? That's the fourth quarter. Are you going to quit then— is it going to be too tough for you—or can people count on you?'

"I had a hard time associating what he meant, but by the time I was 35 all of those things had happened to me—except for my wife running off with a shoe salesman. One of the great things that came out of the Junction days was the belief that everyone had in each other.

"Out of that group of 10 seniors, all 10 wives we have are still the first. Isn't that amazing?"

Pardee met Phyllis, his wife since 1957, on a blind date while he was a senior at A&M and she was at TCU.

"Jack is a generous and loving husband," Phyllis Pardee said. "I just thank the Lord every day that I have him, because my husband has taught me so many things about life and being a good Christian. He's at peace all of the time, and I believe he was born that way."

The couple had five children: Steven, Judee, Anne, Susan and Ted, and 12 grandchildren. After graduation Pardee set sail on a highly successful NFL career with the Rams and Redskins, but much like his father, he dealt with an affliction early in his life. But it was cancer, not arthritis.

"I was 28 years old and had just finished an All-Pro season and my career was going well, and suddenly I was confronted with this," said Pardee, who checked out a mole on his arm after reading a story by famed Houston sports writer Mickey Herskowitz in 1964.

Herskowitz had told of how Houston Astros pitcher Jim Umbricht had lost the zip on his fastball and doctors had discovered cancer when checking out a hurt groin.

"They traced it to a black mole on his foot, and in describing that, gosh, it sounded just like a deal I had, except mine was on my arm," Pardee said. "And it turned out to be cancer."

While doctors caught Pardee's cancer in time (Umbricht had died from the affliction), the disease brought about much introspection on his part.

"Suddenly there were a lot more important things in life than making a little money or playing football or whatever," he said. "I was always trying to get a better cave to live in and all of the things you work for, and then I didn't even know how much longer I had to live. That's also when I decided I wanted to be a coach."

But Pardee still had plenty of ball left in him, and he played another seven seasons, even winning NFC Defensive Player of the Year honors in 1972 with Washington, at age 36. The Redskins and their famed "Over-the-Hill Gang" lost to Miami that season in the Super Bowl, and Pardee retired to enter coaching full-time. But President Richard Nixon, who invited the Redskins to the White House on occasion, urged Pardee to play another year or two.

"You're too young," Nixon insisted. "You don't need to be retiring yet."

"But my body said yes, I did," Pardee said, smiling.

Pardee spent 11 years in the NFL as a head coach with the Bears, Redskins and Oilers, compiling an 87-77 record and producing five playoff teams. He last coached in the league in 1994 and now describes himself as a "full-time rancher" on his 615 acres near Gause, Texas, not too far northwest of Bryan-College Station.

"I didn't quit working," Pardee said, grinning. "I just quit getting paid."

Pardee realized many of his old teammates still like to get together on the golf course, but he never was much for the sport.

"This is my golf course," he said of his beautiful ranch. "This is my country club."

And for a brilliant, brisk afternoon in 1956 in Austin, Jack Pardee absolutely owned 85 yards of prime Texas turf on a dazzling kick return, as Texas A&M busted the reputed Memorial Stadium Jinx.

Jack Pardee succumbed to cancer on April 1, 2013, at the age of 76.

CHAPTER 5

JOHN DAVID CROW

Name: John David Crow
Born: July 8, 1935 in Marion, La.
Hometown: Springhill, La.
Current Residence: College Station, Texas
Occupation: Retired from the NFL, A&M athletics administration
Position: Running Back
Height: 6'2"
Playing Weight: 215 pounds
Years lettered: 1955-57
Accomplishments: Paul Bryant's lone Heisman Trophy winner; All-American in 1957, two-time All-Conference (1956-57); member of the National Football Foundation and Texas Sports Halls of Fame; rushed for 562 yards as a senior to go with five interceptions; first-round pick of the Chicago Cardinals in 1958; four-time Pro Bowler with the Cardinals; led the NFL with a 5.9 yards per rush average in 1960; served as Texas A&M's associate athletics director from 1983-89 and as A&M's athletics director from 1989-93.
Nickname: Ol' Crow
The Game: Texas A&M at Arkansas, Nov. 2, 1957

John David Crow. *Photo courtesy of Texas A&M Athletic Media Relations*

THE LIFE OF YOUNG JOHN DAVID CROW

John David Crow, who earned Texas A&M's lone Heisman Trophy primarily because of a tough, barreling running style, fought hard for ground from the first moment he tried gasping for breath on July 8, 1935.

"When I was born my navel cord was wrapped around my head, and it damaged a nerve," says Crow, who grew up in North Louisiana near the Arkansas border. "I've never been able to move the left side of my face, except for the top of my eyelid."

John David's mother, Velma, may have coddled him a bit because of the birth problems she had with the third of her four children, but he was still the son of Harry Crow—a tough man who'd weathered and even bettered the family's lot during the Great Depression.

"My father had 11 brothers and sisters and they grew up in Bastrop, in Northeast Louisiana, and I don't know whether any of the children graduated from high school or not," Crow says. "I know that he didn't. He was about 20 years old when the Depression hit, and he and my mother had a pretty tough road until he got a job with International Paper Company, right after I was born.

"His first job at the paper mill was pitching pulp wood out of box cars, and 44 years later he retired as superintendent of the wood yard. He was hardworking and a tough disciplinarian who didn't spare the belt, and my mother didn't spare the switches. We came up in a household where it was, 'no, ma'am,' and 'yes, sir.' It was understood among the children that, No. 1, hard work solves most every problem that you have, and, No. 2, finish everything you start. You also knew that if you'd done something wrong, you'd be punished."

Following the lead of his older brother Raymond—who played college football at nearby Magnolia A&M, just across the state line in Arkansas— John David began punishing Springhill High's opposition every Friday night on the gridiron, thus earning the attention of Division I schools.

Raymond had played at Magnolia (which later became Southern State) for Coach Elmer Smith, a likeable sort who'd accepted an assistant's slot with Texas A&M newcomer Paul Bryant in 1954. That's how John David wound up as The Bear's most prized recruit in Bryant's four seasons in Aggieland.

"I didn't really know anything about A&M, and I knew even less about Coach Bryant," Crow says. "We had one television station out of Shreveport, and we all had antennas sticking out of the top of our houses as high as you could get them, for better reception. I didn't know much about any colleges, except for Magnolia A&M."

After Smith and Bryant had persuaded the broad-shouldered, swivel-hipped back to College Station, John David had one last item of business to take care of in Springhill: marrying his high school sweetheart, Carolyn Gilliam.

"She was Miss Lumberjack, the beauty queen of Springhill High," Crow says, smiling. "And to me, she's still Miss Lumberjack."

Aggies, too, have Carolyn—whom John David married on July 2, 1954—as much as Elmer Smith to thank for getting the eventual Heisman Trophy winner to College Station. Had Crow stayed single, he likely would've attended Arkansas and stared across the sidelines at Bryant from 1955-57.

"I grew up right on the Arkansas state line, and if they'd have accepted married players [by offering a 'married scholarship'—in other words, help provide for off-campus housing] I'd probably have gone to the University of Arkansas, for sure," Crow says. "But the way everything turned out, there couldn't have been a better place for me to go than Texas A&M."

THE SCENE

Coach Paul "Bear" Bryant possessed an extremely long memory— one that extended even past prior victories against teams, to losses or ties to that same opponent. John David Crow found out as much at practice in November 1957, on the day before the top-ranked Aggies' game at Arkansas, when Bryant reprimanded the senior in front of the team for laughing on a bus ride over to Fayetteville.

Back in 1955.

"We'd gone to Arkansas that year, when I was a sophomore, and played them to a tie," Crow says. "We'd stayed in Bentonville [Ark.] the night before the game, and then took a bus over to Fayetteville. And on that bus ride, I laughed at some little joke, and I'll never forget the look I got from Coach Bryant. He slowly turned around and just stared at me, and my first thought was, 'My gosh, he's going to kill me!' But that incident was never brought up, and later that day the game wound up 7-7."

The Razorbacks visited Kyle Field the next year, and A&M promptly whipped Arkansas 27-0 en route to the Aggies' first Southwest Conference title in 15 years. Two years following the tie at Arkansas and after the Friday practice before another game in Fayetteville, the Aggies took a knee in the grass around Bryant for his customary talk. That's when the intimidating coach caught the attention of Crow, the best player on a No. 1 team that had held four opponents scoreless in dashing to a 6-0 record.

"You owe us a game," Bryant said, in slow, measured tones while never removing a stern gaze from the startled Crow. "You were having so much fun on the trip the last time we came up here that you forgot to play."

"It was the first time it had ever been mentioned," Crow says, smiling a bit in disbelief about that Nov. 1, 1957 afternoon. "And it was two years after the fact."

*   *   *   *   *

About the same moment half a world away, the Russians were preparing to launch a little dog named "Laika" 1,056 miles into space aboard Sputnik II—as earth's first living creature to orbit the planet. Had the pup (a sacrificial lamb, as it turns out) scooted over in her satellite doghouse, Crow might have hopped in if afforded the opportunity— anything to escape Bryant's glare.

"Of course, everybody looked at me, wondering how'd I react," Crow says of Bryant regurgitating a two-year-old, apparently untimely, giggle. "I didn't do anything—I just tried to play as hard as I could the next day."

The gruff coach, an Arkansas native, may not have fully realized it when he told Crow "you owe us a game" in 1957, but the A&M-Arkansas contest loomed every bit as large to Crow, because he'd almost played for the Razorbacks.

Regardless, Bryant's premeditated strike on the conscientious youngster apparently paid dividends, as the headline two days later in the Bryan-College Station paper trumpeted, "John Crow Plays Like All-American." Of course, that's how the Springhill, La., native had played most of his career at Texas A&M, all laughing matters aside.

THE SETTING

B y late 1957 the archrival Russians had jetted in front of the USA in the space race through the launch of the Sputnik satellites, prompting Americans to fear the Soviet Union planned to soon land on the moon, and claim it by stamping a big red star on its surface.

Lyndon Johnson, then the United States Senate majority leader, told a Houston gathering in December '57 that it was time for the American space program to move into "high gear."

"Rockets to the moon are just over the horizon. Space ships are only a few years away, and most of us will live to see them," Johnson said. (The United States won the race to the moon in 1969.)

Space race aside, many Aggies, meanwhile, simply hoped to see Texas A&M finally vie for another national championship, an idea that—before Bryant's arrival in 1954—seemed about as feasible as jumping over the moon. But halfway through the 1957 season the undefeated (and unsmiling, based on Bryant's admonition) Aggies owned the Associated Press poll pole position as they rolled into Fayetteville on Nov. 2.

A&M, in fact, hadn't lost in 16 contests, as the Aggies tied Houston 14-14 in 1956, and finished that probation-laced season 9-0-1. The vaunted Aggies defense, led by end Bobby Marks and All-American tackle Charles Krueger, had only allowed three touchdowns in its six games so far in 1957, which had propelled A&M into the top spot in the AP slot. Rare air, indeed, for a program that hadn't even finished in the Top 25 from 1942-54.

"Coach Bryant is The Man who came to A&M to produce winning football teams," wrote Charles Carder of the *Bryan-College Station Eagle*, "and has lived up to every detail of the plan."

Meanwhile, Arkansas, which had just whipped sixth-ranked Ole

Miss but also had lost to Texas the week prior, was 2-1 in SWC play and anticipating a record crowd of 31,000 to greet the Aggies as part of its Homecoming festivities.

"The Aggies have overwhelmed just about everyone on their schedule, and you certainly can't improve on that," Arkansas coach Jack Mitchell said in the days before the A&M game. "I didn't think any team in the country could hold TCU and Baylor scoreless."

Part of A&M's toughness, at least, was credited to a small patch of scarred earth—soberly enclosed by a wooden fence—adjacent to Kyle Field that Bryant had dubbed the "challenge circle." Here, a player in a white (second-team) jersey could challenge a player in a maroon (first-team) jersey for his position, and on down the line among the depth chart. As part of the drill and with the entire squad watching, the challenger had to win four of six blocking battles with the first-teamer to earn a change of jersey.

"It didn't happen very often, but the opportunity was there for players, and you knew you could try it if you liked," Crow says. "But somehow or another, it seemed the best player wound up getting that maroon jersey back before the game."

While the "challenge circle" got plenty of notoriety for supposedly helping make the Aggies tough, really, it was simply Bryant's grueling practices that did the trick. Crow, who as a freshman didn't make the infamous Junction journey, had his own brush with mortality thanks to Bryant's exhausting drills. It was August 1956, on a day hot enough to boil chili at parched Kyle Field.

"That's the closest I've come to leaving this world," Crow says. "We'd gone through a normal, long, hard practice and hadn't done too well, but there were people in the stands because it was a scrimmage, and so Coach Bryant dismissed us so the fans would leave.

"So we went into the locker room and I was sitting in a metal chair in the shower and letting water run over me when a manager came up.

"'Put your gear back on,' he said, as I looked up in disbelief.

"'The Man said put 'em back on,' he repeated. So we all got dressed and went back out there and Coach Bryant told us to take a knee, but I didn't kneel because I didn't think I could get up if I did.

"And I'd [dizzily] look at Coach Bryant, and then at that tunnel on the north end of Kyle, and then back at him, and then at that tunnel … and I didn't hear a thing, but I figured he was chewing us up for not playing well. Then he put a ball on the 40-yard line and said, 'OK, offense! We're going to take this damn ball down and score!'

"I remember thinking, 'Hell, you might kill me, but you ain't going to make me quit, by God.' We scored on that drive and turned around to start back the other way, and I don't remember anything after that."

Crow collapsed near the north end zone. When he came to three hours later, the first face he saw wasn't God's—but the mug of a man whom any Texas A&M player of that era considered a mighty decent replica: Coach Bryant.

"I woke up in the infirmary and the first thing I saw was Coach Bryant at the foot of my bed—Carolyn was sitting next to me—and he was extremely concerned," Crow says.

"John David," said a confounded Bryant, who called the rest of his players by their last names, "why didn't you tell me you were tired?"

The next day before practice Bryant told the players that if they felt dizzy to take a knee and rest.

"Nobody really believed that was OK," Crow says, laughing. "Nobody ever did it, anyway."

Years later at a 1982 reunion, Bryant admitted that Crow's collapse scared the Bear out of him.

"I should have known that John David would never complain," Bryant said.

"He just didn't have any quit in him."

Especially with so much on the line, as it was that fair day in Fayetteville, when Texas A&M lived up to its top ranking by squeaking past Arkansas 7-6. Thanks, also, in part to a missed field goal (wide left) from the 12-yard line in the second quarter by Arkansas kicker Freddy Akers, the same Fred Akers who later coached 10 years at the University of Texas.

THE GAME OF MY LIFE
By John David Crow

In the 1955 game in Fayetteville we'd tied the Razorbacks, and we knew that you'd better take your lunch when playing Arkansas there—because you were going to be in for a battle. Two years later we trailed for the first time all year, when Arkansas scored in the first quarter on a one-yard quarterback sneak.

We fought back in the second quarter when I scored on a 12-yard sweep, and the extra point of our kicker, Loyd Taylor, meant the difference in the game in a scoreless second half. We'd had a chance to pad our lead in the fourth quarter on a play we could all laugh about later—because we'd won.

In the huddle and with us deep in Arkansas territory and leading 7-6, our quarterback, Roddy Osborne, called for a pass play on a rollout, and we all just looked at him.

"Doggone, I'm not gonna throw the thing," Osborne said of protecting our one-point lead. "I just want to take up some more time."

John David Crow, who later became Texas A&M athletic director, earned the school's only Heisman Trophy in 1957, when he rushed for 562 yards on 129 carries. *Photo courtesy of Texas A&M Athletic Media Relations*

So on the presumably fake pass play I ran out into the flat and started waving my hands like crazy, to help fool the defense because it looked like I was wide open. And, lo and behold, Osborne threw the cotton-picking thing, and Razorbacks defender Don Horton came across and intercepted it. I turned and gave chase, as did Roddy, who wound up catching him. Horton was a helluva lot faster than Roddy and just about anybody on our team. The saying goes amongst us that Horton was just running for a touchdown, and Osborne was running for his life, because Coach Bryant would have killed him.

Horton returned the ball 64 yards, and Arkansas threatened to score again when I was fortunate enough to make the play that sticks out most in my entire college career, when I was playing defensive back. Their quarterback, George Walker, threw a pass that I intercepted on the goal line with less than a minute remaining in the game. It was a shock that Arkansas threw the ball, because we felt like they had a chance to kick a field goal for the win. Of course, they'd already missed a field goal in the second quarter.

By game's end we were still ranked No. 1 and still had a chance to win the national championship. And, yes, we could laugh all we wanted in the locker room afterward.

GAME RESULTS

Paul Bryant was all grins after Texas A&M pushed its record to 7-0 and solidified its top ranking with its 7-6 victory at Arkansas. Asked the main reason for his team's win, Bryant nodded and pointed at No. 44.

"The good Lord, a group of fine boys and Ol' Crow," Bryant said. "You don't have to be a Phi Beta Kappa to see that Crow was all over the place. The biggest play of the game was his interception of Walker's pass there at the end."

So, too, were the good times at A&M under Bryant nearing an end, as a story of his impending departure for his alma mater Alabama—where he heard "mama calling"—was reported on the day before A&M's game at Rice on Nov. 16.

Bryant tersely denied the reports from his perch in Houston's Shamrock Hilton hotel on that Friday, that he'd bow out of his $15,000-a-year job at A&M at season's end, and dash east.

The top-ranked Aggies, stunned by the strong rumors, fell to Rice 7-6 and Texas 9-7 (in Darrell Royal's first year in Austin) before closing out the season with a 3-0 loss in the Gator Bowl to Tennessee.

"I'd like to say Coach Bryant's leaving was the reason we went from being the No. 1 team in the nation to third in the conference," Crow says, "but those were all good teams that beat us, as well."

Bryant, too, had pitched Crow for the Hesman Trophy, admonishing voters with the idea that they ought "to do away with the thing" if they didn't vote for Ol' Crow. Sure enough, Crow won the coveted trophy with 1,183 points, nearly doubling that of runner-up Alex Karras, a tackle from Iowa.

Meanwhile following the season, a retrospective Bryant departed Texas A&M for Alabama, where he'd win an amazing five national championships as the legendary Crimson Tide coach.

"It has been one of my great privileges to have had the honor of being an Aggie for the past four years, and sharing in the great traditions of Aggieland," Bryant said in his departing words. "I shall always cherish the many memories of my association with the players, and they will forever hold a special place in my heart."

Including, of course, one tough-as-pulp-wood Louisiana boy named

John David Crow, the only player ever to win the Heisman Trophy under Paul "Bear" Bryant.

WHAT BECAME OF JOHN DAVID CROW?

The tear in his father's eye meant more to John David Crow than any fancy New York ceremony.

"I was home from school for the holidays when I found out I'd won the Heisman, and Mother said we needed to go tell Daddy," Crow says. "And so we went to the paper mill, and he got a little aggravated when he first saw us, because he didn't know why we were there. But when we told him that I'd won the Heisman, that was the first time I'd ever seen any emotion from him, and that meant as much to me as anything. People talk about Coach Bryant being a Bear—a tough man—but, shoot, he wasn't any tougher than my Dad.

"Coach Bryant could have kicked me in the butt a lot of times and he wouldn't have caught up to my Dad. But, let me tell you, I appreciate my upbringing, and it made me so proud at that moment to make my father and mother proud."

Crow figures his Heisman acceptance speech to be the shortest on record.

"I looked up there and saw that cluster of microphones, with ABC and CBS and all of those, but the one that really caught my eye was called Movietone News," Crow says. "I'd seen that in the theater in Springhill, and it hit me that I'd be watched throughout all of the movie houses, including back home. I hadn't prepared for the speech, so I turned to the Downtown Athletic Club president, who was sitting next to me, and asked him what I should say."

"John," George Hall told him, "get up there, say what you've got to say, don't forget to say thank you, and sit down."

So Crow thanked his teammates, his wife and his parents, and quickly sat back down. Four decades later, he's still thanking his wife for nearly 50 years of wonderful marriage.

"Whatever credit I get for doing anything, she deserves a lot more than I do," Crow says. "She's been the stabilizer for our family and has been very, very good for me."

John and Carolyn had three children, John David Jr., Annalisa and Jeannie. The family suffered a heartbreaking loss when John Jr. died in a car accident on Sept. 10, 1994.

"I pray for every person who's lost a child," Crow says. "Because we know how hard it is."

*   *   *   *   *

Crow, a first-round draft pick of the Chicago Cardinals in 1957, led the NFL with a 5.9-yard per rush average in 1960. He played 11 seasons in the league before entering coaching and private business (he served as Northeast Louisiana University's athletics director and head coach from 1975-80). In 1983 Crow became associate athletics director at his alma mater, Texas A&M. Six years later, he succeeded Jackie Sherrill as A&M athletics director, a position Crow served in for four years before accepting a fund-raiser role with the university.

"Coming back to A&M and eventually serving as athletics director … that's the ultimate for any athlete who played at a college," says Crow, who retired from the university in June 2001. "Hopefully I'll always be a part of Texas A&M. I've been fortunate to have never really had to divorce myself from football."

Paul Bryant, of course, would expect nothing less of his lone Heisman Trophy winner.

"John David," the revered coach said after Crow won All-America honors in 1957, "has only a burning desire to win."

CHAPTER 6

EDD HARGETT

Name: Edward Eugene Hargett
Born: June 26, 1947
Hometown: Linden, Texas
Current Residence: Crockett, Texas
Occupation: Manager of an electrical co-op
Position: Quarterback
Height: 6'
Playing Weight: 185 pounds
Years Lettered: 1966-68
Accomplishments: Two-time All-Conference (1967 and '68); all-time school leader in total offensive yards in a game (418 against SMU in 1968); 16th-round draft pick of the New Orleans Saints in 1969; completed 205 of 437 passes over four-year NFL career.
The Game: Texas A&M at Texas Tech, Oct. 14, 1967

THE LIFE OF YOUNG EDD HARGETT

Young Edd Hargett had three older siblings—all boys—who grew into college football players, but they rarely messed with li'l brother. Mama wouldn't let 'em.

Edd Hargett. *Photo courtesy of Texas A&M Athletic Media Relations*

"I was the baby and supposed to be mama's little girl, so she wouldn't let them beat me around too much," Hargett says, laughing. "Besides, they were quite a bit older, so they didn't hardly fool with me."

His fledgling football skills sharpened by the heavy influence of his athletic siblings, young Edd excelled early on the fields of the deep Northeast Texas town of Linden—near the Arkansas and Louisiana borders.

"If you could walk and chew gum in Linden," Hargett says of the same small hometown in which musician Don Henley grew up, "you played football."

Henley, who graduated in 1965 in the same class as Hargett, played in the school band at the football games, and Henley's own band, The Four Speeds, played around Northeast Texas.

And while the talented musician later made a career of singing with The Eagles, Hargett soared with the eagles as the best high school quarterback in those parts in the mid-1960s. And by his senior year, the Southwest Conference's Arkansas—to the northeast—and Texas A&M—to the southwest—had come knocking.

Hargett had even wrecked his knee late in his senior year on an inspiring play against the archrival Atlanta Rabbits, but the recruiters didn't back off. Childhood friend Tony McDuffie, now the chief of juvenile justice in Cass County, recalls the night a valiant Edd scored on one leg.

"Edd took the ball around left end, where I was playing, and tore up his knee on the run," McDuffie says. "But instead of going down, he hopped on one foot a good seven or eight yards for a touchdown."

Edd's older brother by four years, George, had played for the Aggies starting in the early 1960s, which wasn't necessarily an enticing thing, since the combined record of George's A&M teams under Jim Myers and then Hank Foldberg was 9-19-2 from 1961-63.

"I'd pretty much made up my mind that I was going to Arkansas," Hargett says.

"The Aggies just hadn't been very good. The recruiting was different then, too. One of Arkansas's assistants, Bill Pace, had become a friend of mine and had come to seven of my high school games my senior year."

Plus, a Longview, Texas, sports writer and devout Razorbacks fan named Van Thomas had pointed Hargett's nose toward Fayetteville. And Little Rock. Or wherever else the Razorbacks happened to be playing that fall of 1964.

"Van would come by and pick me up on Saturday mornings," Hargett says. "And so I watched Arkansas play quite a bit that year, including in the Cotton Bowl against Nebraska [a 10-7 Razorbacks win]."

But everything changed for Hargett when longtime A&M assistant Elmer Smith, who also recruited his brother and had recruited John David Crow to Aggieland in 1954, showed up at his door with a renewed enthusiasm in courting the slingin' quarterback.

"He'd been there before to make his pitch, but it just seemed like he wasn't that enthused about it—that he was just doing his job," Hargett says. "But on this visit, you could see that he was excited about Gene Stallings taking over from Foldberg—and not long after that Coach Stallings showed up to recruit me."

And that was enough to convince a grounded, passing quarterback from Linden, Texas, to pack his bags and light out for Aggieland—in the exact opposite direction of Fayetteville, Ark.

THE SCENE

Billy Hobbs earned All-America honors in both 1967 and 1968 as one tough son-of-a-gun linebacker for the Aggies. A few Texas Tech fans startlingly found out from whom he inherited his mettle on a mid-October day in Lubbock, in a breakthrough game for Texas A&M under Coach Gene Stallings.

"Hobbs's mother and brothers were there in the crowd and some Texas Tech fans were sitting right behind her," says Edd Hargett, a record-setting A&M quarterback from 1966-68. "And they were carrying on and ragging the Aggies the entire game. Afterward, Billy's brothers lost their mother in the crowd while heading for the exits. They turned around, searching for her, and there she was—this little ol' woman pointing her finger right in some guy's chest, just lettin' him have it."

The Aggies, and little Mrs. Hobbs, finally had something to pound their chests about—in a near lost season that spun 180 degrees on a desperation drive just minutes before Billy's mom shared her feelings with a stunned Red Raider.

"We started that season 0-4," Hargett says, smiling a bit at the fateful turn of events that began on a sweet evening in West Texas. "But we really believed we should have been 3-1."

That wasn't just wishful thinking on the part of the '67 Aggies, who lost three of their first four contests by a combined eight points. A&M had struggled in its first two seasons under its former all-conference end in Stallings, compiling 3-7 and 4-5-1 records in 1965 and '66, respectively.

The rugged coach, in searching for something to spark his team—or possibly just to appease the press—claimed that he was going to change the basic principles of the A&M passing game following the 0-4 start.

A&M hadn't won a Southwest Conference title since Stallings's senior year of 1956 under Paul Bryant, and alumni grumblings were taking root midway through the '67 season.

"I never really did believe in the dropback pass," Stallings said before the Texas Tech game of why the Aggies would abandon the old standby in favor of constant rollouts by Hargett. "When you get caught on a dropback, you really lose eight or 10 yards. Besides, it takes a lot of work to protect the passer.

"On a rollout, we'll be running away from half of the rush, and that should help."

*   *   *   *   *

Elsewhere around the nation in the fall of 1967, thousands of young people were running away from the government's draft for the controversial Vietnam War by burning their draft cards or blocking the paths into draft induction centers.

That type of rebellion hardly was fathomed on the conservative and militarily-inclined Texas A&M campus of about 11,500 students behind university president and World War II hero James Earl Rudder.

"At Texas A&M in 1967 there wasn't any unrest," Hargett says, "because General Rudder didn't allow any unrest."

On a couple of fronts, however, Rudder served as a catalyst for change at Texas A&M—in terms of switching the name of the budding place (from Agricultural and Mechanical College of Texas to Texas A&M University) and allowing women into the classroom on a full-time basis. The former took place in 1963, to a low rumble. The latter occurred in 1964, to an audible roar from some tradition-entrenched alumni and students.

"Having been a football coach before, Earl knew the Aggies' football coach was probably having trouble recruiting because so many of the football players wanted to go where the girls were," says Rudder's widow, Margaret Rudder, of why her husband suddenly supported such a drastic change on campus.

A *Bryan-College Station Eagle* article once reported how Rudder, who assumed the university presidency in 1959, dangled an Aggie by his feet out an office window for the mere suggestion that women should attend Texas A&M.

Many Aggies would have liked to do Rudder the same—had they the mettle—for his allowing "Maggies" (a derisive name for women students) into the classroom. Margaret Rudder clearly remembers the day her husband announced the change in policy in G. Rollie White Coliseum.

"They booed him," she says of the very un-Aggie thing to do.

And in the midst of that same night, Margaret Rudder awoke to the startling sounds of some Corps of Cadets members gathered outside the president's home on campus, astonishingly burning World War II hero Earl Rudder in effigy.

"I just saw the flames out there and you could hear the kids," Rudder says of when she peeked out the window. "It liked to have scared me to death."

As for the general?

"He turned over and went back to sleep," Margaret says. "Earl was always pretty calm. After what he went through in World War II [leading a fierce attack on Pointe du Hoc on the beaches of Normandy during the D-Day invasion], that was a small matter."

Turbulent times, indeed—although at A&M for much different reasons than elsewhere, as protests about Vietnam grew legs across the nation, and sometimes violent civil rights movements took hold.

And those citizens over the benchmark age of 30—who'd witnessed the eventual (and overwhelmingly necessary) success of World War II—could only scratch their short hair at this largely unkempt slew of American youth.

"Quite simply," *New York Times* columnist Russell Baker sighed, "we've produced a generation of garrulous young windbags."

One such young man certainly was not Edd Hargett, a clean-cut, married fellow who appreciated his lot in life and certainly respected his elders. Especially that day in Lubbock, when li'l Mrs. Hobbs had the Aggies' backs in one of their three biggest wins of the 1960s—victories that all came in the same extraordinary season.

THE SETTING

Certainly Edd Hargett never pictured this circus scene when Gene Stallings sat in his living room back in Linden and pitched all the good things that were to come under his regime. No, sir, Hargett never imagined this.

"Two of our bigger free spirits were [receivers] Tommy Maxwell and Bob Long, and both were hurt during a practice," Hargett says, in recounting a comical (to everyone but its participants) story from his senior year.

"Bob had a hurt shoulder, and Tommy a pulled leg muscle. And they were just jogging and having a good time over to the side, and Coach Stallings saw them over there and got mad.

"And so he made Tommy roll down the field on his side, while Bob ran circles around him. I think that made Tommy's muscle get well pretty quick."

In fact, when ESPN's *The Junction Boys* movie came out in the fall of 2002 about that grueling 10 days in South Texas for Bear Bryant's 1954 team, Larry Stegent immediately placed a call to his old quarterback.

"When are they going to make a DeWare Fieldhouse movie?" Stegent, an A&M tailback from 1967-69, jokingly asked Hargett. "We went through that stuff for three years."

Says Hargett of Stallings, "He was just a very tough, disciplined coach who thought a lot like Coach Bryant."

*   *   *   *   *

In the late 1960s, a lot of people were trying to think a little differently when it came to college football. At the same time Texas A&M and Texas Tech were gearing up for their 12th clash as Southwest Conference foes on October 14, 1967, noted Dallas sports writer Blackie Sherrod expounded to a gathering in San Antonio about his guesses on the future of college football.

Sherrod said at the meeting that he expected "super" conferences to form in the near future, to combat the growing popularity of professional football. He also said a "national championship playoff" could result from the same efforts to win back college fans. Lastly, Sherrod said, fans' interests were growing away from who'd just win conference each year to who was placing among the top of the national rankings.

"Early on in college football, and even then, it was more about who won conference," Hargett says.

"Of course, you'd have liked to go undefeated and been named national champions, but it wasn't really as big a deal as it is today."

At that point in October 1967, A&M gladly would have accepted its first conference title in 11 seasons—especially following an 0-4 start to what was thought to be a promising year—in a season that regained its varnish with a slick 28-24 win in Lubbock.

And, yes, Hargett consistently rolled out against Tech to find open receivers and scramble—but he'd done that all year anyway. This time, however, one particular dash helped lead to an oasis of a season in an otherwise desert of conference titles—both in the many years before and after for Aggies football.

THE GAME OF MY LIFE
By Edd Hargett

Texas Tech was riding high going into its game against us, because they'd defeated Texas in Austin two weeks earlier. But I'd also bet

Texas Tech's coach, J. T. King, had some awful flashbacks to 1962 on our final drive of the '67 Tech game. In '62, Tech kicked a field goal with 19 seconds remaining to lead 3-0 at Kyle Field. Then the Red Raiders kicked to Danny McIlhany three yards deep into the end zone, and he returned the ball 100 yards, something only four other Aggies have ever done.

Two seconds remained on the clock when A&M beat Tech on that day, but five years later we somehow managed to beat that by scoring with no seconds left. Our final touchdown came on a 59-yard drive, the biggest play occurring on fourth and 15 from the Tech 43-yard line. That's when Bob Long made an incredible, 28-yard catch among a bunch of Tech defenders, giving us a first down with three seconds remaining on the Red Raiders' 15-yard line.

My kids have watched that film clip and said, "Aw, Dad, that was just the luckiest throw." And I said, "Hey, there wasn't but just one little ol' spot you could throw it to, right where Bob was."

But really, it was a great catch. Bob jumped up and pulled the ball out of the air to get us down there within striking distance.

"How he caught the ball," one writer said, "may never be known."

My kids have wondered, as well, why the films of those ol' games are all run in slow motion—or so they seem. Anyway, we got down to the 15-yard line with only three seconds left and trailing 24-21, and Coach Stallings elected to go for it, because a tie just wouldn't have done us much good if we were angling for the Cotton Bowl. We were only 0-1 in league play, but we needed a win that season in a big way.

We capped the drive by scoring on the same play—called Pass 62—that we'd scored our other three touchdowns that day on. And I became the fourth different guy to score. Pass 62 was a fake to the tailback on a counter, and the fullback slipped out in the flat. The tight end came across, and the split end curled. The tailback went through the fake, and if there wasn't anyone to block, he released and got on down the field.

Honestly, I don't know why we'd fake a running play with three seconds left on the 15-yard line, other than it gave us a chance to get a lot of people in that zone and maybe find an opening there. Funny thing, Tech has always said there should have been a penalty called on that play, and my response is that there *was* a penalty called. The Red Raiders were offsides.

Just before our center snapped the ball, I saw their guy jump and the flag go down, so I knew that we had a free play. After the play unfolded on that little semi-roll I'd always do, I could either force a pass or run. I ran. Tech only rushed three people, they weren't really coming upfield, and we had most of our receivers off to the left side. When I looked back to the right, there was only Larry Stegent and one defender over there—the one Tech fans claimed got clipped—and so I sprinted that way.

After I cleared the line of scrimmage it was fairly wide open on that

Edd Hargett, who passed the 1967 Aggies to their first Southwest Conference title since 1956, threw 40 touchdown passes from 1966- 68. *Photo courtesy of Texas A&M Athletic Media Relations*

side of the field, and once I scored I just kept going, right into the locker room, because the final gun had sounded. I waited for the rest of the team to follow, but no one did. Turns out that the guy Stegent blocked, defensive end George Cox, had a knee injury, and it took a while to get him off the field. I watched us finally kick the extra point—why we even had to kick it is still a mystery—from the tunnel.

About the same time, Mrs. Hobbs was giving that ol' boy an earful up in the stands about our 28-24 victory, our first of seven straight wins that season.

GAME RESULTS

The Aggies didn't lose another game that year, including beating rival Texas 10-7 at Kyle Field on Nov. 23, 1967, before a record crowd of 49,200 in what Stallings had dubbed a "wild and woolly" season. Two days before the Thanksgiving Day contest against UT, Stallings wasn't sure his boys had another victory in 'em—and maybe were getting a little fat from five straight wins after the four losses.

"We had a lousy practice on Monday," Stallings growled, sounding every bit the part of Paul Bryant. "It looked like we were getting ready for prom."

"That was a great line," Hargett says. "Just more of his psychology to try and fire us up. That was a year where we had played on Saturday [an 18-3 victory at Rice] and turned around and played four days later against Texas. We didn't have much time to get ready."

If the giddy Aggies truly were acting like they preparing for prom instead of the Longhorns, then Hargett and Long again wound up kings of the dance, as the quarterback hooked up with the receiver on an 80-yard touchdown pass in the fourth quarter.

The decisive play came only 16 seconds after UT had gone in front 7-3 on a two-yard quarterback sneak, and it seemed as if the Longhorns would extend their mortifying 10-game winning streak over the Aggies. The Aggies had tried the same pass play immediately before, when Hargett threw incomplete to the tight end. That's when Long grabbed Hargett in the huddle.

"Their safety is cheating up," Long said. "I can get behind him!"

"So we ran the play again," Hargett says. "It was a little bootleg, and when I turned and looked to the tight end—who I was still going to throw to if he was open—the Texas safety [Ronnie Ehrig] had come up a little bit, and sure enough, Bob had gotten behind him."

Hargett connected with Long 30 yards through the air, and the receiver sprinted another 50 yards for the touchdown.

"Of course," Long later recounted of that fateful moment in the huddle when he had pleaded that he was open, "I pretty much came back to the huddle and said that every play."

Stallings labeled the victory over the Longhorns "the happiest moment in my athletic career." The Aggies hadn't beaten UT since 1956, when Stallings and the Junction Boys prevailed in Austin 34-21 in Bear Bryant's lone win over the Longhorns as A&M coach.

"I think it was the happiest moment in all of our athletic careers," Hargett says.

"People remember that Texas Tech game because it was so thrilling, but we had to beat Texas to get into the Cotton Bowl. And we hadn't beaten Texas in a long time."

The surging Aggies then rolled to a 20-16 victory over Paul "Bear" Bryant's Alabama Crimson Tide in the 1968 Cotton Bowl, cementing one of the school's sweetest seasons—and also Stallings's lone winning record (7-4) in Aggieland.

Wild and woolly, indeed.

WHAT BECAME OF EDD HARGETT?

Women hardly attended Texas A&M when Gene Stallings recruited Edd Hargett in 1965. That detail often hurt in recruiting, which university president Earl Rudder used in his reasoning for allowing women into the classroom. Such an item, however, didn't matter one iota to Hargett.

"I had a steady girlfriend in high school," Edd says with a smile, "who turned out to be my wife."

Edd and his love, Shirley, married as college undergraduates, while so many of his teammates were enjoying Aggieland's nightlife, catching such acts as B. J. Thomas and Johnny Cash when they ventured through town.

"We were young when we married, but we just kind of grew up together," says Shirley Hargett, who often plays golf with her husband. "And from the beginning, we had common goals in life."

Edd and Shirley have three children—Amy, Tedd and Thadd—and four grandchildren. Edd, who majored in electrical engineering and is now manager of a co-op in Crockett, played in the NFL for four years with the New Orleans Saints. He retired from the league in 1973 and put his degree to good use.

Edd plays a little golf and has stayed active with the university, but in his spare time he mainly dotes over his grandkids. Having such little ones around in your 50s certainly seems a reward for marrying young—as Edd Hargett in so many ways seemed opposite of folks' often single-minded impressions of the "wild and woolly" 1960s.

"We felt like we could handle marriage at an early age," Edd says, smiling, "and we've handled it for 36 years."

CHAPTER 7

DAVE ELMENDORF

Name: David Cole Elmendorf
Born: June 20, 1949 in San Antonio, Texas
Hometown: Houston, Texas
Current Residence: Nomangee, Texas
Occupation: Managing director of a Bryan country club community
Position: Safety
Height: 6'1"
Playing Weight: 190 pounds
Years lettered: 1968-70
Accomplishments: All-American in 1970; two-time All-Conference (1969-70); intercepted six passes and returned 23 kicks for 457 yards as a senior; All-American in baseball as well; member of the National Football Foundation Hall of Fame; third-round pick of the Los Angeles Rams in 1971; an All-Pro in L.A. with 27 career interceptions.
Nickname: Elmo
The Game: Wichita State at Texas A&M, Sept. 12, 1970

Dave Elmendorf. *Cushing Memorial Library*

THE LIFE OF YOUNG DAVE ELMENDORF

Fresh off slapping the bow on a standout two-sport career at Houston's Westbury High, Dave Elmendorf trotted down the Kyle Field stands on Thanksgiving Day 1967. At that moment, among his fellow freshmen, he figured life to be pretty darn good.

"Imagine my glee—and, of course, freshmen weren't eligible to play back then—when we beat Texas at Kyle Field to win the Southwest Conference championship," Elmendorf says. "A year earlier I'd narrowed my choices down to Texas A&M and Texas, and I'm thinking, 'Boy, did I make the right decision.'

"The rest is history, of course. We won a total of eight games my three years at A&M, and Texas won a national championship and part of another one."

Like most anyone, Elmendorf has a few regrets in life. For starters, he never responded to a pleasant letter from actor Ozzie Nelson that read in part, "Please let us know when you're coming out here so we can at least get you started with a home-cooked meal," after the Los Angeles Rams selected "Elmo" in the 1971 NFL draft.

"I'd met Ozzie Nelson at a college awards function, and I got so busy I never got in touch with him when I moved to L.A.," Elmendorf says. "I wish I had. Just to have Ozzie Nelson as a friend would've been a lot of fun."

One thing Elmendorf certainly does not regret, however, is choosing Texas A&M over Texas, regardless of the schools' records of that era.

"I went to the right place for me, no question," Elmendorf says. "If you keep things in the proper perspective, I got an education at the university that I wanted to be a part of—even though we didn't win very many games."

Elmendorf certainly was used to playing the role of a winner. During his senior year at Westbury, he rushed for 653 yards, scored 100 points, had 28 receptions for 447 yards and picked off eight passes—amazing numbers considering he nearly quit the high school team going into his sophomore year. Perspective, it seems, has certainly played a role in Elmendorf's career, starting as a ninth grader in Houston.

"I had a disease called Osgood-Schlatter's, where your bones grow faster than your joints, and I could hardly run," Elmendorf says. "That was certainly a tough time as a young man, because I'd played sports all of my life."

Osgood-Schlatter's is an extremely painful irritation of the shinbone, just below the kneecap, most common in active youngsters. It usually goes away within a year or two, as it did with Elmendorf. Young Dave never forgot the pain involved, however, and how it nearly stopped his sporting career.

The son of an Aggie with an electrical engineering degree, Elmendorf placed as much emphasis on his academics as his athletics, having learned at a mighty young age how sports can abruptly end due to injury. That's one reason Elmendorf became a baseball Academic All-American at Texas A&M—and a pure pleasure for tough-minded football coach Gene Stallings on the gridiron.

"I just wanted to drop you a note," Stallings wrote in a Dec. 16, 1970, letter to Ed and Patricia Elmendorf about the third of their four children, "[to let you know] what a pleasure it has been working with Dave for the past four years. [Earning All-American honors at defensive back] is even more of a compliment considering the win-loss record we had this year."

THE SCENE

The new artificial turf of Kyle Field in late summer of 1970 had captured the Aggies' attention at least as much as season-opening opponent Wichita State.

"Texas and Arkansas had it, and so it made us look like we were behind because we didn't," says Gene Stallings, A&M's head coach from 1965-71 who also served as the school's athletics director from 1967-71. "You needed it primarily for recruiting. Of course, later on everybody went back to grass."

Dave Elmendorf, senior star safety for the Aggies and onetime owner of a couple of painful shinbones, didn't care for the fake stuff.

"The Astrodome had just opened about five years before, and Astroturf was the next big thing," Elmendorf says. "If you had Astroturf, you were something special."

For their part the Aggies, owners of successive 3-7 records in 1968 and '69, were hardly anything special—especially as archrival Texas won its second national championship in '69 under Darrell Royal. Texas A&M, a proud institution at that point dealing with issues on multiple fronts—from blending more women into the onetime all-male college to fully integrating the football team—recorded only one winning season from 1958-73.

"I went to school at A&M from 1968 to 1972, and if memory serves, in four years we won 13 football games," says Rick Perry, Texas governor and one-time Aggie yell leader.

Perry's memory serves, all right, and the smallest number of wins in that span came in 1970, when the Aggies finished 2-9 following a mighty promising start. But, in so many ways, there may not have been a more pivotal season for Texas A&M in that era than the 1970 campaign. During that season, an African American player finally busted into the Aggies' lineup, and women began arriving at A&M in quantifiable numbers.

And, sadly, the 1970 season was marred by a tragic event involving an opponent. It was an accident that certainly put a seemingly dismal era into stark perspective for a conscientious young man named Dave Elmendorf.

THE SETTING

Man landed on the moon (July 20, 1969) before an African American man landed in the Texas A&M starting lineup (Sept. 12, 1970 against Wichita State). Same goes for the University of Texas, as offensive lineman Julius Whittier became the first black player to suit up for the Longhorns, also in 1970.

"It was important for the ultimate success of the game," Dave Elmendorf says of the "about-time" integration occurring on football fields across the South at that time at sometimes begrudging universities. "Colleges simply couldn't continue to discriminate against black players because there were so many good black players out there."

One such player was former walk-on Hugh McElroy, a wiry receiver who burst onto the Aggieland gridiron scene by catching a team-leading three passes for 67 yards in the 1970 season opener against Wichita State. Although he followed in the footsteps of J. T. Reynolds and Sam Williams (black players who practiced but rarely touched the field for the Aggies from 1967-68), McElroy became the first African American in history to start a game for the Aggies on that day.

But that game also became shockingly important for another reason, when less than three weeks later one of two chartered Wichita State planes crashed near Silver Plume, Colo., killing 31 people—including the head coach, the athletics director, and 14 football players. The Shockers were en route to a game at Utah State.

The 2-1 Aggies found out about the crash on their way to a practice at Michigan Stadium, as A&M prepared to play the vaunted Wolverines for the first time in history.

"It tore up our whole team," Aggies fullback Doug Neill said in the days after the crash. "They were really a great bunch of guys. They never started any fights or gave anyone a hard time. It shook me up to think of all those faces I saw across the line—and I'm wondering if they're dead or not.

"Man, we'd do anything possible to help Wichita State, if we could."

Turns out the Aggies nobly did, in an otherwise miserable season that ended with nine consecutive defeats.

THE GAME OF MY LIFE
By Dave Elmendorf

We played maybe the toughest schedule in the nation my senior year, with conference games against national powers Texas and Arkansas along with non-conference road games at LSU, Ohio State and Michigan. And those non-conference games were all in a row, as a matter of fact. A&M wasn't much of a big-time program back then, so in some ways to become one you had to schedule tough games like that.

We won the LSU game in an upset 20-18 when Hugh McElroy raced 79 yards for a touchdown in the closing seconds. Afterward and as a team captain, I presented Hugh with the game ball. He'd won the game for us, essentially, on that play, so presenting him with the ball in the locker room frankly was a no-brainer.

Things had started so promisingly that season, with the LSU road win that was preceded by the victory over Wichita State in the opener. In that game, we set a then-school record for total offense with 534 yards.

We started the year 2-0, but then lost at Ohio State (56-13) and Michigan (14-10). Wichita State's plane had crashed the day before our loss to the Wolverines. It was a close game and a tough loss to take, but something like that plane crash where people are killed really gives you a perspective on athletics, and where they rank—where sports rank in the game of life.

Don't misunderstand that statement. Athletics have been my life and I love them to death, but I also have always kept sports in their proper place. And if you realize athletics aren't life and death, it helps you handle the pressures of playing the game.

*   *   *   *   *

After such a tough season, Coach Stallings came up with a wonderful and fitting idea: donate the $5,000 set aside for our football banquet to the Wichita State football fund.

So the four senior co-captains—punter Jimmy Sheffield, guards Winston Beam and Jimmy Parker, and myself—flew to Wichita, Kan., in

Before becoming an All-Pro safety for the Los Angeles Rams, Dave Elmendorf (36) intercepted six passes and returned 23 kicks for 457 yards as an A&M senior. *Aggieland Yearbook.*

January 1971 to present WSU with the donation. It was the right thing to do, and looking back, I'm so glad that we did.

The Texas Legislature even passed a resolution commending Texas A&M for the fact that we'd given up our banquet to help out the Wichita State football program, and I've still got that certificate hanging on my wall.

EPILOGUE

A woman from Wichita, Kan., tossed and turned one night in 1982 in her Silver Plume, Colo., motel room, 12 years after a Wichita State plane crashed at the base of nearby Mount Trelease, killing 31 of the 40 onboard, including 14 football players. One victim was a young man named Ron Johnson from Platte City, Kan.

In a fitful dream, the woman saw a blond boy walking away from her, asking her to follow. The next day while visiting the crash site with her husband in a sort of pilgrimage, the woman found a half-buried charred ring with the initials "RGJ" inside. Upon seeing a picture of Ronald Gene Johnson in the days following, she told her astonished husband that it was the boy from the dream.

The woman delivered the precious ring to Ron Johnson's parents, in a story relayed in the *Kansas City Star* in 1995.

"It's a miracle," said the mother of Ron Johnson, who'd given her son the ring as a gift and received it back a dozen years after he'd died.

The Wichita State football program never quite recovered from the crash and disbanded in 1986 for financial reasons. But back in 1970, amazingly, after canceling their game with Utah State, the Shockers played out their schedule with the remaining players (the team's other chartered plane had landed safely in Utah), in honor of their dead and wounded.

In that spirited contest between Texas A&M and Wichita State at Kyle Field on Sept. 12, 1970, a good-natured and vivacious young man named Ron Johnson collected 10 tackles for the underdog yet valiant Wichita State Shockers. It was a game that Dave Elmendorf and his Texas A&M teammates will never forget—a game that put some awfully tough seasons for Texas A&M football into crystal-clear perspective.

WHAT BECAME OF DAVE ELMENDORF?

Dave Elmendorf had a couple of examples of culture shock in moving from College Station to Los Angeles as a third-round pick of the Rams in 1971. One was playing football with more than one African American teammate.

"This was a totally different era, and it was a real learning experience to not only play with a number of black players, but to become good friends with black players," Elmendorf says. "It was a learning experience that was comfortable and positive."

The other bit of culture shock? Moving from Aggieland to Actorland.

"My rookie year I played in a golf tournament, and guess who I was paired with? Fred MacMurray, the father on *My Three Sons*," Elmendorf says, still a bit wide-eyed at his brush with the kindly actor. "I mean, I was playing golf with him, and he was just as nice in person as on TV.

"That's one of the things I found out when I crossed paths with a few actors out there—who they are is who they are. Fred was the same on the golf course as he was on the TV show."

The same may be said of Elmendorf, although for his part he's the same in his office (as managing director of the Miramont development in Bryan) as on its surrounding golf course. As genuine as the day he presented Hugh McElroy with the game ball following A&M's win at LSU in 1970.

"I attribute that act solely to Dave Elmendorf," a grateful McElroy says. "He was the team captain, and everyone reacted in a very positive manner."

Elmendorf, who also served as an A&M football broadcaster for a dozen years, and his wife, Mamie, live on about 300 acres near Normangee, Texas, and in his precious spare time he enjoys hunting and fishing. And, of course, he loves to play golf.

"From our ninth fairway at Miramont," Elmendorf says, smiling, "there's a great view of Kyle Field."

Kyle Field is a landmark with lights bright enough to top anything in Los Angeles, apparently, as the All-Pro Elmendorf wrapped up his nine-year NFL career in the 1980 Super Bowl, and then made his way back home.

CHAPTER 8

HUGH
McELROY

Name: Hugh Thomas McElroy Jr.
Born: Jan. 2, 1950
Hometown: Houston, Texas
Current Residence: Houston, Texas
Occupation: Director of Sales & Marketing for J & E Associates
Position: Receiver
Height: 5'8"
Playing Weight: 170 pounds
Years lettered: 1970-71
Accomplishments: Walked on the Aggies' football team in 1969, played sparingly on special teams and a little bit at receiver. Earned a football scholarship in 1970.
Nickname: Mac
The Game: Texas A&M at LSU, Sept. 19, 1970

THE LIFE OF YOUNG HUGH McELROY

In many ways Hugh McElroy seemed the perfect candidate at staunch Texas A&M to help slash through years of racial separation and into the Aggies' starting lineup in 1970—the same year that the

Hugh McElroy. *Photo courtesy of Texas A&M Athletic Media Relations*

University of Texas suited up its first African American player, offensive lineman Julius Whittier.

"First of all, I knew that everything that came to my mind didn't have to come out of my mouth," says McElroy, the first African American to ever start a football game for the Aggies. "I was probably the forerunner to what you'd call being politically correct. I also kept myself from being duped into being a lightning rod for either side of the race issue."

One time, however, McElroy's diplomacy slipped—and quite by accident. What might one expect from a soon-to-be freshman?

"Two of my [Houston Worthing] high school classmates, Sidney Chachere and Edgar Harvey, were being recruited for the A&M track team," McElroy says. "Sidney had this little Volkswagen bug, and he knew he was going to A&M, and so he had an Aggies sticker in the windshield. So we're driving on this highway in Houston, and a car passes by with a young white guy and his girlfriend in it.

"Suddenly the guy looks over at me and sticks his thumb up and starts 'gigging.' I didn't know what it meant, and I thought he was saying, 'Up yours!' Man, did I light in to that guy—yelling out the window and so forth. Sidney starts yelling,—'No, Mac, no! That's the A&M sign!'

"I leaned back in the seat and started laughing. Poor guy was only trying to be friendly—which is the A&M way—and Sidney and I were laughing so hard about the whole thing he was gone before we could try and tell him what had happened."

Though McElroy's tact had innocently slipped on that pre-Texas A&M occasion, it came in awfully handy on others while in Aggieland, as McElroy dealt with being the only black player on the football team—although three African Americans participated on the track team.

"There was a lot of news about the riots in Los Angeles in 1968 and others around that time, and many of the clippings, of course, showed policemen beating blacks and using their attack dogs and those kinds of things," McElroy says. "One night some of the football players were at Sbisa Dining Hall eating dinner and the discussion turned to the riots. And a teammate said, 'Hey, did you see those cops beating that nigger?'

"I just kept eating. Everyone else at the table just kind of looked at him like, 'Hey, man, Mac's at the table.'"

The apprehensive teammate glanced down the table and caught McElroy's eye.

"Mac, man, I'm sorry."

"For what?"

"You didn't hear what I said?"

"Yeah, I heard you, but you wouldn't be apologizing unless you thought I was a nigger."

The best way to handle any similar situation, McElroy still contends, is as he did that day: civilly twist such a comment on the offender.

"You just take it and turn it the other way around, instead of jumping up and going crazy," he says. "That guy and I have a good relationship to this day."

Of course, that wasn't the lone incident McElroy dealt with as the only African American on the football team.

"There were several opportunities to start something over comments made and such, if that's what I was after," he says, "but it never was."

Long before such occasions McElroy, who measured five foot eight and 170 pounds at A&M, had learned from his grandmother, Bessie Chapman, that outer appearances had nothing to do with a person's character or heart.

"I was always smaller than everyone else physically, but my grandmother instilled in me that had nothing to do with anything—that you're only smaller than everyone else if you measure from the outside in," he says. "If you measure from the inside out, then it's a different story."

McElroy was born and raised in Houston, an only child mostly reared by his grandmother. His parents divorced when he was a little boy, and his mother moved to Galveston as a registered nurse.

"She could get more overtime and extra work there in an effort to save money and put me through school," McElroy says. "I stayed with my grandmother in Houston. I had five or six cousins living with me as well. I should say we were living with them. In any case, we were together most of the time."

McElroy, a member of the National Honor Society at Worthing, set out at A&M to become a technical writer, because journalism had played—and continues to play—a strong role in his family. His uncle, George McElroy, was the *Houston Post's* first African American writer and also the first minority of any race to write a regular column at a major Houston newspaper.

George McElroy also taught journalism at the University of Houston, Texas Southern and the city's public schools. And Hugh McElroy's first cousin, Kathleen McElroy, is an A&M graduate and assistant editor of the *New York Times*.

Hugh McElroy, meanwhile, wound up an industrial technology major. And on McElroy's questionnaire for the Texas A&M sports information department in 1970, he couldn't describe his greatest athletic thrill.

"None," he wrote. "Always in someone else's shadow."

A sizeable shadow, anyway.

"All through junior high and high school I was on the football team, but I never lettered and never made a touchdown because I played behind a guy people might recall by the name of Clifford Branch," McElroy says, smiling. "We played the same position in every sport."

Cliff Branch became one of the Oakland Raiders' most prolific receivers in team history. But for many Aggies of that generation, the name Hugh McElroy is even more memorable. Especially after what happened on Sept. 19, 1970.

THE SCENE

Texas A&M introduced artificial turf to Kyle Field in 1970, but that was only the second biggest change to Aggies football that year. The first? Hugh "Mac" McElroy. The fleet, wiry receiver became the first African American to start for the Aggies, as well as the first to score a touchdown.

McElroy wasn't the first black player to suit up for the Aggies, however, or even the second. J. T. Reynolds and Sam Williams had preceded him beginning in 1967, but neither had started and each played sparingly, mostly on special teams. By 1969 both had left the team (Williams graduated that year and Reynolds graduated in 1970).

In 1967 in the season opener against SMU, a wayward fan turned loose a couple of black cats on Kyle Field, because receiver Jerry LeVias—the Southwest Conference's first black scholarship football player—had come to town with the Mustangs. Ironically, that game also marked the first time an African American took the field for A&M, when Reynolds played sparingly on special teams for the Aggies (and with none of LeVias's fanfare).

"I've had several public speaking opportunities where the consensus of the crowd mistakenly thought that I was the first black to play for A&M," McElroy says. "I always try to publicly acknowledge that J. T. and Sammy were on the team and sweated and bled just like everybody else, they just didn't get the opportunity to play. I must lay a lot of recognition at their feet, because if they hadn't gone through what they did, I may not have had the character and stamina to last.

"My part was easy, because I got to play for my practice. They had the tough part. They toiled in anonymity."

Gene Stallings, A&M head coach from 1965-71, says he always recruited based on the "importance of getting the very best player that we could."

"I never considered a player a black player or a white player," Stallings says. "I never thought along those lines, and I still don't. I tried to recruit minority players to A&M, but that was sort of hard to do in those days. There wasn't just a whole lot to do in College Station, and a lot of people didn't want to be in the Cadet Corps. We tried to recruit the best player that we could find."

Stallings didn't have to recruit the first black to start for the Aggies, however, as Hugh McElroy mostly just fell in his lap. McElroy, an A&M track athlete, tried out for the team in the spring of 1968. But an old hamstring injury flared up during his audition, and Stallings suggested to McElroy that he not bother returning for two-a-days.

A year later, McElroy tried out again at the behest of a bunch of his "back yard" football buddies, with Reynolds and Williams having already left the team.

"I talked to J. T. and Sammy about trying out, because we were—and still are—close," McElroy says. "Their approach was, sooner or later the door has got to open."

America at that time was opening up—quickly and sometimes violently—in the battlefield of civil rights. While the Vietnam War raged on, President Lyndon Johnson of Texas had moved rapidly—at least historically speaking—to try and bring equality to minorities.

The Civil Rights Act of 1964 prohibited discrimination in public quarters, including restaurants and hotels. The Voting Rights Act of 1965 fortified punishments for interference with voters' rights. And the Civil Rights Act of 1968 forbade discrimination on issues of housing.

But Johnson, whipped by the unpopularity of Vietnam coupled with the most unrest in the homeland since the Civil War, elected not to seek the Democratic nomination in 1968, and his vice president, Hubert Humphrey, lost the election by a slim margin to Republican Richard Nixon.

Two years later and around the same time McElroy prepared to earn his first start for the Aggies, in September 1970, Nixon shied from even speaking on college campuses because of incessant heckling seemingly every time he opened his mouth.

"It's a sad day when a great university can't hear controversial speakers—and any man in political life is controversial," Nixon muttered.

"It was a very cynical time," McElroy says. "It was a me-generation and for the most part—certainly not as much on the A&M campus— a drug-induced time. There was an awful lot of pessimism toward the government, mainly because of such an unpopular war going on."

THE SETTING

The claim went in a newspaper in 1970 that Baton Rouge, home of Louisiana State University, "is the only place in the country where you can walk out onto the field at halftime and get stoned just by breathing the air."

Enter into that setting the preacher of the A&M Church of Christ, Bob Davidson, who'd been prodded to attend the Texas A&M-LSU game in Baton Rouge. Especially since one of his congregants, Hugh McElroy, was a starting split end for the Aggies.

Davidson had first turned down the chance to make the trek from College Station across the swamps to Southeast Louisiana, insisting that he had a sermon to prepare for Sunday.

"You can work on it on the way," his friends insisted.

Davidson thus did, and even took his Bible to Tiger Stadium, where he was stopped at the turnstile.

"Whatcha got in the bag?" the gate attendant inquired.

"A Bible," Davidson replied.

"Yeah, right—lemme see."

So Davidson, smiling a bit, opened his black bag to reveal a Bible.

"Whoo, whee," the attendant replied, shaking his head. "A Bible, in this stadium? That's a first. Y'all Aggies must really want to win this one bad."

They did. A&M had finished 3-7 in successive seasons under Stallings in 1968 and '69, but 1970 was thought to hold promise behind flashy quarterback Lex James and safety Dave Elmendorf. A&M opened the '70 season with a 41-14 beating of Wichita State at Kyle Field, and its next game was at LSU, where the Aggies hadn't won since 1956 under Bear Bryant. In fact, A&M played nine consecutive games at LSU prior to the 1970 contest and hadn't won any of them, although the '66 Aggies managed a 7-7 tie.

"LSU never came to College Station because, quite honestly, we could go over there and lose and make more money than we could if we had won in College Station," McElroy says. "It was a financial situation."

Whatever the situation, it left Stallings in a bad mood even after the win over Wichita State. LSU returned 32 lettermen that year from a 9-1 nationally ranked team.

"I wish we were home or playing them on a neutral field such as Bogoda, Powderly or Texarkana—anywhere but Baton Rouge," Stallings half-joked in the days before the game.

Asked which movie his team would watch on Friday night, as per custom before road games, Stallings shook his head.

"It won't be a horror show," he said. "They'll get that on Saturday night when they play LSU."

Says McElroy, "There was a grain of truth to that. We weren't given much of a chance, and I remember that no Texas newspapers—outside of the Bryan-College Station paper—even bothered coming over to cover the game, it was supposed to be so lopsided."

But this A&M-LSU script would have a happy ending for Aggies, as Hugh McElroy raced 79 yards for a touchdown on a wild pass play with 13 seconds remaining, staking the Aggies to a stunning—and sobering for a crowd of 67,590 at Tiger Stadium—20-18 victory.

"Hugh McElroy catches that pass, and boom! Touchdown!" Stallings says, still grinning at the memory. "What a great win that was!"

THE GAME OF MY LIFE
By Hugh McElroy

I've had people tell me there are two things that they remember from that era—where they were when John F. Kennedy died, and where they were when I caught that pass. Now, that's scary.

We'd called a play to our tight end, Homer May. So when we snapped the ball, I just kind of ran out and turned around to look and see what had happened, and then—Oh my gosh!—here comes the ball.

I can't even say that I'd run a route, because my number hadn't been called in the huddle. I just ran a half-baked decoy pattern and turned around about 10 yards inside the sideline, and Lex James had fired the ball at me. Lex, now, he was cool under pressure. Not only was he good, but he had that Joe Namath-like confident air about him—minus the fur coats and pantyhose, of course.

So, under a rush, Lex threw in my direction and an LSU defender leaped for the ball but missed—it went right through his hands—and I caught it and spun to the outside. From there, it was just a race to the end zone.

There was no way they were going to catch me at that point. We'd played too hard and come too far. One guy had a fairly decent angle, but he just didn't have the speed.

We finished that game with minus-42 yards rushing, although we threw for 314 yards. I wound up with six catches for 180 yards, a huge chunk of that, of course, coming on our final offensive play. The next week a reporter asked Coach Stallings about that play.

"You get McElroy out in the open field and let him wiggle, and they just might miss him," Stallings said. "If someone else caught it out in the open field he may not wiggle quite as well."

That statement was hindsight on Coach's part. In 1969, when I was hardly playing, and would go against the first-team offense and do that little wiggle he was talking about and score, that didn't make Coach Stallings very happy.

"The shortest distance between two points," he'd yell, "is a straight line!"

One time I told him, "But, Coach, I'm like water. I diffuse to the point of least resistance."

In 1970, Hugh McElroy became the first African American player to both start and score a touchdown for the Aggies. He's shown here scoring that remarkable touchdown at LSU that gave the Aggies a stunning 20-18 victory. *Aggieland Yearbook*

I kind of muttered that one under my breath, though. Coach always did say there wasn't but one vote cast, and that was his.

After the LSU game and in a jubilant locker room, team captain Dave Elmendorf—our star safety—grabbed a football and said something I'll never forget.

"It's appropriate that Mac gets this game ball," Elmendorf said, adding that the LSU game marked quite a milestone for black football players at Texas A&M.

I don't think it was a team decision to award me the game ball, but I also think no one minded when Dave did that. Everyone reacted very positively. People should also remember that Dave intercepted a pass deep in our territory right at the end of the game to preserve our first win at LSU since the Bear Bryant days.

And it's a game—one that Coach Stallings called "one of the great wins in Texas A&M football history"—I've got preserved in my memory forever.

GAME RESULTS

Texas A&M's win over LSU that year served as the season's highlight, considering that the Aggies dropped their next nine games following their 2-0 start. They also played possibly the toughest schedule in the country, as they followed up the win at LSU with road losses at Ohio State (56-13) and Michigan (14-10).

A&M followed that year's 2-9 finish with a 5-6 showing in 1971, and by the 1972 season Emory Bellard had replaced Stallings as head coach. But for one shining moment in 1970—thanks largely to a 79-yard dash by a groundbreaking receiver—the Aggies looked every bit a program on the rise.

"We marched on the field at halftime at LSU, and we were just amazed at how long the grass was," recalls Sigurd Kendall, the Aggie Band's senior commanding officer that year and now a dentist in Bryan.

"It was over the tops of our shoes. When Hugh McElroy caught that pass, my biggest fear was that he was going to trip over the grass. But he scored on an amazing run, and the stadium dropped from loud cheers to deathly quiet. The Aggie Band members rejoiced at first, and then we started trying to figure out how we were going to get out of there alive."

John Platzer of the *Bryan-College Station Eagle* described the winning play, and McElroy, thusly: "Cutting across the center, he was in heavy traffic between three LSU defenders at the Tiger 40. Two of the defenders missed interception attempts and the third tripped as McElroy headed down the sideline with Rocky Self as an escort. The fleet Houston product bested an LSU back in a footrace, and the Aggies were still undefeated.

"… McElroy has been one of the real pleasant surprises on the Aggies this fall, and he's given A&M its biggest home run threat in many years. … On campus, one wouldn't pick him out as a football player. He's quiet and reserved, wears glasses and doesn't attract a lot of attention. But on the football field, he's one man to watch."

Two years after the remarkable touchdown catch, McElroy was living in Morgan City, La., and decided to catch the 1972 A&M-LSU game in Baton Rouge.

"I was working in the oil fields at the time, and [longtime A&M trainer] Billy Pickard had gotten me a sideline pass," McElroy says. "I had a three-piece suit and a hat on, but one of the LSU security guards recognized me and wouldn't let me go on the sidelines until halftime.

"I promised him I had no intentions of putting on a uniform."

WHAT BECAME OF HUGH McELROY?

Hugh McElroy's most shining moment as an Aggie football player occurred at LSU, when he was a junior. His proudest moment took place a year later, as a senior. A&M was playing in McElroy's hometown of Houston at Rice University, and an unexpected visitor settled into a lawnchair on the sidelines, in full military regalia.

"Early on in my life I thought I'd wanted to be a career military man, and my grandfather, Hugh George McElroy, was a heavily decorated soldier," McElroy says. "In fact, in the Institute of Texas Cultures in San Antonio, you'll find his picture hanging on the wall. He fought in the Spanish-American War and World War I, and he won the Croix de Guerre—the French medal for bravery.

"By the time I needed to make a decision on whether to accept a commission to go into the military my junior year at A&M, I had determined that was more of a family dream than a personal dream."

And Grandpa McElroy wasn't happy.

"He told me I was no longer a McElroy," Hugh says, "because every McElroy man had served his country."

His grandfather also had never seen him play football, from junior high on. And then came the A&M-Rice game, as Grandpa McElroy neared 90 years old.

"A lot of our friends and family were going, and they kept asking Grandpa if he wanted to go," McElroy says. "He said he didn't feel up to it. As we were warming up on the field, I waved over to my family sitting in the stands. Suddenly one of the trainers came over and said, 'Your grandpa is here.' He was in a folding chair sitting down on the field, in his campaign uniform, hat and medals and everything.

"After the rest of my family had left for the game he caught a cab and at the gate of Rice Stadium, he told them who he was and who he was there to see. Of course, they believed him. Who else would come up in an old uniform like that? That's how he got in and how he got on the sidelines.

"When he was in his late 80s there was an article in the paper about him wanting to volunteer and go back and serve again [during the Vietnam War]. He was a pretty scrappy guy, and he wasn't the type to come back and say he was sorry, or anything like that, but I took his coming to that game as his way of saying, 'You've done OK by the family name.' Not long after that he passed away."

As for Hugh McElroy, he's lived a hugely productive life in a multitude of businesses, from the oil industry to serving as A&M's associate director of human resources for six years in the 1990s. A father of two—daughters Timisha and Jessica—and a grandfather of two, McElroy is now the director of sales and marketing for J & E Associates in Houston, a janitorial services company.

McElroy, too, will always cherish his trailblazing role at Texas A&M.

"With me having been the first black to start on the football team, there were a lot of people watching, because it was important to them," McElroy says.

"As I look back on it, that's something I'm very proud of, because that won't ever change.

"It's an honor, and not one I take lightly."

And, maybe above all, Mac is certain Grandpa is smiling.

CHAPTER 9

PAT THOMAS

Name: Patrick Shane Thomas
Born: Sept. 1, 1954
Hometown: Plano, Texas
Current Residence: East Amherst, N.Y.
Occupation: NFL Assistant Coach
Position: Cornerback
Height: 5'10"
Playing Weight: 180 pounds
Years lettered: 1972-75
Accomplishments: Two-time All-American and two-time All-Conference (1974-75); third on Texas A&M's all-time interception list with 13; second-round pick of the Los Angeles Rams in 1976; two-time Pro Bowler with the Rams.
Nickname: Road Dog
The Game: Texas A&M at Texas Tech, Oct. 11, 1975

THE LIFE OF YOUNG PAT THOMAS

Pat Thomas, All-Pro NFL cornerback and the first African American All-American football player at Texas A&M, can point to an awful lot of memorable moments in his career. But somewhat surprisingly

Pat Thomas. *Photo courtesy of Texas A&M Athletic Media Relations*

considering his later accomplishments, none stand out more than a stretch of two games during his senior year of high school in the fall of 1971.

That's when Thomas's Plano squad defeated state powerhouses Brownwood and Gregory-Portland en route to the Class 4A state championship. The Gregory-Portland game in particular offered a stunning preview of an annual showdown between Thomas at A&M and quarterback Marty Akins at Texas.

Renowned Texas high school sports writer George Breazeale of the *Austin American-Statesman* labeled the '71 Plano and Gregory-Portland state title contest as the second most memorable game he ever covered.

"Thomas, who rushed for two touchdowns, became an All-America defensive back at A&M, and Akins, primarily a passing quarterback, developed into a brilliant option operator at Texas," Breazeale said.

"That was one heck of a game," Thomas says, smiling at the memory. "Marty and that group were averaging 45 points per game, and we beat them 21-20. We were really underdogs and had barely squeaked past Brownwood the week before. Marty and I were the field-goal kickers for our teams, and the fact that I didn't have to try and kick one at the end was a real blessing, because every extra point for us was a drama.

"In fact, we'd almost lost to Brownwood the week before when I'd missed two field goals, but I kicked one with 21 seconds left from about 20 yards for the win. That was probably the most defining moment out of my football career—on any level, believe it or not."

Thomas, the second of James and Hallie Thomas's four children, expected to attend Oklahoma as a five-foot-10, 180-pound tailback, but the Sooners already possessed a stout runner in future NFL standout Greg Pruitt. So Thomas signed with Texas A&M as part of a group trailblazing role along with seven other African American recruits in 1972.

"The A&M alumni had convinced me that Aggieland was the most special place you could be in the world," Thomas says. "Plus, the football program was so down at that time, we all thought we could come in and start right away."

THE SCENE

The experience of Pat Thomas's first night in College Station was likely to have sent him packing right back to Plano, Texas. As a young lady screamed at Thomas and his fellow freshmen that evening, the guys couldn't figure out who was more startled by the strange ordeal: her, or them.

"Texas A&M had only a few black players come before us," Thomas says. "And suddenly there were eight of us who all signed together. Aggieland at that time was a hard place to get minorities to, trust me. Nobody would come unless you were paying them—either through an athletics scholarship or academic scholarship.

"That was the only way you'd ever get any blacks to Texas A&M in that era."

In 1972, A&M football had recorded only one winning season since 1957—and first-year coach Emory Bellard seemed determined to change that. And one of the best ways to do so, he figured, was to heavily recruit black athletes.

"Our recruiting class came along at the latter part of the introduction of African Americans to college sports in the South," says Ed Simonini, a white player who also was a part of Bellard's first haul. "Texas had just won its national championship in 1969 without any black players, the last time anything like that ever took place. Texas A&M's program was hurting, and when you're hurting it's a lot easier to make changes.

"The players looked at [the sudden wholesale integration under Bellard] as a good thing, because it really improved our team, even if it didn't always go harmoniously. There were problems, but not nearly as many as some other schools in the South."

The first problem came on the incoming class's first night in town in the summer of '72—as evidenced by the woman's howls.

"We'd checked in for training camp, and all of the black guys decided to walk from the dormitory down to this little ice cream place on University Drive," Thomas says. "And as we walked up to a stoplight by the bookstore, there was a white girl and a white guy standing there, waiting to cross the street. And suddenly she turns around and starts screaming and hollering and grabbing on to the guy.

"Apparently at that time if you saw eight black guys together in College Station, people figured there must have been a riot going on or something. I couldn't figure out what the heck was wrong with her, so I asked."

The young woman finally stammered, "I just ... didn't know there were so many blacks in College Station."

Thomas's startling thought, as the couple hurried away, was: "Goodness gracious, what have I got myself into? If this is a sign of things to come—if this is what the next four years are going to be like—Lord, have mercy."

Fortunately it wasn't, mostly, for the groundbreaking class of eight African American football players.

"At that time things really started growing at Texas A&M," Thomas says of the university expanding from about 15,000 students in 1972 to 25,000 four years later. "And we were national figures by the time we left."

For good reason: An amazing 21 of the 22 starters on the 1975 team—Thomas's senior year—played in the NFL, and the Aggies jetted to a No. 2 ranking late in that season. Meanwhile Thomas had grown into Texas A&M's first black All-American, and probably somewhere up in the Kyle Field stands, that young woman at the stoplight was yelling in favor of Thomas and the university's budding program.

THE SETTING

B lacks and whites may have had a few differences as they adjusted to each other's company on the Aggies' football team in the early to mid-1970s, but one mutual interest in particular always signified smooth sailing: the choice of pregame music.

"There was a group of us seniors, guys like Ed Simonini, Jackie Williams, Garth Ten Napel and myself, who'd all get together in Cain Hall before football games and turn up the music really loud before heading over to the stadium," Pat Thomas says. "We felt like we were invincible, because of the spirit that we shared among one another."

The choice of tunes? Jazz legend Harvey Mason. Always Harvey Mason.

"It was the drums and the horns and everything—it just grooved," Thomas says. "It wasn't like rap or anything like that."

Meanwhile the Texas A&M defense, behind that groovin' bunch, had absolutely dominated its competition for much of the 1975 season. Through the Aggies' first 10 games that year, no opponent scored more than 14 points against A&M's pre-"Wrecking Crew" wrecking crew.

"Our success wasn't based so much on our raw talent as our desire," Thomas says. "We fought and fought to win, and anybody you put in the game you knew would die for the team. That's the way we played and that's what we believed in. It's easy to have a championship-caliber defense on a team when you know that everyone, regardless of his athletic ability, will die for that common cause."

Texas A&M's rugged and innovative defensive coordinator, Melvin Robertson, made the Aggies even tougher.

"He used to spit on people all of the time when he talked to them," Thomas says, still grimacing a bit at the memory. "That's why they called him Mad Dog. Plus, he had a glass eye that stayed steady, and that other eye—boy, it'd be darting all over the place. And when he talked, he was always chewing and spitting all in your face when he'd be explaining some defense.

"All you could do was stand there and take it. You just acted like it didn't happen, and once he walked away you'd wipe the spit off. He was a great coach, though."

*   *   *   *   *

One of the sources of Robertson's incessant saliva, too, may have been up-and-coming voluptuous beauty Dolly Parton, named the Country Music Association's Female Entertainer of the Year about the same time Texas A&M was bouncing around its league opponents in the fall of 1975.

In a classic television moment, Parton's dress popped open when she earned the entertainer award, and a CMA audience member lent her a fur to cover up the transgression.

"My hair is out of the '60s, my clothes are from the '50s and my shoes are from the '40s," Parton, 29, said before the show. "I like looking like I came out of a fairy tale."

The Aggies' stellar defense, ranked No. 1 nationally for part of 1975, seemed straight out of a fairy tale for long-suffering Texas A&M fans, as well. And none of its members were more flamboyant than safety Lester Hayes, who, in a move to possibly one-up the well-endowed Parton, sported a hood ornament on his green-and-white sedan unlike any other in Aggieland in the mid-1970s—or since.

"It was a big ol' eagle, probably stood about a foot tall," Thomas says, laughing. "You could see it for a mile."

If you didn't see Hayes first.

"My cousin, Jackie Williams, had nicknamed Lester 'Freeze,'" Thomas says. "Lester was just so *cold.* He tried to dress real hip, but really, he was just one of those guys from Houston who grew up with all of those cowboys. He'd wear real loud colors, and he always had on hats and glasses.

"The rest of the guys dressed pretty normally, with regular collared shirts and tennis shoes or what have you, but Lester dressed like a pimp most of the time."

While Thomas didn't bother offering Hayes any fashion advice, there were early signs of Thomas's coaching future when he and Jackie Williams, A&M's starting safety, helped convert Hayes from linebacker to safety while in college.

"We took Lester under our wing and taught him how to study film and backpedal and things like that, and we were constantly having to work with him," Thomas says of the future All-American at safety and All-Pro cornerback with the Oakland Raiders.

"And, shoot, he ended up better than all of us."

THE GAME OF MY LIFE
By Pat Thomas

Our first two years in the program we finished 3-8 and then 5-6 under Coach Bellard, but you could certainly see signs of progress for Aggies football—especially when we finished 8-3 in 1974. The following year we were really on a roll going into Lubbock, with a lot to prove even though we were 4-0 and had outscored our first four opponents—Mississippi, LSU, Illinois and Kansas State—99-22.

Some K-State guys had even said after we beat them 10-0, "They're not in the class of the Big Eight." Funny that A&M and three other old Southwest Conference teams would join forces with the Big Eight about two decades later and form the Big 12 Conference—and the Aggies have done just fine in that league.

The battle for respect in 1975 seemed never-ending for a program that had been down for so long, and we had a chance to earn a little in a nationally televised game at Texas Tech. The Red Raiders, at least, were acting as if it was a big-time challenge to play Texas A&M.

"I think A&M should be in the NFL," Tech coach Steve Sloan joked. "Maybe the Central Division."

It's not nearly as big a deal for the Aggies to be on national TV now, but back then it was huge—and we didn't want to squander an opportunity to showcase our rising program, especially in our conference opener that year.

We didn't, as our featured running back, Bubba Bean, put Tech away on a 94-yard sprint—still the second longest touchdown run in A&M history—early in the second half, and we never looked back. We'd gotten over the hump in what was expected to be a tough league road game, and were finally on a winning streak that we'd all hoped for as incoming freshmen, back in 1972.

GAME RESULTS

Texas A&M's 38-9 romp over Texas Tech served as a springboard for five more SWC wins, including a huge triumph over Texas—the first time A&M had defeated the Longhorns since 1967. The Aggies, ranked second in the nation, would lose badly at Arkansas, 31-6, to close out the regular season, but A&M still made its first bowl in eight years that pivotal season.

"We hadn't been to a bowl game our entire four years there, and we had worked our butts off to get the program back on track," Thomas says.

In 1974 cornerback Pat Thomas became the Aggies' first black All-American. He later played in two Pro Bowls for the Los Angeles Rams. *Photo courtesy of Texas A&M Athletic Media Relations*

The Aggies lost 20-0 to USC in the Liberty Bowl in John McKay's final game as Trojans coach.

"It's strange to say, but winning the game didn't seem as important as just being there for us," Thomas says. "We had turned bowl week into one big party—to celebrate Texas A&M finally making it back to one."

For his part Jackie Williams labeled the end of the 1975 season a huge downer.

"After the Arkansas loss, it was a letdown," Williams said. "We wanted the Cotton Bowl or nothing."

Bellard would lead the Aggies to two more lesser bowls over the next two seasons—the Sun and the Bluebonnet—before he abruptly resigned midway through the 1978 season. Bellard said that he quit because the university president and board of regents were about to ask him to give up coaching and concentrate on his athletics director duties.

A&M wouldn't play in another bowl following the 1978 season until 1981, in Tom Wilson's final year as head coach.

WHAT BECAME OF PAT THOMAS?

Pat Thomas and the rest of the 1975 Aggies each got a Liberty Bowl watch for their participation in the Memphis, Tenn., event, and Thomas promptly gave it to his father, James.

"I gave him all of my things of that nature—the watches, rings…" Thomas says. "I felt like they belonged to him, because he's the one who inspired me to play sports. And when I played, I played for my mom and dad, because without their guidance, I wouldn't have been able to accomplish those goals."

Pat Thomas also grew up under the influence of a mighty grandfather, James Thomas Sr., a legendary man in Plano.

"There's a school named for him—James Thomas Elementary," Thomas says, smiling. "Plano is less than one percent minority, but the people there got together and decided they wanted to name a school in his honor. My grandfather had shined shoes in downtown Plano, and he helped the community greatly during the Depression. He basically fed and clothed the whole black community during that time."

Meanwhile Pat has carried the Thomas family banner proudly, as he wrapped up a two-time All-America career at Texas A&M in 1975, and then played in two Pro Bowls in a seven-year NFL career with the Los Angeles Rams.

Pat and his life's love—wife Lenith—have three children: Patrick Jr., Tamara and Joshua. He also has an older daughter, Heather Taylor. Pat, who as a player never figured he'd get into coaching because he was too much of a perfectionist (and thus, would be too hard on his players), has served as defensive backs coach for the Buffalo Bills, Indianapolis Colts and Houston Oilers since 1990.

But as much success as he's had in the NFL, Thomas will always hold a special place at Texas A&M, as a groundbreaking All-American on one heck of a defense in the mid 1970s.

"It didn't take long for people to get the message," A&M All-American linebacker Ed Simonini says of how much African-Americans were bettering once-stubborn and segregated football programs across the South during that era. "It's hard, too, to argue against simply the right thing to do."

CHAPTER 10

ED
SIMONINI

Name: Edward Clyde Simonini
Born: Feb. 2, 1954
Hometown: Las Vegas, Nevada
Current Residence: Tulsa, Okla.
Occupation: Director of Distributors for Hilti Latin America LTD
Position: Linebacker
Height: 6'
Playing Weight: 215 pounds
Years lettered: 1972-75
Accomplishments: All-American in 1975; four-time All-Conference (1972-75); led the Aggies in tackles for three consecutive seasons (from 1973-75); finalist for the Lombardi Award in 1975; third-round pick of the Baltimore Colts in 1976; played seven years in the NFL for the Colts and the New Orleans Saints; led the Colts in tackles for four consecutive years (1977-80).
Nickname: Weird Ed
The Game: Texas at Texas A&M, Nov. 28, 1975

Ed Simonini. *Photo courtesy of Texas A&M Athletic Media Relations*

THE LIFE OF YOUNG ED SIMONINI

Sixth grader Ed Simonini quickly schemed on how to one-up his older brother, Frank, when Frank arrived home from Abilene (Texas) High School one winter day in 1966 and proudly announced to his family he'd earned a football scholarship to New Mexico State.

"Mom, I'm gonna get two scholarships," young Ed declared. "I'm gonna do better than Frank. I'm gonna get two."

"And I did," Simonini says, laughing. "I had told her I was going to get one for football and one for academics, and I earned a football scholarship to A&M and a scholastic scholarship worth about $1,500."

Ed Simonini, tackling wonder at Texas A&M from 1972-75, learned the art of competition just out of the womb from growing up the youngest of Tom and Pat Simonini's five children.

"There were four boys, and my sister was the oldest," Simonini says.

"There was an awful lot of competition. In a lot of ways, we were your typical Italian family: we'd get loud and noisy when we got together.

"And being the youngest, I got beat up a lot while growing up."

Ed was born in 1954 in Portsmouth, Va.—his father was a navy pilot—and the Simonini family lived in Abilene from 1962-66, where his father headed up a navy reserve unit.

At the same time, Emory Bellard was coaching San Angelo High to a state championship in 1966, and Frank played at rival Abilene. Five years later Ed starred at Valley High in Las Vegas, Nevada, the same school from where Atlanta Braves pitcher Greg Maddux graduated a dozen years later. The Simonini family lived in Vegas from '69 to '72, and when Bellard was hired on in Aggieland, Ed's surname rang a bell with the new A&M staff among potential recruits.

Once at A&M, Simonini and his classmates played a role in a significant part of A&M lore—a slice of history that helped the university expand to one of the nation's largest in lightning-quick time.

"I came to A&M at the same time as the first women's dorm was built on campus: 1972," Simonini says. "I think it made a difference in the recruitment of a lot of players to have more women on campus."

Behind the direction of A&M president and World War II hero Earl Rudder in 1964, the university—somewhat begrudgingly to many—began allowing women into the school on a full-scale basis. But women didn't start attending A&M en masse until the early 1970s.

While the growing presence of females at A&M began dissolving the school's once-rigid standing as strictly an all-male college with strong military leanings, the bilingual Simonini was breaking plenty of the stereotypes of a typical (dumb jock) football player.

"I lived in Italy when I was younger and I actually spoke Italian more than I spoke English," he says of his father's military stationing overseas. "We lived off of base, and the maids and the gardeners all spoke Italian."

Simonini majored in engineering at Texas A&M and finished up his degree at Johns Hopkins University in Baltimore, Md., while playing for the NFL's Colts. In Simonini's time at A&M—from 1972-75—the university grew by bounds.

"When I started at A&M, there were maybe 15,000 students, but that number had grown to about 25,000 by the time I left, which seems like a huge amount," Simonini says. "Now it's up to 44,000, and all of the changes going on at that time just seemed like a prelude of things to come. Girls were on campus, and the development of restaurants and hotels and apartments was just beginning to flourish. The school really, really started to change in the mid-'70s."

And like so many of his peers, Simonini thoroughly enjoyed a good time in his early years in College Station—even if students' social options were a bit limited.

"There pretty much was the Peanut Gallery off of Wellborn Highway—and that was about it," Simonini says, laughing. "It was this little dive where you'd drink beer and eat peanuts and throw the shells on the floor. It was an old wooden floor with a bunch of peanut shells all over the place. Remember, this was 1972.

"Later on there was the Dixie Chicken and a few other places to go, and we had more places to eat and socialize, and it just became a much different environment."

And much like College Station in the early 1970s, Simonini, six foot and 215 pounds, never bowled anyone over on sight alone. It took him roaming the field to impress the opposition and fans—the latter including an impressionable youngster named Jacob Green, who'd one day become A&M's single-season sack leader with 20.

"I chose No. 77 because that was Ed Simonini's number," says Green, a standout defensive end for the Aggies from 1977-79 and a future NFL Pro Bowler. "I wanted to be Ed Simonini, simply because he played the game so hard."

THE SCENE

Ed Simonini, a fierce and spirited linebacker for Texas A&M, evoked quite a sight around the Texas A&M campus for about a week leading up to the 1975 Texas game in College Station. Daily, Simonini sported a T-shirt that pitched a soup—well, sort of.

"The shirt said, 'Campbell's Soup, Umm ... Umm ... good,'" Simonini says, grinning. "It had a picture of Earl Campbell sort of running over me. It was a drawing from a picture taken from the '74 game."

In that game, a 32-3 Texas thumping of the stunned Aggies, the Longhorns' running back and future Heisman Trophy winner Campbell, then a freshman, rushed for 127 yards. Simonini's classmates knew better than to ask why he insisted on wearing the same T-shirt around campus and to practice all week—one that showed an opponent plowing over him.

"No one really talked to me about it," he says. "It's not hard to get the point. It was a reminder for everyone that this is who we've got to stop."

The second-ranked Aggies had plenty of incentive against the No. 5 Longhorns in 1975, starting with the loathsome idea that A&M hadn't beaten its primary rival since 1967—a Texas winning streak of seven games.

Even more embarrassing for the Aggies, in 1974 No. 17 Texas had whipped No. 8 A&M in Austin, dashing the Aggies' hopes of returning to the Cotton Bowl for the first time since the '67 season. A few scribes even dubbed College Station, "Chokesville, USA," following the loss.

"We had a chance to win the Southwest Conference, but we did a poor job and most people said we had choked," Simonini says.

In 1975, Simonini and the rest of the A&M seniors had one final chance to erase a distressing statistic—the Longhorns and coach Darrell Royal had smashed the Aggies and Coach Emory Bellard by at least 29 points in each of the rivals' three previous games.

"It wasn't even a monkey on our back," Simonini says. "It was a huge gorilla."

Royal, who'd already won three national championships at UT, also carried a 17-1 record against the Aggies headed into the '75 game. But 9-0 A&M, which led the nation in total defense behind the likes of Simonini, cornerback Pat Thomas, safety Lester Hayes, middle linebacker Robert Jackson and outside linebacker Garth Ten Napel, promised a tough contest against 9-1 UT.

"I know everyone thinks we've choked against Texas, but that's not going to happen this year," Simonini promised reporters in the days before the game. "This is our biggest game ever. It's about time we showed everyone, especially Texas, how good we play."

*   *   *   *   *

Outside College Station, the mid-1970s marked strange days, indeed, in the time surrounding the UT-A&M football game. Two days before the game a jury in Sacramento, Calif., convicted a Charles Manson follower, Lynette "Squeaky" Fromme, of trying to assassinate President Gerald Ford.

And federal investigators honed in on a few New Jersey Teamsters in the hopes of finding Jimmy Hoffa, the infamous union boss, who'd been missing four months. Hoffa still hasn't been found. And neither has a NCAA Division I football playoff, a hot topic at the 70th Annual NCAA Convention in Kansas City in 1975.

National columnist James Kilpatrick, too, urged readers to take seriously a Ronald Reagan candidacy for President in 1976—even if many folks questioned whether to trust onetime actors in political offices.

Reagan, who once starred as Notre Dame standout George Gipp in 1940's *Knute Rockne, All American*—"Tell them to go in there with all they've got and win one for the Gipper," Reagan declared from his deathbed as Gipp—earned the presidency five years later. Meanwhile the '75 Aggies earned their place in A&M football history on a sunny, beautiful Nov. 28 in College Station.

THE SETTING

Playing for the reserved Emory Bellard—inventor of the Wishbone offense and a mostly undemonstrative sort—didn't come easy for a free spirit like Ed Simonini. For instance, in the fall of 1974, the team hoped to catch the new release *The Longest Yard*—starring Burt Reynolds as a football player turned convict.

In the rebellious flick, Reynolds, as Paul Crewe (with "Mean Machine" stitched across his jersey), organizes a football game of inmates against prison guards. Simonini and the fellows figured it a perfect movie to watch the afternoon before a game. Bellard didn't agree, believing that the players should zero in solely on the task at hand—playing the game the next day.

"I can look back on it now and not be resentful about things like that, but it was tough to take at the time, mainly because you're a teenager, and your emotions are always running high," Simonini says. "But I realize now there wasn't a better guy out there for parents to trust their kids with. Because Coach Bellard, he wouldn't abandon you as a person."

In the weeks before the 1975 Texas game, the local country music stations hadn't abandoned a catchy tune called "That Aggie Joke's On You," penned by Scott Anderson, a Texas Tech graduate who capitalized on A&M's outstanding season.

"Nothing turns an Aggie off more than an Aggie joke, but this year the joke will be on the Southwest Conference, so we wrote this song," Anderson said in pitching the goofy ditty that in part intoned, "Folks can't tell no Aggie jokes this year."

All Campbell's Soup T-shirts and silly songs aside, A&M took its shot at beating Texas for the first time since '67 before a nationally televised ABC-TV audience extremely serious. Despite a 9-0 record for A&M, the 9-1 Longhorns (who'd only lost by a touchdown to No. 3 Oklahoma) were still a one-point favorite—based mostly on the series' recent history.

"I'd be telling a lie," Aggies defensive tackle Edgar Fields shared beforehand, "if I said the Texas game wasn't the biggest of 'em all to me."

A few days later on a supremely sunny day in College Station, the Aggies beat UT 20-10, holding the Longhorns' offense without a touchdown and mighty Earl Campbell to 40 yards on 15 carries before a Kyle Field record crowd of 56,679 delirious fans.

"Umm ... umm ... good," a delirious Simonini thought, as Corps of Cadets members swarmed the team on the field in celebration.

THE GAME OF MY LIFE
By Ed Simonini

The day before the 1975 Texas game we had a light practice, so to just kind of relax and keep ourselves from going crazy, we decided to sight in Garth Ten Napel's new hunting rifle. It was really a beautiful gun, and that was one of the nice things about A&M—a lot of the guys did a lot of hunting and fishing, and you could enjoy those activities not too far out of town.

I was never really big on hunting or fishing, but a lot of the guys were. So we drove several miles outside of the city to this wide-open field, and the guys put up these targets and began shooting the gun. It was Garth, Glenn Bujnoch, Richard Osborne, Blake Schwarz, Ted Ginsberg and myself.

Garth turned to me as I soaked in this Texan ritual.

"Hey, want to shoot the gun?" he said with a half-cocked smile.

I jumped at the chance.

"Sure, what the hell, fine, let me shoot it," I said.

I had nothing better to do.

So I'm looking through the sight and I've got my eyeball right there and I pull the trigger and, BAM! The sight slaps me right across the forehead—and I was bleeding like a stuck pig. My first thought: Am I gonna need stitches? My second thought: Uh-oh, am I gonna be able to play in the game—the most important game in my career?

What the hell had gone wrong? I'd never shot a dern gun before, especially with a scope on it—so I was hunkered down right on top of it. And all of those yahoos were laughing like crazy, because they knew what was going to happen before it happened.

It was Bujnoch and Osborne, after all, who'd nicknamed me "Weird Ed," because I could get pretty strange right before games. There was zero sympathy right after the scope incident, of course. I could have been knocked out with a concussion and they would have laughed and had a great time—thinking it was the funniest thing in the world.

So we got back to College Station and trainer Billy Pickard just went nuts.

"What were you thinking?" Mr. Pickard yelled.

I was thinking it was a good way to blow off steam before our biggest game. I wound up playing that game with a big Band-Aid on my head.

Turns out that rifle blast to the forehead—where I've still got a half-moon scar—forecast a wildly aggressive, physical game. And we won because we were more physical than they were, and that hadn't been the case the year before when Texas won on a cold, rainy, muddy day in Austin.

Ed Simonini (77) led the Aggies in tackles for three consecutive seasons (1973-75) and later excelled at linebacker for the Baltimore Colts. *Photo courtesy of Texas A&M Athletic Media Relations*

During that game, they had worn us down and beat us up. We reversed that in College Station. We held Earl Campbell to only 40 yards, and on one particular draw play just before halftime he broke through the line, and cornerback Pat Thomas stopped him and held him up, and then I came in and hit him and knocked the ball loose. Safety Jackie Williams recovered the fumble. Pat and Jackie were actually cousins, but we all worked as family on that one.

We had a close call midway through the fourth quarter when Texas kicker Russell Erxleben nailed a 47-yarder to close the gap to 17-10. When Erxleben kicked that ball, it just grazed the tips of my fingers. If I had been a little taller or could have jumped a little higher, then we could have blocked it.

But we still hung on for the win. My freshman year Texas had beaten us really bad, 38-3, and after that game I had grabbed Coach Bellard in the locker room.

"Coach, I promise you, we're not going to let this happen again," I said, as he nodded his head.

There had been a lot of freshmen who played back in '72 (the first year freshmen were eligible to play NCAA football), when we were 3-8, who were aiming from that time on to beat Texas—and this had been our last chance. So I grabbed Coach Bellard again in the locker room and hugged his head, squeezing it like a grape.

"I told you we were going to do it! I told you we were going to do it!" I yelled, wildly grinning and feeling no pain from the scope wound on my forehead. "It may have taken a while, but I told you we were going to do it!"

GAME RESULTS

How big was No. 2 Texas A&M's 20-10 win over No. 5 Texas on Nov. 28, 1975? One family of Aggie fans busted out a bottle of champagne in Kyle's upper deck in the victory's waning moments. But the win certainly didn't come easy and was very much in doubt until late in the fourth quarter.

The Aggies, who led 10-7 at halftime and only 17-10 with 7:01 remaining in the game, were greatly aided by running back Bubba Bean's 73-yard sprint in which he used split end Carl Roaches as a lead blocker. UT's Raymond Clayborn tackled Bean at the one-foot line, and a few plays later kicker Tony Franklin's 19-yard field goal put A&M up by the final score with 3:57 to play.

Texas quarterback Marty Akins, already hobbled by a bad knee, left the game for good late in the first quarter—and later returned to the sidelines decked in a blue leisure suit. The Aggies, however, didn't buy into the idea that the missing All-Conference quarterback meant the difference in the game.

"They could have had [national championship-winning quarterback] James Street in there today and it wouldn't have made any difference," said A&M cornerback Pat Thomas, who led an Aggies secondary that collected three interceptions on the day.

Penned Dan Cook of the *San Antonio Express-News*: "The Wishbone only works if you've got a good man in the middle, combined with outside speed and precision. When Akins was carried off, the outside threat was gone so the Aggie linebackers, as later explained by Ed Simonini, moved in half a step and concentrated more on Earl Campbell. Earl only got 40 yards and none came easy, so fierce were Aggie defenders."

A&M, too, had its own problems at quarterback. Mike Jay had subbed for an injured David Shipman, who then subbed for an injured Jay. Darrell Royal, long a coaching legend in the state as well as nationally by then, heaped praise on the Aggies after the game—especially A&M's defense, led by Simonini.

"It would be nice if they could bring another national championship back this way," Royal said in the minutes following only his second loss to A&M in 19 contests.

But it wasn't meant to be for undefeated Texas A&M, as a little more than a week later Arkansas whipped the Aggies 31-6 in Little Rock's War Memorial Stadium, as the surging Razorbacks advanced to the Cotton Bowl. A&M wrapped up its season with a 20-0 loss to USC in the Liberty Bowl, in John McKay's final game as Trojans head coach.

Typically A&M plays archrival Texas in its final regular-season game, but that year ABC-TV had persuaded the Aggies and Arkansas to push their annual Southwest Conference game from early November to Dec. 6.

"Midway through the season, Arkansas wasn't playing that well, but they really came on late," Simonini says. "But, no excuses. The bottom line is the Razorbacks were the better team that day, period."

Still, little smears the memory of 1975's sweet victory over Texas, a game in which years of pent-up A&M frustration evaporated with a single win.

"Garth Ten Napel and I, late that night, were spinning 'doughnuts' in our cars in that commons area between the stadium and Wofford Cain Dormitory," Simonini says, laughing.

"It's all landscaped now, but it was just an old field at the time. He had a Ford Mustang and I had a Pontiac Firebird—a couple of muscle cars—and we were kicking up mud all over the place.

"The wild thing is a campus cop came running out of there with his flashlight, and so we got out of there. We just couldn't help ourselves that night. We were celebrating a big win."

WHAT BECAME OF ED SIMONINI?

A seventh-grade class back in El Paso, Texas, made a lifelong impression on Ed Simonini.

"I always had the desire to live and work in Latin America, and that was in part because of my Texas history class," Simonini says. "I was fascinated by all of those stories about Coronado and the conquistadors."

Simonini learned Spanish by spending three months in Venezuela in 1994, and he's now director of distributors for Hilti Latin America LTD. His office is based in Tulsa, Okla., although he works extensively in countries like Peru, Paraguay, Uruguay, Bolivia and Ecuador.

Simonini, who began working for Hilti in 1986 as a field engineer, retired after seven seasons in the NFL in 1983. He led the Baltimore Colts in tackles for four consecutive years (from 1977-80).

"That sounds wonderful and all of that, but that's not a great accomplishment," an unassuming Simonini says. "It's not something you should strive for, I'll put it that way. There were a couple of years that I led the league in tackles, but that typically means you're on the field a lot. Meaning, No. 1, your offense isn't doing too well, and, No. 2, your defense isn't doing too well, because you're not stopping a lot of people.

"So you're making a lot of tackles, that's true, but it's kind of like the reverse of a football player who's running the ball a lot. Earl Campbell ran the ball a lot when he was playing in the NFL, and it cut short his pro career. There's only so many carries that a running back has, and there's only so many tackles that a defender has, as well."

*   *   *   *   *

Simonini married his wife, the former Karen Christy, on Dec. 30, 1978, and the couple has two children, Ana and Nick, whom they adopted from Guatemala.

"When I was playing for the Colts we were living in Baltimore at the time, and we located an agency that handled international adoptions," Simonini says. "Raising our children has been a wonderful experience."

Simonini attended a Texas A&M football game for the first time in years in the fall of 2002, when unranked A&M stunned No. 1 Oklahoma 30-26 on Nov. 9, 2002, at Kyle Field in R.C. Slocum's final victory as Aggies coach.

"It was a beautiful day, and it very much reminded me of the 1975 game against Texas," Simonini says. "It was clear and sunny with blue skies, and the stands were completely filled. Just a great day to play football. We sat in the stands and I was hoarse by halftime."

Accompanied by his father, nephew and his nephew's friend, Simonini even encountered an unexpected visitor in the traffic and celebration afterward surrounding the stadium.

"We got in the car and people were streaming by and the Aggie Band was marching by and playing, and we had the windows rolled down on the van because it was so nice outside," Simonini says. "We were just north of the stadium when suddenly this guy came up to the passenger window where my dad was sitting and asked, 'Hey, is that where the Aggie Bonfire used to be?' And he's pointing over toward an open field, but the Bonfire actually was last held on the other side of campus.

"Of course my dad is in his 80s and he's got a hearing aid so he said, 'Huh?' And so the guy repeated himself, and in all of the crowd and traffic and for simplicity's sake I just said, 'Yeah, that's where it was.' And suddenly we recognized the man as Barry Switzer, the former Oklahoma coach. He'd coached me in the Hula Bowl when I was a senior, so I hopped out of the van to say hello.

"Out of 80,000-plus people at that game against Oklahoma, we run into Barry Switzer. What are the odds of that? It was a great ending to a great day."

Simonini's impromptu reunion with Switzer took place right by where the vivacious Aggies linebacker had once spun his Firebird in celebratory doughnuts more than a quarter of a century earlier. Ed Simonini, it seemed, had come full circle in Aggieland.

CHAPTER 11

JACOB GREEN

Name: Jacob Carl Green Jr.
Born: Jan. 21, 1957
Hometown: Houston, Texas
Current Residence: Houston, Texas
Occupation: Retired from the NFL, founder of Jaycee's Children's Center in Houston
Position: Defensive End
Height: 6'3"
Playing Weight: 230 pounds
Years lettered: 1977-79
Accomplishments: Two-time All-American and two-time All-Conference (1978-79); school single-season sack leader with 20 in 1979, and school record holder for career fumbles caused (12); first-round pick (10th overall) of the Seattle Seahawks in 1980; played 13 seasons in the NFL and is Seattle's all-time leader for sacks in a game (four in 1986), season (16 in 1983) and career (116); two-time Pro Bowler (1986-87).
Nickname: Sevens
The Game: Texas at Texas A&M, Dec. 1, 1979

Jacob Green. *Photo courtesy of Texas A&M Athletic Media Relations*

THE LIFE OF YOUNG JACOB GREEN

Not-so-little Jacob Green, 13, was well aware he was too young, legally, to drive dump trucks and tractors—but there was much work to be done around Green Brothers Dirt Yard in Houston.

"You've got to do what you've got to do," Green says, grinning at the idea of operating heavy machinery for his father's landscaping company at such a young age.

"I loved that kind of work, anyway. My father owned Green Brothers, and that's where I first started to earn my way in life.

"It was a good, hard honest living, and I met a lot of good people in that business."

But there also was the business of playing football, and Green—one of the best pass rushers ever to play at Texas A&M—quickly established himself as one of the state's most intimidating defenders at Kashmere High in northeast Houston in the mid-1970s.

"Jacob and I have known each other since elementary school, and he's always been extremely competitive," says Jarvis Williams, who attended Kashmere with Green and also played basketball at Texas A&M from 1975-79. "We even had a couple of horses when we were kids that we kept at a nearby stable, and he was always telling me how much faster—and prettier—his was than mine.

"One summer I worked with him over at the dirt yard, and he was operating all of that heavy equipment. It wasn't like he had any choice—he'd probably rather have been somewhere else, like by the pool—but his dad taught him all of that and expected that of Jacob."

The youngest of Jacob Carl Sr. and Tommie Mae Green's two children never wanted for much of anything—save for maybe a bit more poolside time—growing up on Houston's sometimes tough north side.

"My parents did a great job of raising me and preparing me for life," Green says. "I couldn't tell if I grew up on the north side in the 'hood or in [exclusive] River Oaks, because my parents took care of me. They worked hard and did what they had to do to keep my sister and me in line."

Says Jarvis Williams: "Jacob's father was a no-nonsense guy who knew how to love him and discipline him at the same time. That's where Jacob got his grounding—and when Jacob got the to NFL he was able to handle himself and carry himself as a role model, because that's the way he was raised."

But while still in high school and in the fall of 1974, Green had narrowed his college choices to the state's two most prominent programs, having ruled out Oklahoma State and Houston.

"It boiled down to Texas and Texas A&M," Green says. "Texas actually was recruiting another guy at Kashmere named Eddie Day, and Eddie Day was as good as there was. He was as quick and fast as I was and about 10 pounds heavier. He could run about a 4.5 [seconds] in the 40-yard dash. So Texas was recruiting both of us, but Eddie broke his leg his senior year and the Longhorns immediately stopped pursuing him.

"That's when I knew Texas wasn't the place for me."

In turn, it seemed that some skeptics didn't believe A&M was the place for Green, either, based on what they perceived as a lack of talent.

"I distinctly remember not being invited to the high school All-Star game in Houston my senior year," says Green, who'd earned city Most Valuable Player and All-State honors. "So when I came to A&M I had a point to prove from day one that those guys in my recruiting class who played in that game weren't as good as I was. I knew it in my heart."

And Texas A&M coach Emory Bellard, who recruited Green to A&M, knew it as well.

"When you get here, throw your hat in the ring, pardner, and let 'em know what you can do," Bellard reassured Green after he'd signed with A&M.

Green eventually set the school single-season sack record with 20 as a senior in 1979, a number no Aggie has sniffed since.

"There's an art to rushing the passer," Green says. "You've got to study an opponent and find his weakness. My thing was beating a guy off the ball, because once I beat him off the ball then I had a chance to get to the quarterback. Quickness was my asset, and rushing the passer was my trade."

THE SCENE

Team captain Jacob Green couldn't help himself, glancing out among the 40,000 ardent, true-believing supporters staring back at him at the annual Bonfire on the Friday night before the Aggies' 1979 clash with rival Texas—the flashy team with all the "name" guys.

Not only a season of frustrations—5-5 Texas A&M had lost three games to Brigham Young, Texas Tech and Houston by a combined five points earlier in the year—but a career of having to prove himself time and again finally boiled over in Green in one euphoric instant.

Standing at the Bonfire before a huge crowd, down to his final college football game against a glamorous Longhorns team ranked sixth nationally and sporting a shimmering 9-1 record, Green seized the moment.

Peering into all of those trusting faces—the ones who'd stood by this .500 team through it all, Green promised a little sumthin' special to the Aggies faithful that cool Bonfire night.

"We're gonna kick their ass," Green abruptly yelled, and the mass erupted.

"Just like that," Green says, smiling. "The crowd just went wild. It just seemed like everything that could have went wrong that year did, and we had one last chance to prove that we were a good team, as well. So I promised the fans that we'd win. That we'd kick their ass.

"I didn't intend to say that; it was a spontaneous reaction to an emotional moment. I was just gonna say something about beating Texas, but when I told the crowd we were going to kick their ass, everybody whooped. That set my adrenaline to running. I was ready to play right then."

While Aggies defensive coordinator Melvin Robertson enjoyed his star defensive end's bravado, Robertson also knew that promises are useless without fulfillment.

"Jacob, now, you said it," Robertson said, pulling Green aside after the Bonfire. "You better back it up."

"I know, Coach," Green said, nodding his head. "I know."

So full of promise under second-year coach Tom Wilson (who'd replaced Bellard in 1978), the 1979 Aggies lost 18-17 to Brigham Young in the season opener (a Cougars team that wound up 11-1). Then A&M fell 21-20 at Texas Tech in the season's fifth contest and 17-14 against Houston a game later at Kyle Field.

"Let me tell you, we had Brigham Young beat," Green says, still fuming a bit at the memory. "We were up by a couple of touchdowns, and they came back to beat us because we'd put our second-string defense in. We got up and started subbing, and by the time the starters got back in it was too late.

"Their quarterback, Marc Wilson, had gotten hot, and we couldn't shut them down."

Maybe more than any game in the Mormon university's history, BYU's win over No. 9 A&M staked the Cougars program on the college football map. Texas A&M actually played that home game in Rice Stadium, as the university renovated Kyle Field.

The Aggies led 17-10 late in the fourth quarter, but the Cougars scored with 52 seconds remaining, and then gambled—and collected—on a two-point conversion from Wilson to Mike Lacey. The Aggies' mental laces, meanwhile, unraveled at the trepidation of it all, and A&M lost its next game at Baylor, 17-7.

Remarkably, A&M whipped Penn State 27-14 in State College, Pa., in Game 3, but that victory largely was the highlight of the Aggies' season hurtling into their annual showdown with the Longhorns.

"Texas thought it was going to the Sugar Bowl against No. 1 Alabama," Green says, "but we had plans to send them a different route."

*   *   *   *   *

Elsewhere across the nation, President Jimmy Carter wished his 81-year-old mother, Lillian Carter, had chosen a different route in explaining how she'd handle fanatical Iranian leader Ayatollah Khomeini. At the same time as the Aggies and Longhorns suited up for their 86th meeting in history, extremist Iranians held 50 Americans hostages (who were released more than a year later) in the U.S. Embassy in Tehran.

"If I had a million dollars to spare, I'd look for someone to kill him," the stately yet spunky Mrs. Carter said of Khomeini, to wild applause at the Bow Men's Club on the outskirts of Concord, N.H.

The White House quickly responded that "Miss Lillian did not expect anyone to take that comment seriously." But people did—and they cheered. Half a continent away and around the same time, on a much more upbeat and less sober note, 40,000 Aggies yelled for Green, and his own debatable exclamation: "We're gonna kick their ass."

THE SETTING

Emmett Harris, a 1923 Texas A&M graduate, settled into his spot in Section 110 of Kyle Field on Dec. 1, 1979, and recalled watching E. King Gill, the Original 12th Man, receive a summons out of the press box by coach Dana X. Bible.

Gill, a basketball player at A&M who was working as a spotter that day, quickly suited up for the Aggies, using an injured player's uniform in the 1922 Dixie Classic. An Aggies legend was born, although Gill never got in the game.

Little did the elderly Harris know on that December 1979 afternoon that he'd witness another notable moment in Texas A&M football history, one constructed by a bunch of mostly no-name Aggies who'd sometimes plodded and other times burst to a .500 season. On the opposing sidelines, enough household names comprised the Texas roster to fill a house.

"The Texas game is always the biggest game for any A&M senior or for any player for that matter," two-time All-American Jacob Green says. "The two teams on that particular day just don't like each other, regardless of past or future friendships. And I also knew that for the '79 Texas game there were going to be a lot of scouts watching the Longhorns.

"I mean, they had Steve McMichael, Johnnie Johnson, 'Lam' Jones, 'Jam' Jones, Herkie Walls ... they just had a helluva team. And I was mad at the time because I wasn't a finalist for the Outland Trophy and McMichael was. And I had 18 sacks going into that game."

Much like when he was shunned for the high school All-Star game four years earlier, Green prepared to play mad—and like mad—because he wasn't a finalist for the award handed to the nation's top interior lineman. Both McMichael and Green excelled on two superior defenses, as UT entered the game ranked third nationally in total defense.

"Texas's strength is in its personnel," said Aggies coach Tom Wilson, who received a three-year contract extension from the university on the day before the Texas game, despite the team's .500 record. "They're the best technique team on defense that I've ever seen. [UT's defense] has to be compared to the best defensive teams ever, right up there with ones like the 1975 Aggies defense."

But Wilson, in only his first full season and then bearer of a 9-7 overall record, didn't just gush about the opposition beforehand.

"There are a lot of great players in this country right now, but I can't imagine one playing better than Jacob Green," Wilson said.

Green, with plenty of help from his teammates, thus proved the coach prophetic, as the Aggies upset No. 6 Texas 13-7 before a Kyle Field record crowd of 69,017 true-believing fans.

THE GAME OF MY LIFE
By Jacob Green

Right off the bat, Texas tried a reverse on its first possession of the game from its own 40-yard line, and just about everybody on our defense got fooled. Suddenly it was just "Lam" Jones and me—one on one—and I caught him. I can't say that I knew the reverse was coming; I just happened to be in the right place at the right time and I snagged Lam in the backfield. Otherwise, with his breakaway speed, he might have gone all the way.

Believe it or not, that turned the entire tempo of the game, right there. The whole tide shifted, even that early in the game. Now, mind you, we still had our hands full with the Longhorns' offense, and their freshman quarterback, Rick McIvor, had just thrown for 270 yards (then a UT school record) the week before against Baylor.

We knew we had to put plenty of pressure on McIvor, keep him on his heels, and let the secondary do its job in the defensive backfield. It did. I got a couple of more sacks that day, as well.

The biggest play for us on offense came with a couple of minutes remaining in the first half. Our super fast tailback, Curtis Dickey, ran a play that we'd executed in games before—the halfback pass. At the time we were trailing Texas 7-6 and on the Longhorns' 20-yard line. Dickey started to pass, but the receivers were covered, so he just let his athletic ability take over, and he took off for the end zone. Let me tell you, Curtis was as fast as anybody in the country, in track or football.

So when he saw an opening, he was going to take it, and he did. That touchdown gave us a little daylight—but not much. Going into the game we had a goal of a shutout, and in the second half we did shut them out. We knew it was going to be tough to score on Texas, because we had struggled quite a bit on offense that year.

"Make them earn everything they've got!" our defensive players yelled to each other as encouragement before and during the game. Doug Carr, our starting middle linebacker, pulled us together for some urging on Texas's final drive.

"Let's hold 'em one more time!" Carr yelled.

We did. Keith Baldwin, our right defensive end, sacked McIvor on

Jacob Green recorded 20 sacks in 1979, five more than any other Aggie has ever tallied in history. *Aggieland Yearbook*

Texas's final drive to end any hopes of a Longhorns comeback.

Beating Texas made an otherwise disappointing season worth playing—and it was a great way to end my college career. There had been a lot of talking going on at Texas. It seemed like the Horns already had their bags packed for the Sugar Bowl in New Orleans. But we won our bowl game, man, because the Texas game *was* our bowl game. And we ruined their planned party on Bourbon Street.

GAME RESULTS

Texas, the darlings of the Southwest Conference in 1979, wound up playing in the Sun Bowl that season, a 14-7 loss to Washington. Legendary coach Paul "Bear" Bryant won the last of his five national titles that year at Alabama after the Crimson Tide defeated Arkansas 24-9 in the Sugar.

A&M's win also pushed the University of Houston, under coach Bill Yeoman, into the Cotton Bowl for the third time in four years, ahead of Texas. The Cougars' band even played the "Aggie War Hymn" during Houston's 63-0 whipping of Rice on the same Saturday at Rice Stadium.

And while A&M had just given Wilson a three-year extension, the win over Texas proved his final promising big victory, as Jackie Sherrill had replaced the beleaguered coach by the 1982 season.

Aggies senior tailback Curtis Dickey, a future first-round draft pick of the Baltimore Colts, played his final college game with bruised ribs that chilly day in 1979 and had scored the go-ahead touchdown on the 20-yard sprint late in the first half.

"We could lose every game, but to beat Texas makes the whole year," Dickey said afterward, smiling but occasionally grimacing from the sharp pain in his ribs.

"That was one great play," Texas coach Fred Akers said of Dickey running with the ball instead of attempting a halfback pass. "It looked like they were going to throw back to the quarterback, and our people went with him. That left a big hole."

For his part, Green & Co. left a big hole in the hearts of UT, which to that point figured it might still have an outside shot at the national title.

"Jacob Green is a heck of a football player," said the quarterback McIvor, who finished seven of 26 for 112 yards. "He put a lot of pressure on me throughout. You don't find many like him."

And Green, always fighting to prove himself—whether coming out of high school or out of college—had a final message for A&M's critics.

"The Texas defense got all of the pub this year," Green said after the game, allowing a bit of a grin, "but we're pretty good, too."

And, in the end, Green's promise came true: the Aggies had kicked the Longhorns' asses.

WHAT BECAME OF JACOB GREEN?

Jacob Green's school single-season sack record of 20 has withstood the test of time. For the past two decades players have angled for it, only to fall short and, usually, way short. Ray Childress and John Roper—as Green's closest competition—each collected 15 sacks in a season (Roper twice).

"Oh, it's gonna get broken one day," Green says. "But it's gonna take some doing."

Green, who played in two Pro Bowls in 12 years with the Seattle Seahawks, spoke at the annual Aggies-Longhorns lunch in Houston before the game at Kyle Field in November 1999, only days after the Bonfire collapsed in College Station, killing 12 Aggies.

"Steve McMichael called me," Green told the audience through misty eyes of his former college rival. "He just wanted to tell me he was hurting for us. That's what Texans are about, what A&M is about and what UT is about. I just want to say thank you, guys."

Green, one of the best players to ever wear the Maroon and White, never won a Southwest Conference championship at Texas A&M, and he never played in a Super Bowl with the Seahawks. Would he do it all over again—the same way? In the snap of a football, you bet.

"I'd have gone to A&M again in a heartbeat, even if I'd had a chance to win a national title somewhere else, because of the friendships I made and the people I met," he says.

"The same thing with Seattle—I wouldn't change it to any other team."

Following his retirement from the NFL in 1992, Green returned home to Houston and ran his father's durable landscaping business.

"I always did love driving those dump trucks and tractors and such," Green says. "My mom kept the family business going even after my father passed away in 1983. I came back and kept it going for another four years and then got out of that business and started doing what I'm doing now."

What he's doing now is running Jaycee's Children's Center in Houston, a home for teenaged girls that Green established. Green, who has three daughters—Janelle, Jessica and Jillian—with his wife, Janet, opened the home in 1998.

"My sister, Euradell, is a social worker, and she got me involved with this," Green says. "We take these kids in and give them a place to stay for at least six months and try and get them off the streets. These kids just haven't had a break, that's all. That's what we try and provide.

"We give them a place to live, a place to sleep, and a place where they don't have to worry about where their next meal is coming from. We have 26 kids at a time, and it's always full."

Green also is heavily involved in the Fred Hutchinson Cancer Research Center in Seattle, a foundation he's raised hundreds of thousands of dollars for since his father died of cancer early in Green's Seahawks playing career.

Meanwhile daughter Janelle has continued Green's strong A&M legacy as a member of the perennially powerful Aggies soccer team starting in 2002. Green, who once happily and ardently drove dump trucks for his father at age 13, has much of which to be proud, after successfully tackling so many heavy loads in life.

"Growing up and coming from the north side of Houston and the 'hood, so to speak, there were many temptations," Green says. "But I wanted to try and be something. That was a key to success, and my parents simply raising me right. The best thing you can do is keep your nose clean, your head straight, and do the right thing."

CHAPTER 12

12th Man
Kickoff Team

Blessed be the tie that binds—a tie that Jackie Sherrill unwittingly, but so beautifully, forged for Ray and James Barrett from high atop the Aggie Bonfire stack that cool fall evening in 1982. Sherrill, in his first year as Texas A&M coach and near the end of a 5-6 season, had wandered by Bonfire, and wound up staying for a few hours to help with its construction in the days before it was to burn.

"The way those guys worked," Sherrill said at the time, "I wanted some of them on my team."

Thus, Sherrill created the 12th Man Kickoff Team—comprised of Corps of Cadets members and other plain ol' Texas A&M students—that would cover kickoffs at home games. And in doing so, Sherrill helped a son become more like his father.

"So many boys want to follow in their dad's footsteps," James Barrett says. "And I'd seen over the years the friendships my dad had kept through playing football for the Aggies. Suddenly, when Coach Sherrill formed the 12th Man Kickoff Team, I had the opportunity to be more like my dad."

Ray Barrett, one of Paul "Bear" Bryant's Junction Boys, had walked on the Aggies' football team in 1952 as a five foot ten, 200-pound guard. Ray was reminded of exactly how much times have changed in half a century on the gridiron when he attended the annual Maroon and White

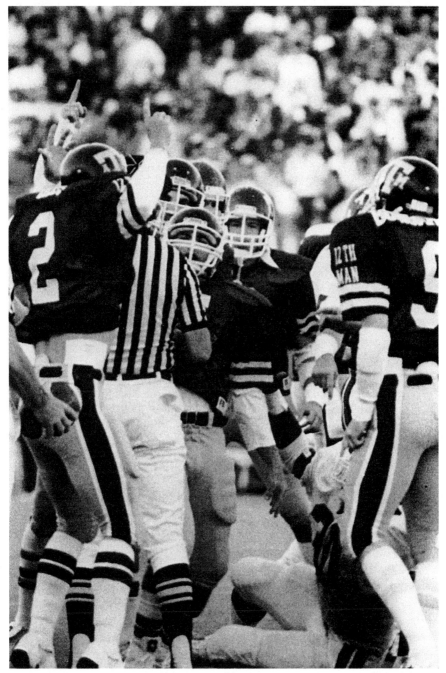

The Aggies' 12th Man Kickoff Team, a brainchild of Coach Jackie Sherrill, celebrates a fourth-quarter fumble recovery against Arkansas in 1983. *Aggieland Yearbook.*

game in the spring of 2003.

Lo and behold, another Barrett was wearing No. 60—Ray's old number—but this fellow was six-foot-four, 310-pound Mason Barrett, also an offensive lineman.

"Our biggest guy back then was about 220 pounds," Ray says, smiling, of the Junction days. "The kids just got a lot bigger and faster over the years."

That's why in the early 1980s and at about his father's size at 195 pounds, James Barrett realized he had no chance to earn a football scholarship to Texas A&M, although he'd starred as a linebacker at Rankin High School in West Texas.

So James enrolled as a regular Texas A&M student—he always wanted to be an Aggie, just like his dad—and then one day heard about the new coach, Jackie Sherrill, soliciting volunteers for a kickoff team.

"It was a chance of a lifetime," James says. "To get the chance to play for the Aggies meant so much to me, especially since my father had done the same."

James, along with 251 other students (including two women), showed up for the first tryouts. The coaches whittled that number to 16 by the summer, in preparation for the Kickoff Team's first adventure on Sept. 3, 1983, against California at Kyle Field.

"I guess everybody's got their fingers crossed," A&M scholarship center Matt Darwin said a couple of days before the Kickoff Team's debut.

Stunningly to many, the 12th Man team worked spectacularly in both its first year and the seasons to come under Jackie Sherrill. In that first year, in fact, the Aggies kickoff team allowed just 13.1 yards per return, compared to the varsity's 18.8 the same season on road games (the 12th Man didn't travel).

"The 12th Man was just a bunch of marginally talented kids having a lot of fun," says Sean Page, a San Antonio lawyer and a Kickoff Team member from 1985-87. "We always knew we were one touchdown away from going back to the scrap heap."

Sherrill had formed the Kickoff Team to make students feel more connected with the program.

"The [scholarship] football players are excited because they know it's not taking anything away from them," Sherrill said when he created the Kickoff Team. "And the students are excited because they know it might be their roommate down there, covering a kickoff. It's an extension of yourself."

Sherrill had the last part right, anyway: Students were excited. The scholarship football players, however, weren't always as thrilled.

"The Aggies had an awful lot of talent at that time," Page says.

"And then they had us. But after games when we were walking out of the locker room and such, alumni and students and fans wanted to talk to us—because we were like them.

"A lot of times the scholarship players were like, 'Why are these blocking dummies getting all of the glory?'"

The "blocking dummies" also played some backup positions on the team during practice, as NCAA scholarship limits and injuries hindered college football teams' depths. Page was once playing defensive back in practice and smacked scholarship receiver Greg Dillon, who was flying across the middle.

"Dillon went crazy," Page says.

The next day, an assistant coach specially requested that Page serve as a running back in a blocking drill on a grass field adjacent to Kyle Field. That's when Rich Siler, a 240-pounder and a future NFL tight end, fiercely planted the 5'9", 165-pound Page into a fence surrounding the practice field during the drill.

"I got my ass handed to me," Page says. "I had a big ol' scrape mark on my body from that fence."

But it wasn't *all* fun and games for the Kickoff Team, as the gang took its job of shutting down return men extremely seriously, and the gung-ho bunch didn't allow a kickoff return for a touchdown from 1983-89.

But in 1990, Texas Tech's Rodney Blackshear returned a kick for a TD, vanquishing the mystique. And in 1991 Aggies coach R.C. Slocum—who had called Sherrill's Kickoff Team "a stroke of genius" when Slocum took over the program in late 1988—shaved down the on-field squad to one walk-on player (wearing No. 12) who runs down on kickoffs.

Still, that lone player (several 12th Men are on the roster, and usually one plays a game) gives Aggies plenty of reason to yell for "one of their own."

"In a lot of ways," Aggies tight end Dan Campbell once said of when the 12th Man makes a play, "it's almost like the crowd made the tackle."

The 12th Man's most infamous tackle took place at the 1988 Cotton Bowl, a 35-10 Aggies win over Notre Dame. In the fourth quarter, the 12th Man Kickoff Team tackled Heisman Trophy winner Tim Brown, and then 12th Man Warren Barhorst stole Brown's hand towel off of his uniform. Brown then chased down a giddy and unsuspecting Barhorst and tackled him, touching off a bench-clearing tussle that earned Notre Dame a 15-yard penalty.

"They must have had something planned on the sideline," said a fuming Brown, who'd gotten the towel (which he recovered) with his

Ray and James Barrett share a moment at the Texas A&M Athletic Sports Museum in 2001. *Texas A&M Lettermen's Association*

initials and number on it from a teammate's girlfriend.

Barhorst played dumb afterward about swiping the towel.

"In all of the excitement of tackling a Heisman Trophy winner like Tim Brown, I had a hand on his towel and took it," Barhorst said, with a straight face. "When I started to run off the field he tackled me."

The 12th Man Kickoff Team created several such memorable moments through its unbridled enthusiasm in playing a game usually reserved for the biggest and fastest of athletes. That's why it was so special for James Barrett, diagnosed in 1999 with the crippling Amyotrophic Lateral Sclerosis (ALS)—or Lou Gehrig's Disease—to get that chance back in 1983 to be more like his father, who played in a different era.

"There's a bond between the Junction Boys that even I, as my father's son, can't figure out," James Barrett says. "We believe the 12th Man Kickoff Team has the same type of bond."

CHAPTER 13

RAY CHILDRESS

Name: Raymond Clay Childress Jr.
Born: Oct. 20, 1962
Hometown: Dallas, Texas
Current Residence: Houston, Texas
Occupation: Auto Dealer
Position: Defensive End
Height: 6'6"
Playing Weight: 270 pounds
Years lettered: 1981-84
Accomplishments: Two-time All-American and two-time All-Conference (1983-84); 25 sacks over his finals two seasons, including 15 as a junior; Lombardi Award finalist as a senior; second player picked in the 1985 draft; five-time Pro Bowler in 11 seasons with the Houston Oilers.
The Game: TCU at Texas A&M, Nov. 24, 1984

THE LIFE OF YOUNG RAY CHILDRESS

Ray Childress grew up in Memphis, Tenn., a huge Ole Miss and Alabama fan—literally. Childress, one of the best defensive linemen to ever play at Texas A&M, stood six foot six and 262 pounds in high school

Ray Childress. *Photo courtesy of Texas A&M Athletic Media Relations*

and earned the nickname "Manchild" among teammates and coaches.

When Childress's family moved from Memphis to the Dallas suburb of Richardson—his father, who was in the construction business, found that market more lucrative—during his sophomore year in high school, his collegiate interests changed as well.

"Then the schools you heard about were Texas A&M and Texas," Childress says.

At Richardson's Pearce High School, Childress specialized in terrorizing the passer, and that never changed over his outstanding college and professional careers. Childress credits his mother and father, Ray and Marie, for giving him such a focused, single-minded mentality.

"They instilled in me a work ethic and an understanding that to be successful you've got to be dedicated and you've got to stay after it," Childress says. "And that was the attitude I took to rushing the passer. When the ball was snapped, I'd just go upfield. It still irritates me when I listen to these commentators who actually played the game or coached the game, and they talk about these defensive linemen who are offsides, and they can't believe it because all he has to do is watch the ball.

"That's not reality. That's like saying a receiver should never drop a pass. A great defensive lineman isn't going to wait on anything. You've got to get into a good rhythm and get a quick start off of the ball.

"That's why every once in a while a guy is going to be offsides, but hopefully by the end of the game he's produced enough good plays to make up for that."

The tall, lean Childress produced enough good plays to catch the eye of recruiters nationwide, and he chose the Aggies under coach Tom Wilson over Texas and Nebraska.

Jackie Sherrill, the deposed Wilson's replacement in January 1982, arrived at A&M a year after Childress, and the former Pitt coach quickly grew to appreciate the mentality of the quiet giant in the Western wear whom he'd inherited.

"Ray Childress plays as hard as he can play," Sherrill said while in his second year at A&M. "He's a very polite young man, but there's an awful lot of intensity in him."

An intensity that Jackie Sherrill—another man with an awful lot of intensity in him—further appreciated a year later in a pivotal 1984 game against TCU.

THE SCENE

J ackie Sherrill cut to the chase—as he so often did—in discussing upcoming opponent Texas Christian University that November day of 1984.

"No two places are the same," Sherrill simply said when asked why A&M's season had gone south to that point, as opposed to why he figured upstart TCU was busily sizing itself for purple "Cinderella" slippers.

Sherrill, in his third year at Texas A&M—and likely faced with a third consecutive season with a mediocre record—might have waxed more eloquent and expounded more exponentially had his tenure in Aggieland gone any better. Then again, maybe not.

"When Jackie Sherrill got to A&M in 1982, he had a very brash personality," says Childress. "He had wonderful leadership skills, but I don't think he had great communication skills—at least not at first. He yelled and screamed a lot and demanded a lot out of people.

"But toward the end of that third year—which was my senior year— Jackie's communication skills were much better, and people had stopped resisting some of the coaching philosophy that he wanted to put in place. And when that happened, we just exploded."

By "people," Childress means Sherrill's players and even some of his assistant coaches. Many A&M fans and the media, however, seemed a more reluctant sell, considering Sherrill had finished 5-6 in 1982, 5-5-1 a year later and to that point in 1984—careening into the TCU game with only the Texas game to follow—4-5. One Houston columnist had even called for Sherrill's job, something the high-priced coach didn't take kindly to.

On Jan. 19, 1982, A&M had lured the 38-year-old Sherrill from the University of Pittsburgh with a six-year contract worth around $287,000 a year—numbers then unheard of for a college football coach.

"No president or chancellor or professors at any university that I know of, including our chancellor, are paid anywhere near that much," groaned Ed Bozik, assistant chancellor at Pitt.

A&M's courtship of Sherrill, who'd played on a couple of national champions for Paul "Bear" Bryant at Alabama in 1964 and '65, had attracted detractors from the beginning. University president Frank Vandiver threatened to resign because he'd given Wilson the oft-dreaded "vote of confidence" in November 1981, and then the school's big money went above his head and ran off Wilson.

"Can the Aggies buy respect?" read a headline in a February 1982 *Newsweek* article that began, "How many Aggies does it take to hire a football coach?" Sherrill wasn't even A&M's first choice. Michigan's Bo Schembechler had turned down a 10-year, $2 million contract offer only days before the Aggies hired Sherrill, whose Pitt team (behind quarterback Dan Marino) had finished No. 2 in the country in 1981.

The Houston Astros, a little more than an hour down Highway 6 from College Station, had taken plenty of heat in 1980 for signing pitcher Nolan Ryan to a $1 million per year contract. Now, critics were zeroing in on A&M—the nation's fastest growing university—for letting money talk so loudly in college athletics.

"The regents reach in where they have no place, spend over a million dollars on a football coach, and we find ourselves the butt of national jokes," said Angelique Copeland, student editor of A&M's *Battalion* newspaper, in 1982. "This is not the kind of reputation A&M should be building."

*   *   *   *   *

Three football seasons into his hire, Jackie Sherrill had yet to notch a winning year at A&M. As comedian Eddie Murphy yukked it up at the Schulman Theatre on 29th Street with his *Beverly Hills Cop*, hardly anyone was laughing around Bryan-College Station late in the fall of 1984.

At least when it came to football. The 4-5 Aggies, who'd only had one losing season in their past eight prior to Sherrill's arrival, seemed in a spiral with two games remaining in '84. Worse yet, affable TCU coach Jim Wacker and his surprising Horned Frogs were 8-2, and fighting for a Cotton Bowl slot. The media had picked the Aggies that year to finish near the top of the Southwest Conference under Sherrill, but things had gone awry.

"We had just gotten beat at Arkansas 28-0 before the TCU game, and we only had two games left in my senior year," Ray Childress says. "The TCU players were saying a lot of things in the papers about how they hadn't won at Kyle Field in forever, but that they were going to turn that around.

"No way were the A&M seniors going to let that happen. No way."

Sherrill did some great—and not-so-good—things at A&M before he left the school in late 1988. By the time he'd split College Station in a cloud of NCAA troubles, many Aggies still sighed, "Good thing we had Jackie Sherrill to get this program going again." Good thing, too, Jackie Sherrill had Ray Childress.

THE SETTING

Kyle Field hadn't held such a small crowd for an A&M game in a decade and likely will never again.

"It wasn't well attended," Childress says of the 1984 TCU-A&M game.

"But we didn't let that distract us."

Ironic, too, that a man who'd become one of A&M's most revered former athletes would then play a defining and most memorable game in such a setting—before 38,209 fans in a half-empty stadium. In the week prior to Texas A&M's collision with TCU, the Texas Longhorns had sucker-punched Cinderella, whose dainty slippers featured cleats.

"But Cinderella's not dead," declared upbeat TCU coach Jim Wacker. "Not even close."

TCU had earned the nickname of the fairy-tale heroine after running its record to 8-2 and a Top 15 ranking in 1984, only a season after finishing 1-8-2. The Horned Frogs still had a shot at winning the Southwest Conference, although UT had just whipped their behinds 44-23 in Fort Worth.

But winning the conference meant winning at Kyle Field, where the Horned Frogs hadn't earned a victory since 1972. TCU hadn't even beaten the Aggies in 11 consecutive contests, no matter the site. But that still didn't stop the Horned Frogs from chatting up the idea things would be different in 1984, because of the two teams' directions to that point in the season.

"They hadn't been to a Cotton Bowl in about a jillion years [actually, since 1958], but things were supposed to be different that year for TCU," Childress says. "People were saying they were going to come down to College Station and have their way with us. I didn't think so."

Plus, the Horned Frogs were threatening to mess with the Bear. Paul Bryant wasn't quite as revered in College Station as Tuscaloosa, Ala., but A&M certainly enjoyed its ties to that whole Junction trip in 1954, and an SWC title in 1956.

Bryant's '54 Aggies team finished 1-9, but followed that season with a 7-2-1 mark, setting a Southwest Conference record for biggest improvement by a team from one season to the next. TCU, which finished 1-8-2 in 1983, would complete a seven-game improvement with a win at A&M, besting the Bear's 6.5.

Finally, TCU's Kenneth Davis—a mostly unknown player until that year—was angling for the national rushing title, needing 178 yards against the Aggies to surpass Ohio State's Keith Byars. To do so, he'd have to slip past Childress, who as the '84 team played worse seemed to play better, in collecting a whopping 26 tackles in the shutout loss at Arkansas the week prior.

A couple of days before the TCU game, a fed-up Childress no longer could stand the Aggies' continued mediocrity. In a locker room tirade aimed squarely at his underachieving teammates, Childress vowed that the Aggies would not—could not—lose to TCU.

"He must have had a hard rock to sleep on instead of a pillow the night before, because—lemme tell you—he really had a problem that day," says Doug Williams, the Aggies' starting right tackle at the time and a future NFL player. "Ray was one of those quiet guys who usually just went about his business, and it took a lot to flip his switch.

"But once that switch got turned on, you better get the hell out of the way."

The fiery Sherrill, a Duncan, Okla., native, also, had admonished his players around the same time with a bit of coaching-on-the-edge wisdom.

"Y'all keep going like this," Sherrill angrily told his 4-5 team, "and you're gonna lose your scholarships—and get my ass fired."

The Aggies responded to both Sherrill and Childress—with history claiming the latter's blazing speech having served as a swivel point in the program—by whipping No. 17 TCU 35-21 before A&M's smallest home crowd since the TCU game 10 years earlier. That seemingly insignificant 1984 game—in the scheme of things, anyway—set the stage for huge audiences to come at Kyle Field, from that moment on.

THE GAME OF MY LIFE
By Ray Childress

The seniors were near the end of our season, and it hadn't gone as we'd liked or as expected. When you reach finalities such as that, you're just grabbing on to everything and throwing stuff you don't want away and just moving on.

The Arkansas game a week before the TCU game was kind of a turning point for us, in the sense that we'd just gotten whipped by four touchdowns.

"Let's take the gloves off against TCU," we told each other in the locker room before the game. "Let's just get after it and see what we can do."

I was playing mad at that point, but that's pretty much how I played anyway. When the center snapped the ball, I'd just go after it. The whole team played that way against the Horned Frogs. We just dominated and manhandled TCU, which had come in cocky and overconfident.

Our seniors realized that we only had two games left in our college careers, and we didn't want to end them with a couple of losses. We showed a lot of pride and took care of business, 35-21.

Ray Childress, a two-time All-American, tallied 25 career sacks from 1981-94, a school record for a non-linebacker. *Aggieland Yearbook*

GAME RESULTS

On the same day Boston College quarterback Doug Flutie tossed a 60-yard Hail Mary to win at Miami in one of the most recognized plays in college football history, across the Gulf of Mexico the Aggies had first marked their territory as a perennially ferocious defensive team.

Texas A&M's two-touchdown win over TCU sealed its first victory over a Division I-A team with a winning record that year. Meanwhile Ray Childress also made TCU pay for his lack of serious consideration for the Outland Trophy or the Lombardi Award—and a disappointing year in general.

Childress, who refused to quit on the season even after the 28-0 loss at Arkansas, finished with 14 tackles (10 unassisted), forced a fumble and swatted down a pass against TCU. He also popped two different TCU quarterbacks—sending one to the showers and splitting the other from the ball—in the fourth quarter as A&M protected a 28-21 lead.

"We just couldn't block Childress," TCU coach Jim Wacker said. "He dominated the line of scrimmage, and he was a big reason they played tougher than we did. I can tell you this—we haven't gone against anyone like Ray Childress before. He's tremendous."

Said Horned Frogs running back Kenneth Davis, who finished with 141 hard-earned yards (37 shy of the number he needed to win the national rushing title): "Childress must have played the best game he's ever played."

And, to paraphrase Davis, Childress gave the best speech he ever gave (a short list, indeed) in the days before the game, in sparking a defensive demolition tradition that's carried on since.

While A&M's win over TCU doesn't receive the notoriety of some of the school's bigger victories in history, the Aggies' shocking 37-12 victory at Texas a week later probably wouldn't have been possible without it. The Aggies led that game 30-0 in the third quarter, and jetted on to Sherrill's most prolific win to that point in Aggieland.

"Everything started against TCU," Childress says, "and it carried over to the Texas game. We played absolutely reckless defense against the Longhorns, and were just whipping people physically. It wouldn't have mattered who we played that day; we'd have won."

Going into the game, Texas had a shot at a share of its 23rd Southwest Conference championship. Instead the Longhorns got a fistful of Aggies, who scored their most points ever against UT to that point. About the only bad thing to come from the A&M-UT game that year for the Aggies were a bunch of T-shirts some students sold that blared "Horn Busters" across their front, a rip-off of the popular movie and song of the time, *Ghostbusters.*

"I'm in shock over this," UT senior defensive tackle Tony Degrate said, shaking his head (about the game, not the T-shirts).

And Sherrill, who wouldn't lose again to rival Texas, took a moment to rip all of his program's non-believers. That group included a reporter who'd joked in the press box before the UT game that A&M was replacing its Astroturf with paper, because the Aggies always looked better on paper.

"There were a lot of things going against us," said Sherrill, who wound up with his first winning record (6-5) at A&M. "The press jumped ship, some former students jumped ship, some fans jumped ship, but our players made a decision to keep going."

Sherrill pointed to one player in particular who led the way and got the ship steaming ahead as A&M built a reputation as a defensive force behind Sherrill and then-defensive coordinator R.C. Slocum: Childress.

"It's a shame we didn't win enough games earlier so our players could get the recognition they deserve," Sherrill said. "Ray Childress is the best football player in the country, no question."

WHAT BECAME OF RAY CHILDRESS?

One of Ray Childress's biggest thrills in College Station came 13 years to the month after he'd helped whip TCU at Kyle Field. Former President George Bush requested that Childress introduce dignitaries at the dedication of Bush's Presidential Library and Museum in November 1997.

"It was amazing to see," Childress says. "Four United States presidents and six former first ladies attended. It was like a movie set. Watching all of them walk onto the stage at the same time was unbelievable, and it was great for that community—and still is today."

Childress adds that he didn't realize the "magnitude of the task" when asked to introduce the bigwigs at the outdoor event on a sunny fall afternoon in College Station.

"I got to town about 6 o'clock the night before, and I received a list of about 100 names," he says. "The Gulf War had ended several years earlier, and some of the largest sponsors and biggest supporters of the library were Kuwaitis and other Arabic folks—and some of them had four or five names each."

Among the easier names to pronounce were Prince Bandar bin Sultan of Saudi Arabia and Shaikh Saud, minister of information for Kuwait. The name "Arnold Schwarzenegger" (another Bush guest) practically rolled off the tongue in comparison.

"It was a challenge," Childress says. "I spent quite some time with that list. That event was probably one of the most impressive things I've been around."

Childress, too, has put together an impressive professional resume, as he played in five Pro Bowls for the Houston Oilers from 1985-95, after the Oilers made him the No. 2 overall selection of the 1985 NFL Draft.

John McClain of the *Houston Chronicle* once described the big, uncomplicated defensive end thusly: "The only thing Ray Childress might test positive for is Gatorade."

Childress is still prominent around Houston and College Station, as owner and CEO of the Lawrence Marshall auto dealerships halfway between the towns on Highway 6 in Hempstead. He began shooting commercials for Marshall in 1986 and the relationship evolved into his eventual ownership of the large and well-known auto dealer.

Childress married his wife, Kara, a high school classmate and a Texas graduate, while they were still in college, and the couple has four children: Wells, Sloan, Ford and Knox. Childress considers time spent with his family as his main hobby.

"I've tried playing golf, but I'm just not convinced that I like golf," Childress says. "Know what I mean?"

Certainly. A golf ball isn't snapped.

CHAPTER 14

JOHNNY HOLLAND

Name: Johnny Ray Holland
Born: March 11, 1965 in Bellville, Texas
Hometown: Hempstead, Texas
Current Residence: Detroit, Mich.
Occupation: NFL Assistant Coach
Position: Linebacker
Height: 6'2"
Playing Weight: 219 pounds
Years lettered: 1983-86
Accomplishments: Two-time All-American and two-time All-Conference (1985-86); second on Texas A&M's all-time tackles chart with 455; 20 or more tackles in two different games for the Aggies; second-round NFL draft pick of the Green Bay Packers in 1987; totaled more than 100 tackles in six consecutive seasons with the Packers; member of the Packers Hall of Fame.
Nickname: Johnny Rock
The Game: Texas at Texas A&M, Nov. 28, 1985

Johnny Holland. *Photo courtesy of Texas A&M Athletic Media Relations*

THE LIFE OF YOUNG JOHNNY HOLLAND

Johnny Holland didn't much appreciate working construction as a child and teenager in and around Hempstead, Texas—whether it was in the brutal heat of summer or the deep cold of winter.

"My friends would all go to camps and on vacations and such during the summer, whereas I went to work for my dad," says Holland, a standout linebacker and leader of a defense that pushed Texas A&M to its first Cotton Bowl in 18 years in 1985. "My brothers and I hated the summers. I started helping my dad out in about the third or fourth grade—picking up tools and loose lumber and things of that nature. My dad came from a blue-collar background where all he knew was work. And that meant working hard all day in the sun or the cold or the rain.

"On Christmas break we'd work when it was super cold, and during summers we'd be up on a roof or what have you where it was super hot. My dad would just tell us to drink plenty of water."

Now, Johnny Holland can't thank his father enough.

"I tell him now that I appreciate him making us earn our own money," Holland says, smiling. "Because he taught me what work was all about."

Johnny grew up the youngest of Jake Jr. and Irene Holland's eight children in the farming and ranching community of Hempstead, near the Brazos River and 44 miles to the south of College Station. From his father he learned a work ethic; from his two older brothers he attained a love for sports.

"Jake and Alfred would take me to the gym at Prairie View A&M [a nearby college] and then pick me for their basketball teams," Holland says. "So here I was, in the seventh or eighth grade as a little scrawny kid, playing with a bunch of college guys. My brothers helped teach me to compete."

While Holland eventually earned his keep as an NFL linebacker, early on the Hempstead coaches saw a quarterback in the bright-eyed leader.

"I'd shut down the weight room [at night], and Johnny would want the key," said Robert Kinney, Holland's high school coach. "I haven't seen a harder worker than Johnny Holland."

Geographically, Holland grew up in a mighty interesting locale when it came to picking a university as a standout quarterback. Head west on Highway 290, and he'd run right into Austin. Head north on Highway 6, and he'd cruise smack-dab into College Station.

Two more family factors also could have influenced his decision. Holland's cousin, Roosevelt Leaks, the first African American All-American at Texas, had starred as a running back in the early- to mid-70s for the Longhorns—and Holland's sister also had attended UT. Holland, however, followed his heart to Texas A&M. It didn't hurt that College Station seemed a whole lot more like Hempstead than Austin.

"That small-town atmosphere," Holland says, "just drew me right to Texas A&M."

Once in Aggieland in the summer of 1983, Holland spent his freshman two-a-days with six other quarterbacks—a gang that included standout recruit Kevin Murray—but the coaches then gave the Hempstead Kid an option: redshirt, or play his first year on defense and special teams.

"The move to defense excited me, because I could be aggressive and hit," Holland says. "I'd sneak into defensive drills every once in a while my senior year of high school, and our coach would get mad."

None of those other Aggies quarterbacks played in the NFL, while Holland earned a pro paycheck over seven seasons as a standout linebacker for the Green Bay Packers. In retrospect, Holland's shift to defense seems an awfully smart move. The action, too, couldn't have paid bigger dividends for A&M.

As it turned out, the Aggies desperately needed quarterback Kevin Murray on offense and linebacker Johnny Holland on defense, to earn their first trip to a Cotton Bowl in 18 years.

THE SCENE

In the wonderful new world of "glasnost," or openness, United States President Ronald Reagan and Soviet Union leader Mikhail Gorbachev exchanged sugary New Year's greetings on Jan. 1, 1986. It's safe to bet that Jackie Sherrill and Jim Wacker didn't.

A little more than a month earlier Sherrill, Texas A&M's feisty coach, had said his kicker simply mis-hit the ball with the Aggies leading TCU 46-zip late in their November 1985 game, in the week before A&M's annual showdown with archrival Texas. Few believed him, because the play certainly looked and smelled like an onside kick in an eventual 53-6 A&M win.

"That was kind of a strange call at 46-0," Wacker, the Horned Frogs coach, simply said.

Johnny Holland, a standout A&M linebacker from 1983-86, remembers that most ungracious moment.

"Jackie Sherrill and Jim Wacker didn't like each other too much," Holland says. "And any chance our players had to make Jackie Sherrill look better [by playing as hard and scoring as much as possible], we were definitely going to try and do it."

As later explained by 12th Man Kickoff Team member Sean Page, Sherrill had zero to do with the surprise onside kick against TCU, and A&M assistant coach Roy Kokemoor greatly rebuked the kickoff team at a following practice for its scheming behind the coaches' back. Several of the 12th Man members had traveled to Fort Worth for the road game.

By 1985—after a shaky first few years in Aggieland—Jackie Sherrill ("Daddy Aggiebucks" to his detractors) was looking better and better to the A&M faithful. The Aggies were angling for their first outright Southwest Conference title since the Edd Hargett days of 1967, and the point of an onside kick (which A&M recovered) when up on TCU by nearly half a hundred points actually delighted many of the long-suffering fans: No mercy. No prisoners.

At the 76th annual Bonfire on the following Wednesday night before the Texas game, an empowered Sherrill rallied the flock by preaching of a trip to the Southwest Conference's promised land: the Cotton Bowl.

"There are only two people that can take us there," Sherrill bellowed to 50,000 ardent believers. "The players behind me, and you out there."

THE SETTING

Had Texas A&M equipment manager Billy Pickard tossed 85-year-old "Tiny" Keen, a member of the 1921 SWC champion Aggies, a sturdy leather helmet, it seemed as if the old-timer might've checked his eligibility on the day before the 1985 A&M-Texas game.

"We really showed those teasippers and yellowbellies what we had that year," Keen said in hearkening back to '21 (oddly enough, a scoreless tie between A&M and Texas), before bringing the conversation back to the present. "I really like that Coach Sherrill. I attended the Cotton Bowl in '67, and I'm looking forward to going to the Cotton Bowl in '85."

The 1985 game against Texas featured quite possibly the most anticipated buildup for a contest in Aggieland in history (and it certainly didn't end in a scoreless tie). Unbelievably, the only other time the archrivals had played straight up for a trip to the Cotton Bowl came in 1943, when Texas won 27-13, three days before Jackie Sherrill was born.

"I can't think of a bigger game," UT coach Fred Akers said of the 1985 Thanksgiving night matchup between the two 8-2 teams.

Neither could all of those cooped-up Aggie fans, many of whom had heard tales of glory days of Texas A&M football, but had rarely experienced any such true moments themselves.

*   *   *   *   *

As part of something called the Texas Poll in 1985, residents across the state were asked their favorite college football team. Texas received 29 percent of the vote, Texas A&M 14 percent. "No favorite," at 23 percent, even whipped the Aggies by nine percent.

"Aggie fans seem to be concentrated among those with less education, lower incomes or with small-town or rural addresses," wrote Dr. Jim Dyer of the Texas Poll.

Dr. Dyer might have chosen a better way of putting it: Society's underdogs loved the Aggies, who'd only notched one winning season from 1958-73, and hadn't won an outright conference championship for the agricultural and mechanical school since 1967.

Besides, at that point the once underdog but now snarling Aggies were the ones startin' to conduct the educatin' among A&M's and UT's football programs, by winning 10 of 11 games from 1984-94. And no win in the history of A&M-Texas would feature a wider margin of victory by the Aggies than the 1985 game.

The Aggies, had they less class, might have considered blaring this message across the Kyle Field scoreboard: 42-10. Stick those digits in your Texas Poll.

THE GAME OF MY LIFE
By Johnny Holland

We called Jackie Sherrill "Dr. Psyche" because of the way he psyched us up before every game by using motivational tools to bring us together. One of those more memorable instances occurred before the 1985 Texas game, when we were playing the Longhorns for the right to go to the Cotton Bowl. It seems amazing considering our history, but in 1985 Texas and A&M hadn't played for a straight-up Cotton Bowl trip since 1943—a span of 42 years.

So before the game Jackie gave us each a little piece of cow horn—so everybody could put that little piece of horn in their pants and when things got tough we were supposed to rub that little horn as our good luck piece.

It must have worked, because we beat 'em pretty bad that year—which was the start of consistently good things happening for Texas A&M football. We were such an attack defense under defensive coordinator R.C. Slocum—and by that point we had guys who'd been recruited by Jackie who'd played together for two or three years, and things had started clicking.

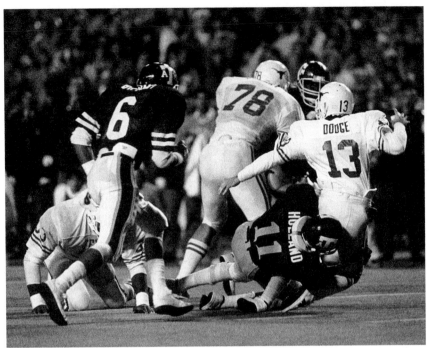

Johnny Holland became the first player in A&M history to record 20 or more tackles in two games. Holland is the second on the school's all-time tackles list with 455. *Photo courtesy of Texas A&M Athletic Media Relations*

Our defensive game plan against Texas was fairly simple—we blitzed the quarterback about 75 percent of the time, put a lot of pressure on their offense, and came up with some big turnovers and some big plays in the game.

In fact, we sacked the Texas quarterback six times and picked off four passes en route to a 42-10 win. The Longhorns' best chance to make a game of it came late in the first quarter, when they had a fourth and goal inside the one-yard line. We only led 7-0 to that point.

We killed a 67-yard Texas drive when running back Edwin Simmons—who was their stud—got the ball, just like we figured. Texas didn't have much of a passing game, and it had a big offensive line to run behind. Cornerback James Flowers and end Rod Saddler wrapped up Simmons short of the goal line when he tried going outside. We had guys diving on that pile from all over—and that moment was definitely the game's turning point. Texas never had a chance after that goal-line stand.

When I first got to Texas A&M, Aggie fans still had the mentality that as long as we beat Texas—no matter what else happened that year—it was a good season. By the time our group left, people expected more. They wanted a winning season *and* for us to beat Texas—and we liked that.

GAME RESULTS

In whipping Texas 42-10, the swaggerin' Aggies played looser than former NFL running back John Riggins at a swanky Washington dinner in 1985. Riggins, the colorful Washington Redskins star, had told Supreme Court Justice Sandra Day O'Connor, "C'mon, Sandy baby, loosen up, you're too tight," before passing out beneath a dinner table.

Suffice to say plenty of Aggies passed out beneath tables in the wee hours of Nov. 29, 1985, celebrating Texas A&M's biggest win in 18 years before a then-Kyle Field record crowd of 77,607—on Jackie Sherrill's 42nd birthday, no less. And one of the biggest reasons for Texas A&M's success that night—and that season—was No. 11 on defense, linebacker Johnny Holland, who collected 14 tackles and an interception.

"You should take a film of Johnny Holland from the Texas game and show it to every high school or junior high linebacker in the country," awed fellow linebacker Todd Howard said after the game. "It's like a textbook."

The Aggies then shifted their teachings to the Jan. 1 Cotton Bowl against Heisman Trophy winner Bo Jackson and the Auburn Tigers.

"Texas A&M is hungry and its fans are hungry," Auburn Coach Pat Dye said. "My biggest concern is that our folks aren't as hungry as A&M."

Sure enough, the Aggies devoured Auburn in the 50th Cotton Bowl 36-16, as Johnny Holland notched two big-time stops of Bo Jackson in the fourth quarter, one on fourth and two on the A&M 28-yard line.

"We weren't just playing the Auburn Tigers that day," Holland says. "We were playing Bo Jackson and the Auburn Tigers. We had running backs on the scout team trying to duplicate him, which was awfully hard to do. Bo had just won the Heisman, and I was really looking forward to playing against him, because he was the best in college football."

Jackson finished with 129 tough yards on 31 carries, while the All-American Holland, a junior, collected a team-high 16 tackles. The exuberant Aggies, who'd averaged an astounding 44 points over their last three games of 1985 against TCU, Texas and Auburn, finished that season ranked sixth nationally. It was their highest tally since 1956's fifth ranking and still hasn't been bested.

"From that '85 season on there have been few letdowns in Texas

A&M football," Johnny Holland says. "It's hard not to say 1985—when we finally made it back to the Cotton Bowl—marked the start of a lot of success since, and we're proud of that."

WHAT BECAME OF JOHNNY HOLLAND?

Johnny Holland loves visiting his hometown of Hempstead every chance he gets—even if his dad sometimes puts him to work.

"He'll always find something for me to do," Holland says, laughing.

In 1994, the always-active Holland was left looking for something to do after retiring from the Green Bay Packers following the discovery of a second herniated disk in his neck. To that point Holland had played seven seasons in the NFL and had recorded at least 100 tackles in six of those seasons. Doctors had discovered a herniated disk in 1992, but Holland returned to record 134 tackles in 1993 on a playoff-bound team. The following off season, doctors discovered another herniated disk, and Holland quietly retired.

"As a kid growing up in a small town, I'd hardly ever met any pro football players, and so I never really thought it was realistic that something like getting drafted could really happen," Holland says.

"It was a blessing to get to play in the NFL for seven seasons, and in a lot of ways Green Bay reminded me of Texas A&M—a small-town, big-time football team with a lot of traditions."

In 2001, the Packers inducted Holland into their Hall of Fame, one of his career highlights. He became a Packers assistant in 1995 under Mike Holmgren and then followed Holmgren to Seattle following the 1999 season. In 2003, Detroit Lions coach Steve Mariucci named Holland one of his defensive assistants.

"I never really figured I'd be a coach, but I still had that hunger to be around football," Holland says. "And once I started coaching, I quickly figured out, man, this is what I'm supposed to be doing. Coaching is the next closest thing to playing."

Holland married his lovely wife, Faith, in August of 1989, and the couple has two children: son Jordan and daughter Joli. And even across the country, Holland still has a way of touching folks from Hempstead. When Houston sportscaster and Hempstead native Mark Berman was interviewing Holland in New Orleans before Super Bowl XXXI between the Packers and Patriots in January 1997, Holland caught the usually unflappable Berman off guard.

"Right in the middle of the interview Johnny started talking about how special my dad—who'd coached him in Little League—was to him," Berman says of the surprise anecdote about his father, the late Hy Berman. "Johnny was saying that he might not be where he is today without my dad, because my dad had helped him keep a focus on sports. I nearly dropped my microphone.

"I knew my dad was a good guy—and sons naturally look up to their fathers—but I never realized just how special he was to others until that moment."

Johnny Holland's heart, it seems, is still as big as Hempstead, Texas—a compliment indeed for a hardworking man who hails from a bountiful, wide-open countryside.

CHAPTER 15

KEVIN MURRAY

Name: Kevin James Murray
Born: June 18, 1964
Hometown: Dallas, Texas
Current Residence: Dallas, Texas
Occupation: Vice President, Technology & Operations Staffing, Bank of America
Position: Quarterback
Height: 6'2"
Playing Weight: 210
Years lettered: 1983-86
Accomplishments: Two-time All-Conference (1985 and '86); all-time school leader in career touchdown passes (48) and season-completion percentage (60.7); in 1985 led Aggies to their first Cotton Bowl since 1967, and the Aggies to successive league titles (1985-86) for the first time since 1940-41.
Nickname: Murray the Magician
The Game: Baylor at Texas A&M, Oct. 18, 1986

Photo courtesy of Texas A&M Athletic Media Relations

THE LIFE OF YOUNG KEVIN MURRAY

Texas A&M fans don't boo—as per Kyle Field tradition—but they sometimes grumble. And young quarterback Kevin Murray heard the grumbling as he stepped into the huddle for a critical—both in the season and in coach Jackie Sherrill's legacy—third-quarter drive.

The Aggies were trailing little Arkansas State in the third game of the 1984 season, and at that point things weren't going well for Texas A&M in general. The Aggies had attracted national headlines—and a fancy *Sports Illustrated* spread—when they'd lured Sherrill from Pittsburgh before the 1982 season.

Now they were attracting much smaller headlines—and lots of snickering—for their continued mediocrity even with the high-priced coach onboard, and falling behind Arkansas State at home obviously wasn't what the Aggies had in mind in trying to right the ship.

Murray, then a sophomore, and Sherrill shared a special bond: part father-son, part mentor-pupil. It was Sherrill who'd lured Murray to College Station from North Dallas High School, when he'd strongly considered Oklahoma or hometown SMU. Murray also had played in the rookie league with the Milwaukee Brewers organization in 1982, but when Sherrill wound up at A&M, Murray reevaluated his choices.

"I took a chance on Jackie and knowing his history—that he'd coached Dan Marino at Pitt, and Marino was always my favorite quarterback—I believed he was going to throw the football," Murray says. "When Coach Sherrill came to A&M, the program was totally unstable. ... I wanted to throw the football, and I wanted to play a key role in turning things around."

Turns out Murray, one of the best quarterbacks to ever play at A&M, did both, as Sherrill named him the team's starting QB five games into his freshman year of 1983, and the Aggies closed out that season 4-2-1 over their final seven games.

But in this third game against Arkansas State the next season, things looked dire indeed for Sherrill and the Aggies. Suddenly, however, "Murray the Magician" came alive, and the Aggies rallied for a 22-21 win.

But on a key drive at the end of the third quarter, Murray landed awkwardly on his right ankle, which shattered on Kyle's artificial turf near the Arkansas State four-yard line. Many A&M fans, so ecstatic about their quarterback of the future—and present—wondered if the strong-armed, fleet-footed QB would ever be the same. But Murray never did.

"I was hardheaded," he says. "You couldn't tell me I wasn't going to play any more. All I could think of was that I needed to get my job back, and so I came back for spring drills and competed on one leg."

The ankle noticeably bothered Murray in the 1985 season opener at

Alabama, a 23-10 loss, but the resilient quarterback made an indelible impression on that football-loving state with his toughness on that day. Later on that season, he'd make an even bigger imprint on the state of Alabama, in the 1986 Cotton Bowl.

That year the Aggies won their first outright Southwest Conference title since 1967 and whipped the Auburn Tigers and Heisman Trophy winner Bo Jackson 36-16 in the Cotton Bowl in Dallas.

Jackson, who rushed for 129 hard-earned yards on 31 carries, earned game offensive MVP honors in a 20-point loss, as Sherrill fought for his standout quarterback who'd thrown for a then-Cotton Bowl record 292 yards in his hometown.

"We have a player who set a passing record and was on the winning team," Sherrill said after the game in arguing for the man he considered the true MVP. "Who would you take?"

But Murray spent little time reveling in the what-ifs—or even the big-time bowl victory. He already was thinking ahead to the next season and particularly to one game: Baylor. The only league loss in A&M's run to the 1985 SWC title had come in Waco, and Murray already was bent on revenge against the Bears.

THE SCENE

The most popular movie of 1984 generated $239 million at the box office, and *Ghostbusters* certainly possessed staying power, thanks partly to its huge success at those newfangled video rental stores. Plus, the logo made famous by *Ghostbusters*—the familiar red circle and slash—was about as synonymous with the 1980s as Rubik's Cubes, Pac-Man and the "We are the World" music video.

Everyone, it seemed, considered himself a "buster" of some sort. One of the cruder (and most popular) T-shirts of the day read, "No Fat Chicks," replete with the red circle and slash. But that odd edict was nothing—at least in Murray's eyes—to what Baylor's defense, for grins, had begun calling itself: Murray Busters.

In the '85 loss in Waco, Murray tossed three interceptions and Sherrill even benched him in the fourth quarter for backup Craig Stump. That, coupled with Baylor's apparent Murray-busting, provided the proud quarterback with plenty of incentive springing into the '86 season.

"It was frustrating having to sit on that performance for 365 days," Murray says. "But we all know what happened during the Baylor game of '86—that's one so many Aggies still love to talk about."

Indeed. Dave Campbell's *Texas Football* magazine proclaimed in 1990 that A&M's comeback victory keyed by Murray was the SWC's "Game of the Decade."

"We had about 75,000 fans packed into Kyle Field that day," says Aggies linebacker Johnny Holland. "But there are probably 150,000 or more Aggies who claim they were there. It was an amazing game, an amazing day."

THE SETTING

Two of the best games in the Lone Star State's history—regardless of sport—were played within three days and about 100 miles of one another in the fall of 1986. On Oct. 15, the New York Mets beat the Houston Astros in 16 innings in the Astrodome to advance to the World Series.

On Oct. 18 at Kyle Field, Baylor and Texas A&M added even more fireworks for a Southeast Texas fandom still recovering from one of the best playoff games—if not *the* best—in major league history.

While the baseball series had produced a plethora of good pitching, the gridiron classic featured the conference's two-best quarterbacks in Baylor's Cody Carlson and Texas A&M's Kevin Murray.

Murray had earned SWC Offensive Player of the Year honors in 1985, but midway through the '86 season Carlson—a future NFL quarterback— led the league with 1,296 yards passing through the first six games.

Baylor and A&M were expected to contend for the league title, but the Bears had just dropped a game to SMU the week before, giving them a 2-1 league mark.

"There's no question that we have to win," Baylor coach Grant Teaff said in the days beforehand.

Of course, most of Baylor players figured A&M, 2-0 in league play and 4-1 overall, to be the perfect tonic for all that ailed Baylor. BU linebacker Ray Berry, whose brother, Dean, was a member of the Aggies' 12th Man Kickoff Team, fired one more shot at the Aggies the day before the game.

"The Texas A&M game is always very important to Baylor fans," Berry said. "I think we've beaten them six out of the last eight times we've played them. So we'll be ready for them again."

From 1978-85, the little Baptist school on the banks of the Brazos River held a 6-1-1 advantage over the Aggies, including that 20-15 loss in 1985 in Waco. It all added up to one of the biggest challenges in Kevin Murray's career. The Aggies, ranked 11th, needed the win to remain in control of their own destiny in the race to the SWC crown. A&M fans wanted it desperately to finally break Baylor's dominance in the series.

And Kevin Murray, a dismal 13 of 35 with three interceptions in the '85 contest, desired the win for more reasons than anyone.

THE GAME OF MY LIFE
By Kevin Murray

I've never been so mentally prepared for any game in my life as against Baylor in 1986. Our offensive coordinator, Lynn Amadee, and I weren't just on the same page that day, we were on the same freakin' sentence. I had all of the faith in his system, and he had all of the faith in me.

Our game plan against Baylor was to implement a spread offense, to try and take their All-American safety, Thomas Everett, out of the game. That said, we started horrendously, and looking back on it Baylor's defense was paying our offensive unit the ultimate respect.

They came up with a defense that you'd only play when afraid. They put everyone they could on the line of scrimmage and said, "We're gonna get him before he can set up and throw the football." Attack, attack, attack, they did—and it caught us off guard.

A defender came free every play, and I had bullets flying past me—it felt like I was back in the *Gunsmoke* days. Baylor's secondary was particularly stout and we had only one receiver, Rod Harris, who could probably make a move and outrun guys in their secondary.

Everything in our offense was predicated on timing, and Baylor certainly disrupted that. By the time we had adjusted, we were down 17-0 in the second quarter.

Early in that quarter we had 20 yards of total offense and not a single first down. But we didn't panic, because these were the two best teams in the conference, and it was obvious they didn't have any respect for us. Their mentality seemed, "Let's knock Murray out of the game, period."

It didn't work. We struck twice in the second quarter to make it 17-14, and by the start of the fourth quarter, they were leading 27-17, but we knew we still had 15 minutes to make a little magic.

I never saw our first score of the fourth quarter, because I was on my back when Keith Woodside caught a touchdown pass in the back of the end zone to make it 27-24. A Baylor field goal then made it 30-24, and our final drive was on.

On that series, we converted three crucial third-down plays en route to their end zone—none bigger than the final third-down conversion. We

Kevin Murray, who in 1985 guided the Aggies to their first conference title in 10 years, threw a school-record 48 touchdown passes from 1983-86. *Photo courtesy of Texas A&M Athletic Media Relations*

were perched on the Baylor four-yard line, on a third and goal with about four minutes remaining.

A field goal wouldn't cut it, because with their offense there weren't any guarantees we'd get the ball back. We figured this showdown was for the ballgame—and so did they.

I expected an all-out blitz, and that's exactly what I got. As one of their linebackers, Robert Watters, barreled down on me, I kept the focus upfield, knowing I was about to get hit. With Watters wrapped around me, I fired a pass to Tony Thompson, who first juggled the ball and then caught it. I was on my back—again—but heard the crowd erupt. Magic. That was, by far, the toughest battle any of us had ever played in.

You don't come back from a 17-0 deficit against teams that good—you simply don't. But we did on that day.

GAME RESULTS

Texas A&M's amazing 31-30 victory against Baylor helped eventually lift the Aggies to their second consecutive SWC title and seemed to have a rather devastating impact on the Bears.

Aggie fans, at least, may make the argument that Baylor never quite recovered from the stunning loss, considering the Bears hadn't defeated A&M since 1985 going into the 2003 season.

"For our fans, Texas is always the big game," Murray says. "But for the players, we all knew that year Baylor was the most important game of the season. If we were going to win another championship, we knew we were going to have to shut up those trash-talking Bears."

And Murray certainly did on that unforgettable, sun-drenched day, as he grew from a leader of the Aggies into a legend of Aggieland.

"There's no question that his performance was probably the best I've ever seen from a quarterback," said A&M coach Jackie Sherrill, who played with Joe Namath at Alabama and coached Dan Marino at Pitt.

A&M's mystifying comeback certainly left venerable Baylor coach Grant Teaff shaking his head—especially because of that savvy Aggies quarterback from Dallas.

"Spell it M-U-R-R-A-Y," Teaff said. "On third down he was just incredible, and he did the miracle things necessary to win."

The Aggies really didn't need any miracles on that Saturday afternoon. All they needed was simply a Murray, who in the span of three memorable quarters became an all-time Baylor Buster.

WHAT BECAME OF KEVIN MURRAY?

K evin Murray still possesses a flair for the dramatic, but these days it's limited to the golf course—where he sports a remarkable drive (off the tees). And unlike in his younger, sometimes more abrasive youth, Murray finds more humor in daily living.

"Being a father makes you learn to laugh at yourself," Murray says.

Murray and his lovely wife, Missy, have three children: daughter Precious and sons Kevin Jr. and Kyler.

To his children, Murray is a father, friend, coach and hero—not because of his success many years ago on a football field, but rather because of his life now. Murray, a vice president with Bank of America in Dallas, stays busy with his job, but he's rarely too busy for his family.

"My family keeps things in perspective," he says. "They don't care if I have a good day or a bad day at work. They're always happy to see Daddy and always ready to play."

Murray once wanted to continue playing football after college. He opted for the NFL following his junior year at A&M—having led the Aggies to consecutive league titles for the first time since 1940-41—but failed all of his physicals. Murray briefly considered a career in the Canadian Football League before settling into his business career.

"My football dreams ended at the age of 22," he says.

"I'm not one of those fathers who lives vicariously through his kids. I coach my kids and teach my kids, but I don't force things on them. My wife and I want only the best for them, and maybe one day the best thing for them will be attending Texas A&M. I have so many great memories of my time at A&M."

Likewise, Murray the Magician—on an enchanting 1986 day at Kyle Field—produced one of the greatest memories in Texas A&M football history.

CHAPTER 16

BUCKY RICHARDSON

Name: John Powell Richardson
Born: Feb. 7, 1969
Hometown: Baton Rouge, La.
Current Residence: Houston, Texas
Current Occupation: Sales Representative for Environmental Improvements Incorporated
Position: Quarterback
Height: 6'2"
Playing Weight: 215 pounds
Years lettered: 1987-88, 90-91
Accomplishments: All-conference in 1991; Aggie Heart Award winner in 1991; eighth-round NFL draft pick of the Houston Oilers in 1992; started four games for the Oilers in 1994 at quarterback.
Nickname: Bucky
The Game: Texas at Texas A&M, Nov. 26, 1987

Bucky Richardson. *Photo courtesy of Texas A&M Athletic Media Relations*

THE LIFE OF YOUNG BUCKY RICHARDSON

Once in his life—only once—John Richardson threw up his arms and gave up. He was 10 years old in Baton Rouge, La., and tagged by his Little League teammates with a handle he didn't much care for.

"I fought the nickname 'Bucky' for a year or two and finally I just gave up and said, 'OK, let's just go with it,'" Richardson says.

Besides, there were worse things than being dubbed "Bucky" in the late 1970s, since the nickname stood for scrappy New York Yankees shortstop Bucky Dent. Richardson might have preferred the tag of "Terry," however, for Pittsburgh Steelers great Terry Bradshaw.

"He was a winner and a Louisiana boy," Richardson says. "It was a thrill when he interviewed me at the Cotton Bowl my senior year at A&M."

The handsome Richardson was no stranger to the TV camera, even as a prep star back home in Baton Rouge at Broadmoor High. In fact, one of the city's most revolting (yet humorous to anyone but Louisiana State University fans) moments came when Richardson announced his collegiate intentions live on WBRZ-TV in Baton Rouge.

Three days before the signing date in 1987, Richardson told the world—or at least, the city of Baton Rouge—that he intended to play football for ... not hometown LSU, but Texas A&M. The station received a slew of angry phone calls, and Richardson his share of hate mail.

"I'd just always liked the state of Texas," Richardson says of his abrupt decision to attend A&M. "I'd only been there a handful of times while growing up, and I liked the size of it and it just seemed so much nicer than Louisiana. I wanted to venture out somewhere; I didn't want to stay in Baton Rouge my whole life. And, of course, the Aggies were winning conference championships, and that's always attractive to a recruit."

What boiled the Cajuns' blood most about a favorite son splitting the swamps for the higher, drier ground of Southeast Texas? They'd witnessed an NFL player in the making in young Bucky Richardson, the middle of Paul and Suzanne Richardson's three children.

"Bucky didn't start playing quarterback until he was in the 10th grade, and before that he was a running back," childhood friend Mike Arena says. "He always kept that running back mentality. He'd put his head down and try and run over somebody instead of running out of bounds.

"People first really became aware of Bucky when he was in the 11th grade. We had played Baker High, which was state-ranked, the year before, and they'd beaten us about 57 to nuthin'. Baker's coaches were saying before our game the following year that they were going to put in the waterboy and stuff like that, because it was gonna be such a blowout.

"But we beat 'em, and mainly because of Bucky. He ran for a couple of hundred yards and scored a couple of touchdowns, and people started recognizing his talent."

On Richardson's visit to Texas A&M in the fall of 1986, record-setting quarterback and two-time conference player of the year Kevin Murray ushered him around campus.

"Any quarterback following Kevin had big shoes to fill," Richardson says. "He had a great college career and threw for a bunch of yards. We were a lot different type of quarterback, but the end result is winning."

Richardson played his first two years in Aggieland before a knee injury against Texas in the 1988 game sidelined him the entire 1989 season.

"It kind of humbled me in the sense that suddenly I realized that football could be over at any time," Richardson says. "It really made me concentrate on school, and other things besides football. I was so focused on just football in high school and my first couple of years of college.

"The injury actually was a blessing. It gave me a year to mature and grow as a person and get stronger."

Still, the feisty Richardson loathed watching his teammates drill as he stood on the sidelines.

"You're around the football team but you're hurt, and you kind of feel like a deadbeat," he says. "You're taking up space; you can't contribute—you just try to stay out of the way.

"As much confidence as I had in the doctors there, you never know what the future holds when you're going through a rehab like that. It's very humbling and scary. Looking back on it, am I glad I blew my knee out? No. But I am glad I got that extra year of college."

THE SCENE

Leading to its annual showdown with the Aggies in 1987, Texas hadn't bathed its infamous tower in orange—a sign of victory—following a Texas A&M game since 1983. So some UT fans chose to soak A&M's statue of E. King Gill, the original Aggie 12th Man, in a heavy coat of orange paint—maybe reasoning that must be the next best thing.

A few freshmen from the Corps of Cadets' Squadron 10 spent about three hours on a Sunday afternoon scrubbing away the detestable hue administered in the wee hours of that morning—four days before the Thanksgiving showdown. Meanwhile the Texas football team was trying to scrub away the detestable idea that none of its seniors had ever played on a team that had defeated Texas A&M.

"That was back in the days when they weren't used to getting their asses handed to them by the Aggies," says Richardson. "So they were having a hard time digesting all of that."

The Longhorns had never lost four consecutive games to A&M, meaning that forlorn gang of Texas seniors had a good shot at becoming the first class in school history never to win at least a game against their archrivals.

"I've knotted my stomach from thinking about that," UT safety Gerard Senegal said in the days before the game. "This is my last chance. I'm willing to go out and give 500 percent."

The Aggies had won at about a .500 clip under Tom Wilson in the few years prior to coach Jackie Sherrill's arrival at Texas A&M in 1982. Sherrill, who came to A&M from the University of Pittsburgh, had proven at least one thing after several seasons that so many Aggies still hold dear: He could beat Texas and had done so for three consecutive seasons starting in 1984.

"We're not looking at the past," outspoken Texas safety John Hagy said before the game of A&M's winning streak. "If you do that, you can find periods of 10 years where A&M didn't beat Texas."

True—Texas won every game from 1957-66—but, as the saying goes, that was then and this is now.

"This game isn't just played on the field," groaned UT defensive end Thomas Aldridge. "It's also played in society. Every time you run into an Aggie, he reminds you of it."

The '87 game, too, was for all the Southwest Conference marbles. The winner earned an excursion to the Cotton Bowl. The loser? A less palatable trip to play Pittsburgh in the Bluebonnet Bowl down Highway 290 in Houston. That's why not even an orange-drenched E. King Gill could fire up the Aggies any more than usual against their biggest opponent.

"You don't need anything in particular to get you motivated for that ballgame," Richardson says. "You hear about something like that [the Gill incident] and all of the things that have happened in the past—and the history of the game—play a part, but none in particular."

The 1985 and 1986 A&M teams featured a high-octane offense directed by Kevin Murray, who possessed a rifle arm and a maverick swagger in leading those squads to SWC titles. The '87 team, however, offered a fifth-year senior in the steady but hardly spectacular Craig Stump and a couple of freshmen in Lance Pavlas and Bucky Richardson.

"They're all just fairly average quarterbacks," UT safety Tony Griffin said before the game.

*   *   *   *   *

In terms of scandalous news, 1987 was anything but fairly average. *The Miami Herald* caught married Democratic presidential front-runner

Gary Hart with model Donna Rice on a yacht called "Monkey Business."

About the same time a rock group from Georgia named R.E.M. had recorded a tune called, "It's the End of the World as We Know It"—which almost seemed prophetic. The stock market crashed on the same day (Oct. 19) that United States jets attacked parts of Iran. That prompted comedian Jay Leno—who had yet to succeed Johnny Carson on *The Tonight Show*—to quip that Ronald Reagan was now the first president to start a war and a depression on the same day.

But "Black Monday" aside, the juicy news out of 1987 came from a nation's obsession with likes of Donna Rice, evangelist Jim Bakker's love interest Jessica "I'm not a bimbo" Hahn and shapely Fawn Hall, an adroit paper shredder for Lt. Col. Oliver North early in the Iran-Contra scandal. Even the refined *Wall Street Journal* got in on the act late in '87.

"Crash or no crash," a *Journal* headline declared, "it's certain that 1987 is the Year of the Bimbo."

But that wasn't true for Texas A&M fans. For Texas A&M's faithful, it was the Season of the Bucky.

THE SETTING

Bucky Richardson had played in plenty of rivalry games back home in Louisiana, but nothing had prepared him for A&M-UT.

"I always said that in the weeks prior to this ballgame, and in my whole career at Texas A&M, that this isn't a funny, laughing-type rivalry," he says. "This is a hatred deal. Out there on the field, it's people trying to kill each other."

Or squish each other like a man might a giant cockroach. Speaking of … a year prior to the 1987 Longhorns-Aggies game, UT safety John Hagy had lamented about losing a game—any game—to the Aggies.

"When A&M wins a game," he said, "you're going to hear from every little A&M cockroach in the country."

That quote caught fire and played like fighting words for the A&M faithful. Meanwhile freewheeling Aggies safety Terrance "Chet" Brooks had just nicknamed the A&M defense the "Wrecking Crew" after a rap group, the World Class Wreckin' Cru.

"I think the biggest key," Brooks hooted before the '87 Texas game, "is that they're having to come to what the Wrecking Crew calls the Junkyard."

That objectionable designation never caught on at Texas A&M, for good reason: Aggies consider stately Kyle Field more like a war memorial (55 flags across the stadium's top honor Aggies killed in World War I) than a salvage lot. But Kyle did serve as a wreck of a place to play for opponents under Sherrill and defensive coordinator R.C. Slocum. The A&M defense hadn't allowed a touchdown in its previous nine quarters at home before the '87 Texas game.

The Wrecking Crew, too, had a reputation for carrying an offense that A&M coordinator Lynn Amadee joked had "aged him 10 years" that season, because of a lack of a passing attack. True, the Aggies' offense ranked seventh of eight Southwest Conference teams in 1987, and A&M quarterbacks completed only 44 percent of their passes.

"Shoot, we didn't mind that the defense carried the offense," Richardson says. "I'd take a great defense on my team every time. We played smash-mouth that year and tried to win with defense. That was just the personality of our team."

And in a smash-mouth special for the SWC title, the Aggies marched to their fourth consecutive win against the Longhorns —for the first time in history—20-13 at Kyle Field, on a glorious Thanksgiving night for A&M fans.

THE GAME OF MY LIFE
By Bucky Richardson

Funny, but I didn't even throw a pass in this most memorable game. Craig Stump was quarterbacking most of the way, and then I went in, but I had to go out a couple of times because the Texas defenders kept popping my shoe off in the pile after they'd tackle me.

It came off two or three times—they were definitely taking my shoe off. The shoe just slid off, you didn't have to untie it. Finally, something had to be done so I could stay in the game.

"Tape my shoes to my calves if you have to, I don't want 'em to come off anymore!" I yelled above the amazing volume of the crowd to equipment manager Billy Pickard, who's been at A&M since the Bear Bryant days in the mid 1950s. Mr. Pickard nodded his head and scowled at the opposing sideline.

"Yep, let's get 'em taped," he said.

As a freshman, I figured they'd be trying to knock my head off, not my shoes. I hadn't realized how intense the A&M-t.u. rivalry was, but once we kicked that ball off it was the loudest stadium I've ever been in.

Our big offensive play in the game came in the second quarter when Keith Woodside, a senior tailback, blasted 90 yards for a touchdown on a basic sweep. We weren't even sure that Keith was going to play that week

Bucky Richardson rushed for 2,095 yards from 1987-91, a school record for a quarterback, in leading the Aggies to conference titles in '87 and '91. *Photo courtesy of Texas A&M Athletic Media Relations*

because of a knee injury. That run was one of the most inspiring I've ever seen.

Keith wasn't going to quit until he got it into the end zone, and it was an astounding sight. He must have broken five tackles along the way.

With my shoes securely taped to my ankles and calves, I snapped a 13-13 tie with a little more than four minutes remaining in the game, on a seven-yard touchdown run. It was a speed option to the right, to the strong side, and the defense just overpursued. So I cut back against the grain a little bit and a hole just opened up beautifully, and I went in untouched.

The option, if we executed it the right way and got a block or two downfield, was extremely hard to stop, and the play we scored the final touchdown on isn't designed to fool anybody. It's just a drop step by the quarterback and an option to the right, and of course when the defensive players see that they immediately boogie over to that side of the field, and a lot of times they overpursue.

You've always got to look for that cutback, and that's what I did. When I crossed the goal line, I shot the "hook 'em horns" sign with both of my hands in the air. People still ask me why I did that. There's an easy answer: We were about to win, and that was four in a row, right? I had two fingers on each hand up, and that was my way of saying, "Four in a row!"

I'll never forget all of the cotton flying through the air toward the end of the game, because we were making our third straight trip to the Cotton Bowl—and had beaten Texas, incredibly, four consecutive times for the first time in history.

As for the Longhorns, those guys never once mentioned popping my shoe off.

GAME RESULTS

On the day before Texas A&M's 20-13 victory over Texas on Thanksgiving Day 1987, a woman reported to A&M ticket manager Jim Kotch that her dog ate her game tickets. Kotch replaced them, honoring the noble idea that Aggies never cheat, lie or steal.

A day later Aggies coach Jackie Sherrill concerned himself with a UT player he described as a "cat"—the Longhorns' "Mr. Everything" Eric Metcalf. The Virginian Metcalf, by the way, said before the game that he couldn't figure out why the two Texas schools despised each other so much.

"It's just another game for me," he said.

Metcalf proved Sherrill's concerns valid when he scored on a 50-yard draw late in the second quarter to spring Texas to a 10-7 lead. That play marked UT's lone touchdown against the Aggies.

"Give credit to our crowd," Sherrill said. "This may be one of the toughest places to play in the nation."

Much of that crowd followed the Aggies to Dallas for the Cotton Bowl, where A&M blasted Notre Dame and coach Lou Holtz 35-10 on a chilly Friday afternoon on New Year's Day 1988. Bucky Richardson only completed two of nine passes that day, but he earned offensive Player of the Game honors as the game's leading rusher with 96 yards on 13 attempts.

"Players come to A&M now to play for a national title," a triumphant Sherrill said a day later.

A&M finished 10th in the final Associated Press poll that year, which proved to be its final top 10 ranking in Sherrill's tenure. Sherrill's time as coach was up only a year later following a 7-5 season and NCAA troubles.

WHAT BECAME OF BUCKY RICHARDSON?

A couple of beautiful women, both in their late 70s and avid Texas A&M fans, didn't hesitate in naming their favorite Aggie football player of all time.

"Bucky," Florence Neelley and Priscilla Gougler said in unison, six years after Bucky Richardson had last suited up for the Aggies.

A&M fans seem to remember the popular Richardson as if he wore the Maroon and White only yesterday, because of their undying sentiment for the Baton Rouge Boy who'd found his way to College Station. He was a throwback player who wouldn't have looked out of place in a leather helmet and a running quarterback before it was cool.

"I didn't hook slide and I didn't run out of bounds much," Richardson says. "It's nice that people remember me, and you hope they like the way I played the game. I don't think they remember me because I was the best quarterback they'd ever seen, but I'd like to believe that fans appreciated the way I approached the game and the way I played.

"I was intense, and played hard. You could call it just putting in an honest day's work, and I think people noticed that."

These days Richardson puts in an honest day's work as a sales representative for Environmental Improvements Incorporated in Houston.

"I don't know if I ever want to retire," he says. "I've been doing this for five years now in the water and wastewater industry, and I really enjoy it. Heck, I don't ever see myself not doing anything. I'm not wired that way."

Richardson played a few years for the Houston Oilers, in a special teams and mostly backup quarterback role, and wrapped up his NFL career following his release from the Kansas City Chiefs at the conclusion of the

1996 training camp. His competition for the No. 2 quarterback slot that year was Rich Gannon, 2002 league MVP with the Oakland Raiders.

Richardson thus settled into his sales job in Houston and married the former Tracey Turner of Alvin on March 8, 1997, and the couple has a daughter, Jordan, and a son, John Paul.

"Tracey was a godsend for me," Richardson says. "She's the rock in our family, for sure."

As for Richardson, he served as the rock of an A&M program that won bookend conference championships —in 1987 and '91—in his career, and he'll never forget his playing days in Aggieland.

"Playing football was in my blood, and it taught you how to be unselfish," he says. "It taught you how to be on time and responsible and to follow through with what you said you were going to do.

"Really, football taught me just how to live life."

CHAPTER 17

RICHMOND WEBB

Name: Richmond Jewel Webb Jr.
Born: Jan. 11, 1967
Hometown: Dallas, Texas
Current Residence: Houston, Texas
Occupation: Retired NFL Player
Position: Tackle and Guard
Height: 6'7"
Playing Weight: 280 pounds
Years lettered: 1986-89
Accomplishments: All-Conference in 1989; Aggie Heart Award winner in '89; blocked for the SWC offensive player of the year in 1988, running back Darren Lewis, who gained a school-record 1,692 rushing yards; first-round pick (ninth overall) of the Miami Dolphins in the 1990 NFL draft; seven-time Pro Bowler with the Dolphins; protected quarterback Dan Marino's blind side.
Nickname: Bam-Bam
The Game: Texas A&M at Texas, Nov. 24, 1988

Richmond Webb. *Photo courtesy of Texas A&M Athletic Media Relations*

THE LIFE OF YOUNG RICHMOND WEBB

Richmond Webb kept the business card in his wallet throughout his Texas A&M career—even during his first couple of seasons with the Miami Dolphins—until he lost the billfold. He got the card from Jackie Sherrill when A&M's coach recruited him as a defensive lineman in 1985 out of Dallas.

"I see you coming to Texas A&M, and I see you doing great things for us," Sherrill said, as he slid his business card out of his pocket and wrote "Outland Trophy" on the back of it before a wide-eyed Webb and his parents.

The Outland is awarded annually to the nation's best interior lineman, as selected by the Football Writers Association of America.

"Put this in your wallet," Sherrill said, "and four years from now I'll go with you when you accept the Outland Trophy."

Webb didn't know the Outland from Australia's Outback. But he certainly appreciated this smooth-talking recruiter's confidence in him.

"I still think back to that moment," Webb says, smiling. "I was sitting there as a 17-year-old kid wondering, 'How does this guy know all of this?'

He had a gift for making you believe that you were special and that you'd accomplish whatever you set your mind to."

But Webb, the second of Richmond and Bobbie Webb's four children, had accomplished plenty before Sherrill ever settled onto his couch and coaxed him to College Station. Webb served as senior class president at Dallas's Roosevelt High and humbly says his biggest accomplishment in such a role might have been his class presenting the school with a brand-new speaking podium that year.

Sherrill, meanwhile, got a sturdy lineman in the studious youngster from Dallas, one who signed an A&M scholarship along with high school teammate Aaron Wallace over the likes of Oklahoma, Texas and SMU.

"I didn't have any A&M ties, other than I had spent a week there one time in high school as part of a Fellowship of Christian Athletes camp," Webb says. "It just seemed like the right place for me."

Webb arrived at A&M at about six foot six and 240 pounds, and by the end of his redshirt freshman season the coaches had shifted him from defense to offense. It was a move that one day paid millions for the well-mannered giant from Dallas, who also played basketball at Roosevelt High.

"Richmond and I had gone to school together since the third grade," Wallace says. "We were both on the basketball team in high school and probably didn't score two points between us. But nobody wanted to come inside on us—because we'd jam 'em. They had to beat us from the outside.

"One time Coach Sherrill came to see us play basketball, and so we tried really hard to act like we could play, but we really couldn't. I don't think Coach cared, though—he was there for football."

As for the inspirational business card from Sherrill, Webb never checked with his teammates to see if they also had an Outland, Lombardi, Heisman or some such card in their wallets.

"I didn't want to talk to them about it," Webb says, "because I didn't want to hear something like, 'Man, you believed all of that?' Honestly, I didn't want to know."

Webb never won the Outland—or even made first-team All-American—but he did wind up a first-round draft pick of the Miami Dolphins in 1990 and has a shot at one day becoming Texas A&M's first entrant into the NFL Hall of Fame since Yale Lary.

"I'd rather be a first-round NFL draft pick," Webb says, smiling, "than an All-American any day. I didn't worry too much about all of that stuff, anyway. Winning was the main thing."

THE SCENE

It figures a year that wound up with a game dubbed the "Hurricane Bowl"—a 30-10 loss to Alabama on a nice evening at Kyle Field—registers as possibly Texas A&M's most volatile football season in history. And in the storm's center, more defiant than ever, stood Coach Jackie Sherrill.

Flanked by eight TV crews and a gaggle of newspaper writers, Sherrill calmly sipped on a Diet Coke in the Kyle Field press box three days before the 1988 Texas game and traded barbs with reporters who sniffed the blood seeping from Sherrill's embattled program.

"If I was trying to dodge the issue," Sherrill said of allegations by former player George Smith that Sherrill paid him hush money, "I wouldn't be here today. When I can't handle you guys, it's time for me to get out of the business."

Sherrill, who played Texas A&M's reputation of often possessing an "us against the world" mentality to the hilt, may have lost the affection of the national, state and local media by that point. But he still had his players.

"He was absolutely a players' coach," says Richmond Webb, an offensive lineman on Sherrill's final A&M team in '88 and a future seven-time NFL Pro Bowler at tackle. "He always used some sort of motivation on us. One year he gave each guy a piece of rope and told us that we were each a part of the rope. And, believe me, you didn't want to be the part that broke.

"Another time he gave us a chain link, the next a slice of wood. He told us that you couldn't break all of those pieces of wood—which were cut from the same board—when they were together. But they'd snap individually. That was the team concept that he preached."

Sherrill would have done well to pass out harnesses late in 1988—better for his team to circle the wagons with amidst all of the arrows aimed at College Station based on the hush-money allegations, combined with prior NCAA troubles and what had become an atypically poor season at 6-4.

"Coach Sherrill did a great job of keeping everybody focused on the task at hand," Webb says of that distraction-filled season. "And the thing that we all figured would salvage the season was just beating Texas."

Die Hard, an action-thriller that became actor Bruce Willis's signature flick, was all of the rage in theaters about the time Sherrill was preparing the final time for what became his signature in Aggieland: beating Texas. *Die Hard,* too, might have described a resistant Sherrill's final stand in Aggieland.

THE SETTING

Things were so bad in late 1988 for most all things football in the Lone Star State that even the venerable Tom Landry was on his way out as Dallas Cowboys coach after a 3-13 season. A couple of hours southwest of Big D in College Station, the 6-4 Aggies were preparing for their rival game while the local fire marshal was dubbing the Bonfire a "potential hazard"—for what would a little more than a decade later turn out to be true for the wrong reasons.

"As much fuel that's on it and as much lumber as is there, we couldn't even control it, let alone put it out," the College Station fire marshal said. "Bonfire is well-engineered; it's safe the way they build it, but it's kind of like making dynamite—you're dealing with a potentially dangerous situation. A lot of people get hurt during Bonfire. You wonder sometimes if it's all worth it."

Meanwhile the proverbial flames were licking all around the coattails of Sherrill, who once said of an afternoon spent helping build Bonfire: "In three hours I learned more about A&M than I probably could have learned anywhere else."

Sherrill, however, in 1988 was learning way too much about NCAA investigations while trying to gear up his team up for a strong finish to a stormy season. On Sept. 9 of that year, the NCAA declared the Aggies ineligible for a bowl game and placed the school on two years' probation, citing a sequence of 25 recruiting violations.

Texas A&M, of course, wasn't alone in the Southwest Conference with NCAA violations, as it became the fifth league school to earn probation from the governing body in three years.

A little more than two months after the Aggies received probation, the *Dallas Morning News* reported that former player George Smith received $4,400 in hush money from Sherrill to keep Smith quiet about further recruiting violations not yet reported. Smith, who lettered for A&M in 1982 and '83, later recanted his story, but the damage was done—especially with the Aggies in the midst of a tough season.

"It just didn't seem like what Smith was saying carried any weight," Richmond Webb says. "It seemed like he was trying to benefit [by wanting to sign a book deal] from the school's other problems."

In any case, Sherrill had plenty more than football on his mind as A&M got ready for a trip to Austin. The downtrodden Longhorns, meanwhile, weren't going to a bowl game, either, for different reasons. At 4-6, Texas already was assured of only its second losing season since 1956, and the Longhorns hadn't defeated A&M since 1983.

"The seniors haven't ever beaten A&M," UT coach David McWilliams said. "We'd like to win it from that standpoint."

But even surrounded by the unraveling of his program, Sherrill still could motivate his team to do at least one thing: beat Texas. The Aggies prevailed 28-24 on Thanksgiving night, earning the school's 500th win in its storied history. A milestone victory, of course, that also turned out to be Sherrill's last at A&M.

THE GAME OF MY LIFE
By Richmond Webb

Our biggest challenge that season was to stay motivated even though you knew there was no postseason reward because of the NCAA probation. Of course, there was one thing that would salvage an otherwise tough season: defeating Texas.

And we had a tough guy to help do it: sophomore running back Darren Lewis. I knew the kid was good from having played against him in high school. And then at A&M his freshman year, he just did some incredible things in practice against our defense.

As an offensive lineman, I understood that the skill positions get most of the glory—whether you were a quarterback, running back or receiver. The reward you get as an O-lineman is when a quarterback or running back says, "Hey, without my guys up front, I wouldn't be able to do what I do."

Nobody wants to hear about you making the block, because you don't have the ball. That's understandable. They want to hear about that guy who's got the ball. And Darren, he had the ball plenty against Texas that game, rushing for 212 yards in a true grind-it-out affair. With all of our troubles that season, that game really sticks out in my mind as a high note. Because, at the beginning of the year, that's the one you highlight on the schedule.

GAME RESULTS

Despite all of the season's adversities, Texas A&M beat Texas a record fifth consecutive game (a streak that wound up at six) on that Thanksgiving night before a Memorial Stadium crowd of 77,809. The Aggies—who weren't eligible for the Cotton Bowl—finished up 6-1 in SWC play.

Lewis, who rushed for 102 yards in the first quarter, wound up with a then career-high 212 yards on 38 carries in the 28-24 victory.

Richmond Webb earned most of his renown in the NFL after earning seven trips to the Pro Bowl as an offensive lineman with the Miami Dolphins from 1990-2000. *Photo courtesy of Texas A&M Athletic Media Relations*

"Several times we had him behind the line and he broke tackles and made good gains," David McWilliams said. "He earned a lot of tough yards."

A week later Alabama and linebacker Derrick Thomas blew past the Aggies 30-10 in the "Hurricane Bowl," so dubbed because the Crimson Tide had skipped out on a trip to College Station in mid-September because of the threat of Hurricane Gilbert, which wound up mostly slamming Mexico.

Sherrill, defiant to the end, told reporters after the Alabama game that he'd see them in September. Eleven days later he resigned his post as A&M football coach and athletics director, in the wake of the Smith accusations coupled with the prior NCAA troubles.

"Because of my great love for this school and its people," Sherrill said, "I'm removing myself from my position at Texas A&M ... it's time for us to come to a mutual parting of the ways in order for everyone concerned to get a fresh start."

The university quickly replaced Sherrill with 17-year A&M assistant R.C. Slocum and named the school's 1957 Heisman Trophy winner, John David Crow, as its AD.

"Coach Sherrill had called us all into the meeting room at Kyle Field, told us he'd resigned and got choked up, and so he left," Richmond Webb says. "Coach Slocum and John David Crow then stepped in and tried to ease the guys' minds by telling us everything was going to be OK."

Everything would be OK under Slocum, who'd go on to win four conference championships (three SWC titles and one Big 12 trophy) in his 14 seasons in Aggieland.

Sherrill, following a couple of years in private business, became head coach at Mississippi State on Dec. 9, 1990. And, perhaps most important to many Aggies, A&M continued whipping up on Texas for the next several years under Slocum, who won his first five of six games against the Longhorns—despite winding up with a 7-7 mark against UT.

WHAT BECAME OF RICHMOND WEBB?

Richmond Webb played on three Southwest Conference championship teams at Texas A&M, so his favorite single moment in Aggieland may seem a little surprising. Noble, but surprising.

"I have a ton of football memories," Webb says. "But I think my fondest memory was when I actually got my degree and walked across that stage. At first I'd thought about not even attending the ceremony, but I'm so glad I did. My whole family was there, and that made it extra special."

Webb graduated with a degree in industrial distribution, three years after he'd last suited up for the Aggies. First-round pick of the Miami Dolphins or not, Bobbie Webb wanted to see her son graduate.

"She always stressed education over athletics; both my parents did," Webb says. "Even after my first season in the NFL, she said, 'Mama is happy for you, but you need to get on back down there and finish up school.' So I did."

Webb played 11 years with the Dolphins, his primary job being to protect future Hall of Fame quarterback Dan Marino's blind side.

"Everyone focuses on left tackle along the offensive line because your job is to keep the quarterback—most of whom are right-handed—from taking an unprotected shot," Webb says. "I got to Miami and the first thing I thought was, 'I don't want to be the guy who gets this man knocked out of a game. This is Dan Marino. If something happens to this guy and it's my fault, I'm never going to be able to live it down.'

"So some of my motivation to excel in Miami was partly fear. I didn't want to be the guy who got Dan Marino hurt."

Webb didn't, and he played in an amazing seven consecutive Pro Bowls for the Dolphins from 1990-2000. Webb now resides in Houston with his wife, Chandra, and three daughters: Jasmine, Brianna and Madison. For fun, Webb likes to ride four-wheelers and horses on his 100 acres located west of Houston along Interstate 10 near Schulenburg.

"Everybody was friends with Richmond," former Dolphins teammate Mark Dixon said after Webb signed a contract with the Cincinnati Bengals in 2001. "He's maybe the most impressive person I've ever met, as far as a player and a human being."

CHAPTER 18

AARON WALLACE

Name: Aaron Jon Wallace
Born: April 17, 1967 in Paris, Texas
Hometown: Dallas, Texas
Current Residence: Dallas, Texas
Occupation: Retired from the NFL
Position: Linebacker
Height: 6'4"
Playing Weight: 234
Years lettered: 1986-89
Accomplishments: Two-time All-Conference (1988-89); school's all-time career sack leader with 42; second-round draft pick of the Los Angeles Raiders, played eight years in the NFL; nine sacks in 1990 as member of NFL's all-rookie team.
The Game: Houston at Texas A&M, Oct. 14, 1989

THE LIFE OF YOUNG AARON WALLACE

Aaron Wallace sacked the quarterback on his first play ever for Texas A&M in 1986—and 41 more of those knee-wobbling shots were to come for the young man who'd grow into the Aggies' all-time sack leader.

Aaron Wallace. *Photo courtesy of Texas A&M Athletic Media Relations*

Wallace, the middle of A. J. and Marilyn Wallace's three children, had signed with coach Jackie Sherrill as a six-foot-four, 215-pound linebacker out of Dallas's Roosevelt High School in 1985. And the athletic phenom fit defensive coordinator R.C. Slocum's "Wrecking Crew" scheme —"go get the quarterback, son"—to a tee.

"Coming out of high school I was mainly a pass rusher, and I got to keep doing that at Texas A&M," Wallace says. "I'd just come off of that end, and it came easy to me. After that first year when I had nine sacks, Coach Slocum told me at that pace I'd have a good shot at Jacob Green's career sack record."

Green collected 37 sacks—he also set the school record with 20 in one season—from 1977-79 as a defensive end. Wallace, an outside linebacker, wound up with 42 sacks from 1986-89, along with something just as memorable from his Aggie playing days: half the nickname of the Blitz Brothers.

"That took on a life of its own," Wallace says with a laugh of the handle he shared with fellow outside linebacker John Roper, a tag concocted by the coaching staff in conjunction with the A&M sports information office.

"We were in a position where you had two great pass rushers playing in a system where we weren't confined."

Roper, who tallied 15 sacks each in 1987 and 1988, is third on A&M's all-time sack list with 36—one behind Green. And many observers of Roper—a young man given to blaring nonsensicals at any moment—figured him one potato shy of a full sack.

"Sometimes," fellow linebacker Dana Batiste once said, "you don't think he's playing with a full deck out there. We'll be in the huddle and he'll start talking about cartoons."

Roper, too, in many ways seemed like a character straight off the funny pages. Approached by a *Newsday* reporter before the 1988 Kickoff Classic against Nebraska, Roper brushed off the scribe with, "Ain't talkin! I want to go to McDonald's. It's a nice day for McDonald's." Roper then spit a few times and hurried off into his own odd world.

"I wouldn't call him crazy," Wallace says, "just confident and borderline cocky. He would put on those sunglasses like [Chicago Bears quarterback] Jim McMahon would wear, and Roper knew karate and all of this different kind of stuff. The best word to describe him was eccentric. He'd wear those McMahon shades all day—in meetings, going to class … And he'd tell stories in linebacker meetings that if he wasn't playing football, he'd be a truck driver.

"He just marched to his own beat. One thing I do know—John was a great athlete."

Roper once smashed LSU quarterback Tom Hodson so hard during a 1988 game that he ripped up his own nose. What Wallace saw immediately after made his stomach curdle.

"It was so bad," Wallace says, "you could see the meat in there. The blood was just gushing out of Roper's nose, but that was just a testament to how tough he was. Because they just stitched it up and he was back in there playing, never missing a step."

Following a hugely successful career at A&M, Roper played briefly in the NFL and now lives in Houston. But the Blitz Brothers legend lives on—although Slocum once tried passing down the tag, much as the "Wrecking Crew" moniker has been handed down through the years (sometimes undeservingly so, to less-than-intimidating A&M defenses).

"William Thomas stepped into Roper's place and has done an excellent job with Aaron," Slocum said a year after Roper left for the NFL. "He's allowed us to continue with our same scheme. We still have the Blitz Brothers, just with different people."

History says otherwise, as the Blitz Brothers nickname retired with the Aggieland departures of John Roper and Aaron Wallace.

"You'd be surprised at how many strangers that I run into, and the first person they ask about is John Roper," says Wallace, who occasionally talks to his fellow Blitz Brother. "We're going to be forever linked—that nickname created a two-headed monster."

But Wallace's most shining moment came a year after Roper left College Station, when Wallace beheaded—or at least—"be-helmeted"— a passing monster in Houston's Andre Ware, thus forging an unforgettable moment for the Texas A&M faithful, and fans of the lone remaining Blitz Brother.

THE SCENE

R.C. Slocum possessed a down-home, sometimes self-deprecating humor—one he put to good use in the days before eighth-ranked University of Houston was to roll into town in October 1989, having outscored its opponents through four games by an incredible average of 59 to six.

"It's kind of like when you were a little kid and you went somewhere and cut up," the first-year head coach told reporters. "You knew you were going to get a spanking when you got home, and you spent two or three hours wishing you could go ahead and get that thing over with. We'd like to go on and find out how bad it's going to be."

Privately, Slocum—never one to ruffle opponents' feathers—hummed a different tune to his players. The only spanking he anticipated on the following Saturday was reserved for Cougars junior quarterback Andre Ware, the eventual Heisman Trophy winner that year.

Aggies defensive coordinator Bob Davie and Slocum had devised a defensive scheme that replaced beefier defensive linemen with linebackers and linebackers with defensive backs—to match UH's offensive speed, while still rushing brutes like Aaron Wallace and William Thomas at Ware.

Slocum, of course, wasn't new to scheming up defenses to counter teams' strengths. In the mid 1980s he'd come up with a short-yardage defense the Aggies had dubbed the "Pony," which employed five down linemen, four linebackers and two cornerbacks to successfully counteract the likes of Auburn running back Bo Jackson in the 1986 Cotton Bowl.

"R.C. was really creative," says Johnny Holland, an A&M All-American linebacker in 1985 and '86. "Teams had a really hard time scoring on us in the goal-line area because of R.C. He'd put a lot of big, good athletes on the field in those situations—guys who were hungry to make a play."

Slocum, a true-maroon A&M loyalist although a McNeese State (La.) graduate, had served as an assistant in Aggieland for 16 years when named as Jackie Sherrill's successor on Dec. 12, 1988. By design, the Aggie football players never had much time to be upset that Sherrill had abruptly resigned as Texas A&M coach and athletics director.

"It was a smooth transition," Wallace says. "The defense hardly changed, the only change was in the personality of the head coach. There was more of a cockiness on the team with Coach Sherrill, but then again, part of that was because of the players before us—guys like Kevin Murray. Kevin was just cocky, and the team fed off of that arrogance."

Slocum, a friendly soul, never acted cocky or preached cockiness to his players, but he did exude confidence. And quietly—at least until Texas A&M's Midnight Yell Practice on the night before the UH game—the coach figured he and Davie might have a little sumthin' in store for run-and-shoot Houston on a fall Saturday in Aggieland.

"They think they're coming up here for a track meet," Slocum barked to 40,000 fans in Kyle Field. "But we're going to introduce the run-and-shoot to the blitz-and-destroy!"

Even with a lone Blitz Brother still roaming Kyle's turf—because of all the capable John Roper-replacements on hand, like William Thomas, Slocum was right: the catchy nickname did deserve passing down, based on the continued sacking success of blitzing outside linebackers at Texas A&M through the years. But John Roper and Aaron Wallace, for two, are satisfied that it wasn't.

THE SETTING

The Blitz Brothers were no more by 1989, although the Aggies could have used a zany character like John Roper against a cartoonish, blooming offense called the run-and-shoot, which employed four wideouts, zero tight ends, and no huddles.

Instead of the defunct Blitz Brothers, in fact, Texas A&M got a dose of the Smothers Brothers—and their infamous yo-yo act—on an October 1989 weekend at Rudder Auditorium.

Across Joe Routt Boulevard at Kyle Field, the Aggies were facing a yo-yo act of another sort: No. 8 Houston's incredible offense under the direction of head coach Jack Pardee, a legendary Aggie and Junction Boy who loved the offense's wide-open ways.

Pardee, a one-time NFC Defensive Player of the Year with the Washington Redskins, steadily defended the crazy offense that was putting up record numbers.

"I spent a lot of time on defense," Pardee said before the Houston game at A&M, "and I've always known how hard the pass was to defense. So I didn't have any negative thoughts about the run-and-shoot."

For reasons justifiable. The Cougars, on probation that year for 250 violations between 1978-86 under a different coaching regime, were averaging 647 yards per game through the season's first four games. The next closest in the country? Nebraska at 533. UH also was averaging 560 yards of passing per game, and quarterback Andre Ware's 440 yards per game of total offense would have placed him among the top 20 *teams* in the country to that point.

Many observers had expected Baylor's defense to provide UH with a challenge the week before the A&M game; instead the Cougars had ripped the Bears and then the nation's top-ranked pass defense 66-10. On the same day the Aggies had lost a heartbreaker at Texas Tech 27-24, falling out of the top 25.

"I honestly don't think anyone can stop us," Ware said in the days before the game at A&M.

"The only time our system doesn't work is when we make mistakes and beat ourselves."

Aaron Wallace, William Thomas & Co. might have had a little something to do with the outcome, however, on Oct. 14, 1989, when the unranked Aggies blitzed Ware and then blitzed some more, prevailing 17-13 at Kyle Field in R.C. Slocum's biggest win in his first year as head coach.

THE GAME OF MY LIFE
By Aaron Wallace

The run-and-shoot was a different and explosive offense to line up against, for sure, but in a lot of ways it fit my style. I loved to rush the passer, and about all a quarterback did in the run-and-shoot was throw the ball. I knew that if a guy was going to throw 50 passes in a game, I'd get my licks in.

Sure enough, we wound up sacking Andre Ware six times and picking off three of his passes, and William Thomas had a particularly good game. William was John Roper's replacement at outside linebacker that season, and he had 16 tackles, three and a half sacks and two forced fumbles against Houston—just a great showing against a ranked team.

I'd gone into the game with a sprained toe, but there was no way a bad toe was going to keep me out of this one—so I got a cortisone shot beforehand and kept on rolling. Our defense was never terrified of the

Linebacker Aaron Wallace, Texas A&M's all-time sack leader with 42, hoists Heisman Trophy winner Andre Ware's helmet after a fourth-quarter sack against Houston. *Kathy Young/Texas Aggie Magazine*

run-and-shoot, by any means, because we'd beaten UH the previous two years—we simply had their number. It was just a matter of getting out there and getting after them, and doing what we do best.

We blitzed the entire time I was there, and that's the main reason I went to A&M. We had threats coming from everywhere, and that's what really helped us in that game against Houston. R.C. Slocum and Bob Davie, our defensive coordinator, had the idea to replace our bigger defensive linemen with linebackers like me. We gave away some strength against the run, but we didn't necessarily have to worry about the run against the Cougars. We were able to shoot the gaps and get upfield, because we knew most of the time they'd be passing.

In the fourth quarter, my favorite moment at Kyle Field in my career occurred. Ware dropped back to pass on the Cougars' next to last possession, and with us holding on to the lead, and I got to him. I knew that play also meant that I'd tied Jacob Green for the school's sack record, and that meant an awful lot to me.

As I was bringing Ware down by the head, his helmet popped off. So I grabbed it off the turf and held the helmet straight up in the air, and the crowd went crazy. I threw Andre's helmet back down to him, while he was still lying on the turf. I've heard that spontaneous moment described as similar to a medieval knight triumphantly holding up a severed head.

In a lot of ways it seemed like that to me, too. We wanted to win that game bad. The Cougars had come in ranked eighth and we had just lost at Texas Tech, and we believed we really had something to prove. That play kind of symbolized the entire day. I was never the kind of guy who danced around after a sack or anything, so that reaction with Andre's helmet caught quite a few people off guard—including Coach Davie.

"That was totally out of character," Davie said, grinning. "Helluva play!"

Even Coach Slocum, who always preached for us to let our play do the talking, congratulated me and seemed to enjoy that moment. I know that I did.

GAME RESULTS

Texas A&M honored its 1939 national champions before the 1989 UH-A&M game at Kyle Field, to commemorate the 50th anniversary of the Aggies' lone national championship. Four quarters later any talk of Houston winning its first national title behind the run-and-shoot offense ceased, following the Aggies' 17-13 win over the probation-laced Cougars.

"We tried to counteract their blitzing with the run," a frustrated

Cougars offensive coordinator John Jenkins said.

"We ran the ball more than we ever have and did a good job, but weren't able to handle the rush, and that's what caused the problem."

Andre Ware, who won the Heisman Trophy that year as the Cougars finished 9-2 overall and 6-2 in the Southwest Conference (with losses to A&M and Arkansas), completed 28 of 52 passes for 247 yards and a touchdown against the Aggies.

"They have a hell of a team," Ware simply said of A&M, while also sticking to his belief that the Cougars were "just a couple of plays from breaking it open."

The quarterback, however, is simply lucky Wallace didn't take his head with the helmet on the game's defining moment.

"We treated every play of the game like it was the last," said a triumphant Davie, who later compiled a 35-25 record as Notre Dame head coach from 1997-2001.

The Aggies didn't win the conference in 1989, but their continued reckless style on defense did foreshadow plenty of good times to come under Slocum, who'd win three consecutive SWC championships from 1991-93 and a Big 12 Conference title in 1998.

Houston, meanwhile, never quite got over the top with the run-and-shoot behind Pardee and later John Jenkins, who resigned as Cougars coach in late April 1993 partly because he'd spliced video of topless women into game tape—in what Jenkins had dubbed an "innocent attention getter" for his players.

One of the more obscene attention getters in UH history, however, featured a helmet-less and defeated Andre Ware lying flat on his back while a conquering Aaron Wallace hoisted his innocuous Cougar Red trophy.

WHAT BECAME OF AARON WALLACE?

Aaron Wallace played eight years in the NFL, all with the Raiders, but one of his biggest post-A&M achievements came 13 years after he last suited up for the Maroon and White.

"My sister, Mitzi, had encouraged me to return for my degree once I'd finished up in the NFL," Wallace says. "I just kind of relaxed for a while after I left the league, but then I started helping out with some coaching in Little League, and I got a bug to coach on the high school or college level. And you need a degree for that."

So Wallace first enrolled at a community college so he could earn reentrance into Texas A&M, and he walked across the stage at Reed Arena in the summer of 2002.

"The whole time I was in the NFL it had nagged at me because I knew I hadn't put in the necessary effort to get a degree the first time around," Wallace says. "I knew if I put my mind into it, I could get back into it and get that degree."

Wallace, who has four children: Alyse, Aaron Jr., Tyla, and Aden, has also put his mind to shying away from the sometimes breakneck, reckless life of an NFL player.

"Being away from football caused me to finally come to terms with myself," Wallace says. "I used to party and do all of that stuff that accompanies the lifestyle in the NFL. Now, I'm in a place where I'm really calm and at peace.

"I fulfilled a lot of my football dreams; now I'm trying to spend more time with my kids and live a calmer existence. That other stuff is done; now it's time to move on."

A youthful Aaron Wallace, then seven years old, once told his father of a football dream that became shining reality.

"We had just signed him up to play Little League football," A. J. says, smiling at the memory.

"And Aaron looked up at me and said, 'Dad, I'm gonna play pro football. And when I do, I'm gonna buy you a house.'

"He did both. Isn't that something?"

CHAPTER 19

QUENTIN CORYATT

Name: Quentin John Coryatt
Born: Aug. 1, 1970 in St. Croix, Virgin Islands
Hometown: Baytown, Texas
Current Residences: Houston, Texas and Los Angeles, Cali.
Occupation: Magazine Publisher
Position: Linebacker
Height: 6'4"
Playing Weight: 243 pounds
Years lettered: 1990-91
Accomplishments: All-Conference in 1991; 184 tackles over two years for the Aggies; No. 2 pick overall of the 1992 NFL draft by the Colts; led Indy in tackles in 1993.
Nicknames: The Terminator, Q
The Game: Arkansas at Texas A&M, Nov. 16, 1991

THE LIFE OF YOUNG QUENTIN CORYATT

Quentin Coryatt, born in the Virgin Islands and raised in Baytown, Texas, hadn't seen a snowflake until a numbingly cold

Quentin Coryatt. *Photo courtesy of Texas A&M Athletic Media Relations*

night in Fort Worth, Texas, on Nov. 7, 1991. That's why the stout and usually ferocious Aggies outside linebacker, the guy who made opposing quarterbacks and receivers shiver, rapidly rubbed his arms while trying to warm up just before Texas A&M's kickoff at Texas Christian.

About the same time in a wind chill of 13 degrees, Coryatt spotted what seemed a sympathetic—and nearly frozen—face in A&M defensive coordinator Bob Davie.

"Coach," said Coryatt, his voice rising while shaking, "it's coooold out here! I don't know if I can go out there and play today. I mean, it's snowing!"

That's when Coryatt drew a stare and a response he'll always remember from the man who reminded him so much of the ever-cool Clint Eastwood.

"Q," Davie responded, his voice dropping to a Dirty Harry-like whisper, "Just go out there and play football. Just go out there, son, and fly around, and do what you do best."

Thus charged and amidst those novel snowflakes, Coryatt flew around that night and did what he did best, and TCU receiver Kyle McPherson wound up with a jaw wired shut for the next two months. Many gaping observers considered the spindly receiver lucky.

"Best hit I can ever remember seeing," TCU coach Jim Wacker said. "And in 37 years of coaching, I've seen quite a few."

"The Hit," reverently considered one of the most ferocious of all time on any level of football, occurred on the same day Los Angeles Lakers star Magic Johnson announced that he'd tested positive for the AIDS virus. As for McPherson, he recovered enough to play football again for TCU the next two years—possibly thanks to Coryatt's humanity.

"I could have hit him a lot harder," Coryatt nearly whispers of the prophetic play that shattered McPherson's jaw in three places. "But I didn't."

Funny, too, that it's a game that occurred a little more than a week later against Arkansas that Coryatt remembers more fondly than the 44-7 whipping of TCU on that Thursday night on ESPN. It was, after all, much warmer that evening in College Station.

THE SCENE

A couple of years before Quentin Coryatt literally executed the jaw-smashing success of Texas A&M's Wrecking Crew defense through an act forever known as The Hit, he spent Aggie game days pressing weights and sometimes, a roommate's pants.

Coryatt, a promising linebacker fighting through an early urge to transfer from A&M to a junior college, had sat out his first two years of college ball because of an NCAA punishment for improprieties on his entrance exam.

"I didn't practice my freshman year after the [1988] Baylor game [midway through the year], and I didn't return until spring ball going into my junior year," Coryatt says.

But he never seriously considered quitting the program under seemingly dire circumstances.

"I told myself that A&M is a great school," Coryatt says. "And that I'm gonna stick it out and see what happens."

Sticking it out also meant watching his roommate, fullback Robert Wilson, head off to A&M games while Coryatt holed up in their apartment—or headed over to old DeWare Fieldhouse for an extra workout.

"Man, good luck, have a good game," Coryatt told Wilson every week. "Anything I can do for you?"

"Well," Wilson usually responded with a grin, "you can iron my shirts and my pants."

"You know what?" Coryatt always shot back, shaking his head and smiling, "No problem."

Recruiting fanatics had plenty of problems finding Coryatt on most state top 100 lists, however, while he quietly excelled as a middle linebacker at Baytown's Lee High School in the late 1980s. The Coryatt family had moved from St. Croix, the Virgin Islands, to Baytown when Quentin's father, Irving, got a job as a pipefitter there when Quentin was just beginning elementary school.

But on that bitingly cold evening in Fort Worth—the one where The Hit bared the roots of a receiver's lower teeth—the nation got a firsthand introduction to Quentin Coryatt, a future second overall pick in the NFL draft.

"The funny thing is, a few plays earlier TCU ran the same exact play from a different formation and to our right side," Coryatt says.

"I was about a step away from doing the same exact thing to another receiver—missed him by a hair—and I remember thinking, 'I sure hope they run that play again.'"

The first time the Horned Frogs lined up in that formation – on their first play from scrimmage—A&M cornerback Derrick Frazier intercepted a pass by Matt Vogler and returned it 27 yards for a score. A possession and three plays later, the Horned Frogs lined up three receivers to the right, and receiver Kyle McPherson sprinted about six yards downfield before darting across the middle.

Big mistake.

"They had gone to an empty formation with no backs," Coryatt says. "I knew they couldn't run the ball, outside of a quarterback sneak. As a defensive player, the first thing you look at before huddling up is the down and distance, so you know how far you have to drop and how far they need for a first down.

"Our responsibility was to just look for crossing routes, and on that play, I just happened to be in the right place at the right time. Everyone knows what happened then."

What happened then—as Coryatt knocked out McPherson with his right forearm extended—still holds a soft spot for so many Aggies who either witnessed The Hit in person or on ESPN's Thursday night game of the week. And then watched it become ESPN's hit of the year.

"That was literally smash-mouth football," says former A&M student Brian Bishop, whose handle on the popular website texags.com is "44 The Hit," and whose every post in the football forum includes a video clip of same. "Ask any Aggie about 'The Hit,' and he'll know exactly what you're talking about."

A dark shield screwed on to Coryatt's facemask that hid his eyes—and seemed to accent his bulging muscles—further added to the mystique of the quiet linebacker nicknamed The Terminator.

"I began wearing the shield in the spring of my sophomore year," Coryatt says. "The reason? No one knew what was going on behind there. You didn't know if I looked evil or calm, cool and collected. No one knew what was behind the darkness—and it gave someone the idea that you might destroy the world."

Coryatt's buddy, Derrick Frazier, figured he'd try to emulate the intimidating look, but somehow it just didn't work for a 175-pound cornerback.

"It was something you had to get used to," Coryatt says of the dark shield. "Because when you breathe the hot air just bounces off that mask. And there's spit and sweat inside of there, and it makes it hard to see as well as breathe."

Frazier tried out the Darth Vader look during a practice going into the 1991 season—for about 20 minutes.

"Mr. Pickard!" a frustrated Frazier finally yelled to longtime A&M trainer and equipment manager Billy Pickard, "get this thing off my helmet! I can't breathe! I can't see!"

No doubt McPherson harbored similar thoughts immediately following The Hit. The TCU receiver, however, fought back to play football again and move on to a successful private career—a long way from the night a piece of metal held his split chin and jaws together in a Fort Worth hospital bed. Coryatt and McPherson have never spoken before or since their renowned collision.

"Later, on, I remember having flashbacks," McPherson said, 10 years after The Hit. "Maybe it was the pain. I could just feel how cold the air was. Every now and then I just have these … feelings. I can just see myself and I can feel the pain in my mouth. I get these visions and flashbacks."

The Hit, too, is considered the signature moment of A&M's vaunted Wrecking Crew defense, so nicknamed by safety Terrance "Chet" Brooks in 1987.

"It means a lot to me for people to still have that as a screensaver or video clip or what have you on their computers," Coryatt says. "But there's been plenty of Texas A&M players before or after me who've made plays that could have stood out just as easily."

But none stood out quite like that one, as even Aggies coach R.C. Slocum—who served as defensive coordinator when the Wrecking Crew first earned its name—kept a picture of The Hit in his office.

"It's unfortunate the young man was hurt, but you're trying to make that guy pay for coming in there," Slocum said of how to defend against such an offense. "And that guy certainly paid."

THE SETTING

The unknown, it seemed, had stolen Quentin Coryatt's trademark dark shield in late November 1990. The uncertain future of his older brother, Jason, who had just shipped out to Kuwait to fight in the first Persian Gulf War, laid heavy on Coryatt's mind.

"I got a call just before we climbed on the bus to go play at Texas," Coryatt says.

"Riding on that bus on the way to Austin, I'm thinking about how all of my life, the game of football was something that I took so much pride in. I loved the smell of that grass on a Saturday morning when I was playing Pee-Wee. And here I was, going to play a game which I treated like life or death, depending on its outcome.

"But it wasn't life or death, and my brother fighting in that war really put things in my life in perspective. Riding along in that bus, I was thinking how I could lose my brother, in a war based upon the freedoms and liberty that we have in America."

*   *   *   *   *

Jason Coryatt returned home safely from the first Persian Gulf War, and Baylor coach Grant Teaff might have learned a few lessons from the soldier about comparing war and football. Before the 1990 season at the Southwest Conference kickoff lunch in Dallas, the usually dignified Teaff groaned about losing league charter member Arkansas to the Southeastern Conference beginning with the 1992 season.

"I'm ... thoroughly convinced that the Southeastern Conference is the Iraq of the college football scene in America," Teaff said of the SEC's courtship of the eye-batting Razorbacks.

On Aug. 1, 1990, Arkansas had announced its decision to bolt from the SWC. Two days later, Saddam Hussein's Iraqi forces stormed into Kuwait. A day after Iraq's invasion of its neighbor, Teaff made his debatable comments to a roar of applause from the lunch's crowd.

More than a year later, Coryatt played his best college game against the Razorbacks, as he feasted on the option in Arkansas's final SWC appearance against the Aggies. But Coryatt certainly didn't hold a grudge against the 'Backs for splitting the fabled SWC—he only considers Arkansas ahead of its time.

* 　 * 　 * 　 * 　 *

Sure enough, four years later, the Southwest Conference disbanded, and league lightweights SMU, TCU, Rice and Houston were left looking for a new home. A&M, Texas, Texas Tech and Baylor, meanwhile, joined forces with the Big Eight to form the powerful Big 12. Coryatt wishes he could have played in the new league, to prove a point.

"Defensively, without a doubt, we'd have been unstoppable in the Big 12," he says. "Offensively, we were a little weak when it came to facing bigger opponents."

But not nearly as weak, in most cases, as the Aggies' league competition in the old Southwest Conference.

"There just weren't any powerhouses in the Southwest Conference besides us and Texas," Coryatt says. "The league, as a whole, was just plain weak. Rice? TCU? SMU? Houston? You don't brag about beating those teams. Playing in the SWC to us by then was an injustice, because we had a great team, but nobody could match up with us."

And in mid-November 1991 people figured the 7-1 and surging Aggies to win their final game against escapist Arkansas, before a huge crowd at Kyle Field as A&M angled for its first SWC championship under R.C. Slocum. Only the contest wound up closer than most figured at 13-3, and the Aggies won their final game against the Razorbacks thanks largely to a rugged outside linebacker named Quentin Coryatt.

THE GAME OF MY LIFE
By Quentin Coryatt

Arkansas tried surprising us by coming out in the Wishbone, because the Razorbacks probably figured they couldn't be successful with a passing game against our secondary. We had Kevin Smith and Derrick Frazier on the corners and Patrick Bates and Chris Crooms at the safeties—an awfully stout secondary.

Arkansas figured it was more conducive to just try and pound the ball down our throats, but we had a couple of guys in the middle—one being a freshman in defensive end Sam Adams—who could stuff the run just as well. We prepared all week for the possibility that the Razorbacks would just try to run. Hints afterward by the Arkansas coach, Jack Crowe, that we somehow had stolen their game plan early in the week, were a joke.

We'd seen that offense before, and each of our guys had an assignment. We had a lot of talented and smart players, and we figured out how to stop Arkansas right away.

Had the Razorbacks passed the ball more, we'd have had more interceptions, passes broken up and sacks. But the game's outcome would

Quentin Coryatt broke TCU receiver Kyle McPherson's jaw in three places with "The Hit" in 1991. He later became the No. 2 overall pick of the 1992 NFL draft. *Andy Richardson/A&M Video Lab*

have been exactly the same: we'd have won. Our defense was built on speed and getting to the ball and making big hits, and we thrived on all of those things. Give Bob Davie, our defensive coordinator, credit for that. He knew which players to use in the right situations and how to get the best out of each of us.

If fans loved watching two passing attacks go at it, then they certainly didn't like the Arkansas game that year. The Razorbacks didn't even complete a pass and wound up 0-3 on the game. As for our offense, we were ground-oriented behind Greg Hill and Rodney Thomas.

Even our senior quarterback, Bucky Richardson, was a runner. Our offense got the job done when it had to that year, and Bucky—he was a great leader. But that season it was proven, like the old saying goes, that defense wins championships.

GAME RESULTS

The 1991 Razorbacks-Aggies game better resembled a Bremond-Franklin high school game up Highway 6 than a major college football contest. Neither Arkansas nor Texas A&M completed a pass in the the Aggies' 13-3 win until midway through the third quarter.

A reporter jokingly asked A&M All-American cornerback Kevin Smith, who'd go on to start for two Super Bowl championship teams with the Dallas Cowboys, if he'd even suited up for the Arkansas game.

The grind-it-out special on both sides came a little more than a week after Aggies senior quarterback Bucky Richardson threw for 321 yards—then second on the school's all-time passing list—in the 44-7 win over TCU. Meanwhile Coryatt, not resting on the success of The Hit, finished the Arkansas game with an astounding 20 tackles.

A&M pushed its record to 8-1, its best start to a season since 1975, and capped a 10-1 regular-season campaign by whipping SMU and then beating Texas for the second time in Slocum's three years as head coach.

The longtime A&M assistant also became the first Aggies coach to rip through the Southwest Conference undefeated since Paul "Bear" Bryant did so in 1956. A&M's rock-solid defense, meanwhile, topped a terrific season by claiming the NCAA national total defense title.

"Our defensive philosophy," standout linebacker Marcus Buckley said following the 31-14 win over Texas, "is to run to the ball, and do what we have to do."

The Wrecking Crew carried that philosophy into the Cotton Bowl, but the Aggies' offense never got going against cornerback Terrell Buckley and Florida State in a 10-2 loss to the Seminoles.

"We were just grab-bagging [on offense]," a disgusted Slocum said afterward. "We played well enough on defense to win. I was disappointed offensively that we didn't play more consistently."

That, too, would become Slocum's frustrating signature in his 14 seasons as A&M: good defense, inconsistent offense. Slocum named seven different offensive coordinators in his 14 years as head coach, never quite finding the right combination to finish any higher than seventh overall in the national polls.

WHAT BECAME OF QUENTIN CORYATT

To point to Quentin Coryatt's success at linebacker, one need only step back to those long nights in old DeWare Fieldhouse—since demolished—to see how Coryatt spent his spare time.

"The place for me was DeWare," Coryatt says, bursting into a smile at the memories. "That was truly a great weight room: grungy, nasty, stinky, sweaty. On a typical day I'd eat dinner after practice, study for a few hours and then get to DeWare about 9 p.m. and leave at midnight. Now, this was on top of the workouts I'd do with the football team.

"My teammates were like, 'Man, what's wrong with you? You crazy?'"

Coryatt's drive essentially was his misfortune professionally. After the Colts selected him second overall in the 1992 NFL draft, he led Indy in tackles in 1993, only to subsequently endure four surgeries on his left shoulder and a ripped pectoral muscle. He played his last NFL season in 1999, and later, along with former teammate Derrick Frazier, he started an international magazine called *Controversy*.

"I tried to knock someone out every play," Coryatt says. "My pro career was short because of the injuries and the way I played the game. If I'd have played football as a finesse linebacker, I might have played 15 years.

"But it just wasn't a part of me to go out and try to run around blocks and play without the intensity needed to make my presence known. I feel like I played the game the way it was supposed to be played, and I have no regrets.

"That was my game, and I wouldn't change it."

These days Coryatt, who's single, spends most of his time working in the magazine business, working out, playing pool, reading and playing tennis.

Tennis with The Terminator, anyone?

"Tennis is a great sport," Coryatt says, smiling. "If I could do it all over, I might not have played football—I'd have played tennis."

Imagine, then:

Thus charged and amidst the warmth of Wimbledon, Coryatt flew around that day and did what he did best, and John McEnroe wound up with a jaw wired shut for the next two months—and many gaping observers considered the spindly loudmouth lucky.

Said an awed tennis great Jimmy Connors: "Best hit I can ever remember seeing."

CHAPTER 20

AARON GLENN

Name: Aaron Devone Glenn
Born: July 16, 1972
Hometown: Houston, Texas
Current Residence: Houston, Texas
Occupation: Retired NFL Player
Position: Cornerback
Height: 5'9"
Playing Weight: 181 pounds
Years lettered: 1992-93
Accomplishments: All-American in 1993 and two-time All-Conference (1992-93); 1993 SWC Defensive Player of the Year; led the nation in punt returns as senior, averaging a school-record 19.9 yards per return; broke up a SWC record 20 passes as junior; first-round pick (12th overall) of the New York Jets in 1994; three-time Pro Bowler with the Jets and Houston Texans.
Nickname: Lockdown
The Game: Texas A&M at Texas, Nov. 26, 1992

Aaron Glenn. *Photo courtesy of Texas A&M Athletic Media Relations*

THE LIFE OF YOUNG AARON GLENN

Aaron Glenn, cockier than a swollen rooster, nicknamed himself "Prime Time Jr." at Navarro Junior College in Corsicana, Texas, in a nod to standout NFL cornerback Deion Sanders.

"I play very cocky and confident," Glenn said at the time. "Just like him."

But by the time he arrived at Texas A&M in 1992, Glenn had outgrown his self-anointed handle and opted for a more original tag—at least anywhere east of the Los Angeles Lakers and Magic Johnson—in "Showtime." That nickname lasted about as long as Glenn's first meeting with his new coach in Aggieland, R.C. Slocum.

"At Navarro I was really, really brash," Glenn says. "That had spilled over from my high school days in Houston. I felt I got more out of being a showboat."

Slocum took one look at his new, extremely talented cornerback from the Houston suburb of Humble, Texas (an oxymoron of a hometown, it seemed)—the guy pegged to take All-American Kevin Smith's place—and decided it was time for a talk.

"Coach Slocum had seen tape of me when I'd act up and go into my dance after making a play and all of those things at Navarro," Glenn says.

So the unassuming coach—who preferred action to words, what he considered the A&M way—pulled Glenn aside after practice in the summer of 1992, in the days before the Aggies' season opener against Stanford in the Pigskin Classic.

"You know what, son, you're a helluva player," Slocum said. "But you've got to cut that stuff out after you make a play. It gives you a bad name. You'll get more out of your job just making a play and going back to the huddle than dancing around and what not."

It's advice Glenn never forgot and words of wisdom that he carried over into the NFL.

"From then on I let that nickname 'Showtime' just slide," he says. "It had already started getting out of hand, anyway. People would yell, 'Hey, Showtime!' and I'd say, 'Naah, man, that's not gonna work.' From then on I just kept my mouth shut and made plays and let those speak for themselves."

They certainly did, especially in that 1992 opener—a 10-7 win over Stanford—when Glenn had noticed all of the index fingers pointing his direction from Texas A&M fans beforehand.

"I could heard people saying, 'That's the guy who's going to replace Kevin Smith,'" Glenn says. "I knew I had big shoes to fill."

Smith, who went on to start for two Super Bowl championship teams with the Dallas Cowboys in 1992 and '93, had earned All-America honors at Texas A&M after setting a school record with 20 interceptions from 1988-91.

"Shoot, let the pressure be on me," Glenn told himself out on the field against Stanford, as a little of the "Prime Time Jr." persona bubbled to the surface, even if he mostly kept it to himself. "I'm gonna try and be better than Kevin. I'm gonna try and be the best cornerback ever at Texas A&M."

That was an awfully tall order, considering no college has produced more All-Pro defensive backs than Texas A&M: Yale Lary, Bob Smith, Dave Elmendorf, Pat Thomas, Lester Hayes and Glenn. A&M calls itself "Linebacker U."—but DBU may be at least as appropriate.

"The linebackers are the 'hit' people, and they get the notoriety because of that," says Thomas, a two-time All-American from 1974-75 for the Aggies. "Teams didn't throw as much in the Southwest Conference, as well, so we didn't get a lot of publicity because of that. But when opponents did throw the ball, shoot, that was about the worst thing they could do."

League teams quickly figured that out against Thomas and Lester Hayes & Co. in 1975, and 17 years later the rest of the SWC quickly figured the same about a certain hotshot—a Cornerback Formerly Known as Prime Time Jr.—named Aaron Glenn.

THE SCENE

John Mackovic, in his first year as Texas coach, described the act as malicious—making it seem as if pranksters had chopped off the real Bevo's horns, instead of the fake rack on the emblem at midfield of Memorial Stadium.

"There's a difference in good-natured fun," Mackovic said in the days before Texas A&M and Texas were to square off in Austin on Thanksgiving Day 1992, "and something like this."

UT workers spent most of that Monday repairing the missing horns— vandals had actually cut out the artificial turf while removing the spikes (they "sawed Varsity's horns off," as per the "Aggie War Hymn")—and it cost Texas $7,500 to replace.

In something many Aggies-Longhorns traditionalists found about as offensive, Mackovic skipped the annual Houston Touchdown Club shindig on the day before the game, a coaching custom that dated to 1966. Aggies coach R.C. Slocum, taking part in his 20th A&M-Texas game, went at it alone in Houston.

Slocum, who was raised in Orange, Texas, and had a longstanding relationship with the state's high school coaches, spoke romantically that week of the rivalry's place in Lone Star lore.

"It's a special thing. The people in the barber shop in Brady and the filling station in Orange are talking about the game," Slocum said—surely prompting the outsider Mackovic to wonder, "Where?"

And at that point, the series had become awfully special for A&M, which had won seven of the last eight meetings between the schools going into the 1992 game. The Aggies also were in the running for a national championship at 11-0, although pollsters held what they considered a weak conference schedule against A&M, in voting the Aggies fourth going into the Texas game.

And even Mackovic, new to the state but in the mood to add a little spice to the rivalry, hollered at a UT pep rally, "The Aggies think they're going to be national champs. We want to send them home national chumps!"

Turns out, neither scenario took place, but the Aggies at least got their groove on (literally) following yet another victory over Texas that Thanksgiving night in Austin.

THE SETTING

Aggies junior nose guard and Austin native Lance Teichelman, a good ballplayer and even better quote, broke down the Texas A&M-Texas rivalry to its essentials in the days before the teams were to play for the 99th time on Thanksgiving Day 1992.

"I feel like we're from different sides of the track," Teichelman said. "We're the down-home, tough type of people. They're the rich boys in the weight room doing aerobics."

About the same time Texas A&M fans were hopping mad that 9-1 Florida State had cruised past the 10-0 Aggies to No. 3 two weeks before in the Associated Press polls. That marked the first time since 1962 that a team with a loss passed an unbeaten squad in the polls.

Such a move underscored the Southwest Conference's weak reputation—especially with Arkansas having bolted the SWC following the 1991 season, leaving it an all-Texas conference—and such equations finally added up to the league's demise following the 1995 season.

And at that point in 1992, the Aggies were kings of a dying conference, having won 14 consecutive SWC games, and angling for UT's record of 21 straight SWC wins from 1968-71 (they'd wind up snapping the record and then some).

"Beating A&M ranks right up there with beating Oklahoma," UT running back Adrian Walker said, trying to tweak the Aggies' insecurities about who the Longhorns' true rivals were. "You want the luxury of rubbing it in their face all year."

*   *   *   *   *

About the same time Bill Clinton defeated George Bush in the presidential race, the biggest movie on the big screen in late 1992 featured Kevin Costner as Whitney Houston's no-nonsense bodyguard in the aptly named *The Bodyguard.* In one scene, Houston emotionally belts out Dolly Parton's "I Will Always Love You." Back in College Station, Lance Teichelman felt the polar opposite about the Texas Longhorns.

"I hate them with about everything in my heart," the feisty nose guard said in the days before A&M and Texas strapped 'em on for the 99th time.

For good measure in the minutes before the opening kickoff, a jacked-up A&M squad shoved its way through the Texas band while leaving the field following pregame warmups.

"One of our guys, Wilbert Biggens, even got into a fight with one of the Texas band members," Aaron Glenn says, laughing. "Wilbert was short, but he was really stocky."

It turns out the Longhorns—along with their band—could have used a few bodyguards themselves in another lopsided loss (34-13) to the Aggies, their eighth defeat in nine meetings with their arch-rivals.

THE GAME OF MY LIFE
By Aaron Glenn

It may have seemed like there was an awful lot of bad blood that year in particular between A&M and Texas—and the "cutting off the horns" incident didn't help—but really, it was just typical Aggies-Longhorns pregame hype.

When you got to Texas A&M, you just learned to really dislike Texas—and vice versa. I had a lot of friends on the Texas team—except for that day when we played 'em. It seemed there was something crazy going on every year between our schools, as well. In 1992, someone cut the horns out of their artificial turf. The next year they stole our mascot, Reveille.

[Reveille was recovered just before the 1994 Cotton Bowl, tied to a "No Trespassing" sign near Austin, after missing for a few days. A group calling itself the "Rustlers" had abducted Reveille, with a ransom demand of A&M officials to "say UT is better than them." The Aggies never buckled, however, to that edict.]

We'd had a great season going into the Texas game in running our record to 11-0, with our closest contest a 19-17 win over Texas Tech. Our '92 team possessed an awful lot of talent, and five guys on that roster wound up NFL first-round draft picks [Patrick Bates, Greg Hill, Aaron Glenn, Sam Adams and Reggie Brown].

We had a poised freshman quarterback in Corey Pullig, and the fact that we were a running team behind Greg Hill and Rodney Thomas really helped out Corey. A strong running game will take a lot of pressure off of a quarterback, and that's exactly what it did.

We'd already clinched the Southwest Conference title with a 6-0 record going into the Texas game, but it's true what they say: You can throw the records out when A&M and Texas get together. Plus, we entered the game undefeated and ranked fourth nationally, and we very much figured in the national title hunt. And that game at Texas turned out to be the best one I've ever played.

We led 27-13 late in the fourth quarter when Texas marched the ball downfield to our 11-yard line in seven pretty quick plays. But on first and 11 with about three minutes on the clock, their quarterback, Peter Gardere,

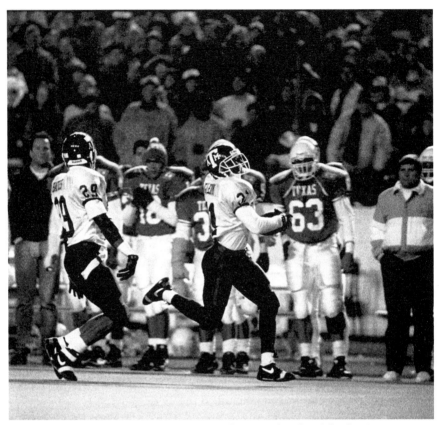

Aaron Glenn, currently a Pro Bowl cornerback with the Houston Texans, led the nation in punt returns as an Aggie senior, averaging a school-record 19.9 yards per return. *Photo courtesy of Texas A&M Athletic Media Relations*

threw my way, and we clinched the win on a 95-yard interception return.

Texas had lined up three receivers on the right side—I played on the left side—and a single guy on my side. Most of the time when you get a single out there you're going to get a fade or a quick pass. At that point I was definitely thinking it wouldn't be a fade, because the receiver [Kenny Neal] really wasn't that big or fast. I guessed slant, and I guessed right. The receiver tried to do a little move and go inside and I just jumped the route, caught it, and was gone.

I couldn't ask for a better way to wrap up my first game against the Longhorns—on a 95-yard interception return in Austin—in one of the best, if not *the* best, rivalries in college football.

GAME RESULTS

An Aggie won the national title in 1992—just not *the* Aggies.
Texas A&M whipped Texas 34-13 on Nov. 26 in Austin and improved to 12-0 for the first time in school history—and then danced on the Longhorns' new midfield emblem afterward in celebration, much to Coach R.C. Slocum's ire. In a year when two powerhouse programs—Alabama and Miami—also finished the regular season undefeated, the Aggies were left out in the cold on New Year's Day, literally and figuratively.

While former A&M coach and All-Conference end Gene Stallings led the Crimson Tide to a 13-0 record and the national championship over the 11-1 Hurricanes, Notre Dame thumped the 12-1 Aggies 28-3 on New Year's Day 1993—striking another blow for the reeling Southwest Conference.

"We need to get better," Slocum said after the 25-point loss. "Our offensive and defensive lines aren't big enough or physical enough. We've got some holes to fill and a ways to go yet."

But the Aggies were never better under Slocum than that season, as they finished seventh in the final polls, with big expectations for the following season. A&M then finished eighth in consecutive years (1993 and '94) and never again cracked the top 10 under Slocum, whose last year came in 2002.

WHAT BECAME OF AARON GLENN?

Aaron Glenn very nearly didn't coax a date out of his eventual wife, Devaney, when they met through a mutual friend at Navarro Junior College in the early 1990s.

"That was when I was in my 'Prime Time Jr.' phase," Aaron says. "She'd come to our games with her friends and I'd be clowning out on the field and all of that. She just figured I was too much. Finally, at one point we were at a get-together, and I offered to walk her home, and she let me. After that I'd walk her to class and things like that.

"We've been together ever since."

Aaron and his love have three children, Aaron II, Tristen, and Reagan, and an oh-so-comfortable living back in his hometown, as Aaron played eight years with the New York Jets before signing with the expansion Houston Texans in 2002.

Aaron even had the pleasure of spending a season in New York with his younger brother, Jason, an All-Conference linebacker for Texas A&M in 2000 who signed with the Jets in 2001.

Aaron, a three-time Pro Bowler, also saw quite an opportunity to really reacquaint himself with Texas A&M, since he suddenly lived year-round a little more than an hour away from his beloved alma mater after signing with the Texans.

And one of his biggest efforts since returning home is promoting more diversity at Texas A&M, something a long line of Aggies truly appreciate.

"Administrators and others can try to get the word out, but there's no better ambassadors for Texas A&M than its athletes," says Seth Dockery, a Dallas businessman who played linebacker for the Aggies from 1988-91. "We all admire that Aaron is taking a stand on something that he feels so strongly about."

Aaron has even started a foundation that will raise scholarship money to afford more minorities the opportunity to attend A&M.

"He's gone above and beyond to help needy students attain their aspirations," said David Prior, A&M's provost and executive vice president. "It's a grand and generous gesture."

The folks back at Navarro Junior College, witness to an awful lot of showboating on Aaron Glenn's part, might be surprised at the undemonstrative philanthropist that he's become. But even then, his future wife, Devaney, saw past the hype and antics of a superbly talented cornerback and into the heart of a good man.

CHAPTER 21

SAM ADAMS

Name: Sam Aaron Adams
Born: June 13, 1973
Hometown: Houston, Texas
Current Residence: Seattle, Wash.
Occupation: Retired NFL Player
Position: Defensive Lineman
Height: 6'4"
Playing Weight: 270 pounds
Years lettered: 1991-93
Accomplishments: All-American in 1993, two-time All-Conference (1992-93); led Aggies in tackles for losses (13), sacks (10.5), forced fumbles (five) and fumble recoveries (three) as a senior; first-round draft pick of the Seattle Seahawks (eighth pick overall) in 1994; two-time NFL Pro Bowler, including with the Super Bowl champion Baltimore Ravens in 2000.
Nickname: Big Papa
The Game: Texas at Texas A&M, Nov. 25, 1993

Sam Adams. *Photo courtesy of Texas A&M Athletic Media Relations*

THE LIFE OF YOUNG SAM ADAMS

S am Adams inherited his work ethic, ample posterior and preschool knowledge of the NFL from his father, Sam Adams Sr., who played a decade for the New England Patriots, New Orleans Saints and Los Angeles Rams. But Junior's athleticism? That's straight from mama.

"My dad's a hard worker," says Adams, a star defensive end for the Aggies from 1991-93. "But my quickness and my talent came from my mama. She played basketball at Prairie View A&M, and that was in the day when the women played three on three. You had to be a good athlete to play that."

There have been few, if any, Texas A&M players who've blended Sam Adams' size (six-foot-four and 270 pounds) and athleticism. For instance, a nondescript box about three feet tall in Texas A&M's Netum Steed weight room helped create an Aggies legend.

"They said Sam hopped right over it," says Dan Campbell, an NFL tight end who's younger than Adams but who'd heard the story from older Aggies teammates. "His feet didn't even touch it. That's unbelievable, considering how big he is."

His teammates wouldn't have been more surprised had Superman himself shown up and leaped over Rudder Tower after Adams executed the move usually reserved for receivers, defensive backs and some linebackers.

"I think it shocked some of the guys that a man of my size could do that," Adams says.

Adams has stunned folks with his athleticism ever since he starred for Cypress-Creek High School in Northwest Houston—back then as a lithe six-foot-four, 266-pounder (his weight has increased to at least 330 pounds in the pros).

"The Good Lord blessed Sam with talent that he didn't give to many," Aggies running back Greg Hill once said of Adams.

Sam Adams Jr., the eldest of Sam and Marilyn Adams's two sons, excelled at just about any sport he put his mind to in junior high and high school, but football was his ticket to a college scholarship and eventual millions in the NFL.

"Sam's the kind of guy who could do whatever he wanted," his high school coach at Cypress Creek, Les Koenning Sr., once said. "He won the state championship in the shot put and barely even worked at it."

Texas A&M coach R.C. Slocum figured Adams to be an early riser, as well, after Slocum received a phone call at 5:30 a.m. from someone claiming to be Adams that recruiting season of 1991.

"Wasn't me," Adams says of the prankster who, posing as Adams, asked Slocum a few trite questions before hanging up. Slocum, however, might've gladly fielded a few early-morning phone calls from Adams during the recruiting season, if it meant getting the Cy-Creek Kid to College Station.

THE SCENE

Sam Adams and his Texas A&M friends liked nothing better than hangin' out with Kelly, Andrea, David, Dylan, Steve, Brenda and Brandon for about an hour every Thursday night in the early 1990s. The most significant number at Texas A&M in late fall 1993 might have been 100—representing the amount of times A&M and Texas had clashed on the football field—but a nearly as significant number for Adams & Co. was 90210.

"We'd all gather to watch *Beverly Hills 90210* every week," Adams says, laughing at the memory of the teenage soap opera with the oft-troubled characters. "We were big fans."

And then Adams's bunch usually tossed in a healthy dose—or possibly unhealthy dose—of *Melrose Place* following *90210*. Those two shows helped elbow Fox amongst the big boys of network television, long dominated by NBC, ABC and CBS.

Meanwhile the Texas A&M football team was the NBC of the Southwest Conference, dominating prime time by stringing together 21 consecutive wins (another important digit that season) in the SWC hurtling into its annual grudge match with the University of Texas in November 1993. Ironically, that number of consecutive league wins also had tied the conference mark held by Texas from 1968-71.

"It'd be sweet to break the record against Texas, knowing those guys had the record," A&M senior star cornerback Aaron Glenn said in the days before the showdown for the SWC title at Kyle Field, adding that the Aggies knew the mark might possibly hold up forever. (Sure enough, it will. The SWC disbanded following the 1995 season. Texas Tech snapped A&M's unbeaten conference streak at 29 games—an all-time SWC record—in '95 in Lubbock.)

While the A&M-Texas game was always big, no matter the teams' records, the one set for Thanksgiving night 1993 was especially huge, considering the winner advanced to the Cotton Bowl as league champion. That had seemed an improbable feat for the Longhorns early in the season, as they'd started 1-3-1. After Texas lost in Austin to Texas Tech 31-22 on Oct. 30 to fall to 2-4-1, the team adopted the motto of, "4-0 or we don't go."

Catchy, one supposes, but not quite *90210* material.

THE SETTING

Famed surgeon Dr. Red Duke, a Texas A&M yell leader in the late 1940s, stood in a concession line at Kyle Field on a bitterly cold night late November night, rubbing his hands together while waiting on a cup of hot chocolate to warm his bones.

"This is not a night for me to play doctor," Duke said of a chance to get away from Houston's renowned Medical Center for a Thanksgiving evening with his family—at the home of the Fightin' Texas Aggies.

The personable Duke had starred as a down-to-earth surgeon with a regular informative segment on news stations across the country and could cast quite a judgment on the heart. And Duke, an Aggie personified, loved what he saw that Thursday night at Kyle Field: the Aggies' heart beat as strongly as any time in the program's proud history on the heels of its third consecutive league title.

A&M's only loss that year was a stunning 44-14 setback at Oklahoma in the second game of the season, but instead of wilting the Aggies had rebounded to win their next eight games by a combined score of 348 to 66. The Aggies' defense, too, featured two upcoming NFL first-round draft picks—and two future Pro Bowl players—in Aaron Glenn and Sam Adams.

"Nobody in the country is better than Sam Adams," second-year Texas coach John Mackovic said before the rivals' 100th meeting. "He's the best I've seen in years one on one, as a pass rusher, and he even leads the team in tackles. That's unheard of for a defensive linemen in this day and age."

Growing more scarce, too, were the "Aggie jokes" long unjustly associated with the school and the program, as by the mid-1990s the flourishing campus had grown into what *Texas Monthly*—an Austin-based magazine—dubbed in its April 1997 issue as "the state's top-rated public university. No kidding."

Adams, too, had a joke of his own for anyone who questioned why he'd chosen Texas A&M in 1991 out of Cy-Creek High School. Ever hear the one about Texas A&M beating Texas nine out of the rivals' last 10 meetings by the end of the 1993 game? Such a streak starkly contrasted the one from 1957-74, when Texas won an astounding 17 of 18 games behind legendary coach Darrell Royal.

"I got sick and tired of hearing about the Longhorns and 'hook 'em' and this and that when I got to A&M," Adams says of UT's 10-2 and 8-0 SWC finish in 1990. "We wanted it to be where when you talked about football in Texas, it no longer included the University of Texas. When we went out on that field, it was to dominate Texas and make it to where they didn't stand a chance. And they didn't, the three years I was there, because we were dead set on being the best."

Adams & Co. watched curiously as several Longhorns, including linebacker and leading tackler Winfred Tubbs, spoke on ESPN about their desire to "avenge" the previous year, when a slew of Aggies had impishly danced on the Longhorns' symbol at midfield following a 34-13 whipping of Texas in Austin.

"They were pretty upset about that," Adams says, failing to suppress a grin. "So they figured they were going to come and return the favor."

Not the least of which was Texas receiver Mike Adams, Sam Adams's cousin who'd reeled in four consecutive 100-yard receiving games prior to the A&M contest, and a man seemingly undaunted by facing two of the nation's best cover corners in Aaron Glenn and Ray Mickens.

"I think I can get open against Darrell Green or Deion Sanders," Adams said of the two NFL greats of the time. "It's a challenge for me and a challenge for [Glenn and Mickens]."

But A&M senior nose guard Lance Teichelman, an overachieving sort from Austin, made the most impassioned plea of the pregame hype among the old rivals—even with Texas as a three-touchdown underdog in a battle for the conference title.

"They hate us and we hate them," Teichelman said, shaking his head and rubbing his fists. "I think if they beat us, it would ruin my life."

Pretty dramatic stuff. Teichelman, in fact, sounded as if making an ardent pitch to star in *Aggieland 77842* (he'd have played the equivalent of *90210* Luke Perry's bad boy Dylan McKay, only about 100 pounds heavier and a whole lot meaner). At least one viewer might have tuned in to such a poignant production: Big Sam Adams, of course.

THE GAME OF MY LIFE
By Sam Adams

It was cold that night against Texas—real cold—but I didn't mind it one bit. My dad had played for the New England Patriots, and I remembered some of those nights at Foxboro Stadium as a child, so I just figured that playing in the cold was part of the job.

We had a great group of running backs at Texas A&M at that time—Greg Hill, Rodney Thomas and Leeland McElroy—probably the best collection in school history. But the thing about that '93 team as a whole—the entire program—was our intensity and drive to try and dominate everyone that we played. And that attitude stemmed from Coach R.C. Slocum right down to the football secretary.

An interesting matchup that game was their receivers on our cornerbacks. Mike Adams, my cousin, and Lovell Pinkney, who was six

Sam Adams, an NFL Pro Bowl defensive lineman, tallied 20.5 sacks over three seasons with the Aggies and never lost a conference game while at Texas A&M. *Photo courtesy of Texas A&M Athletic Media Relations*

foot five and 234 pounds, were a couple of big names for them, and I really enjoyed the idea that we put our shortest player on our defense with the biggest heart, Ray Mickens, on Pinkney. That was fun to watch, and we knew our corners could cover their guys, no matter anyone's height.

And just to show that you never know in football, our biggest play that game wasn't made by our big-time cornerbacks—although they did a great job in holding Adams and Pinkney to a combined 68 receiving yards. Instead, a sophomore backup safety, Dennis Allen, made the play that saved the day against Texas.

There was only 5:55 left on the clock when D. A. intercepted Shea Morenz's pass on a fourth-and-two play from our two-yard line, and we were up 15-9. That play served as a defining moment for our defense, and I'll never forget it. It stands out more than any other in my A&M career.

I was getting a little bit nervous at that point, honestly. The Longhorns were starting to move the ball a bit in the game—and here they were on our two-yard line. On the play, Morenz rolled out to our left—I was at left end—and I wanted to make sure that I didn't get cut by their fullback, Phil Brown. As it turns out, I got upfield, got cut, got back up off the turf and tried to contain Morenz—as linebacker Steve Solari rolled around in containment as well.

That's when Morenz threw the ball, and D. A. read it perfectly and made the biggest play of the game—and in a lot of ways, our college careers. We took over on the three-yard line and drove the length of the field and Terry Venetoulias then kicked a field goal to put Texas away.

I'd almost gotten to Morenz on that play, and it would have been 'game time' had I caught him. Turns out it was game time, though, because of D. A., and the way we all worked together to make that happen. That's how we got things done—by working together—because we were the Wrecking Crew.

GAME RESULTS

Texas coach John Mackovic took plenty of heat for his playcalling on fourth and two from the A&M two-yard line, when Aggies safety Dennis Allen stepped in and intercepted an errant Shea Morenz pass with the Longhorns trailing by six late in the game.

"It was an option play where the quarterback could run, pass or pitch the ball," Mackovic explained of the 18-9 loss to Texas A&M. "The quarterback decided not to toss it, but passed it instead, and it just didn't happen."

The Aggies, too, got a big boost when blazing return man Leeland McElroy returned a kick 100 yards in the second quarter, with A&M trailing 6-0. After fielding the kick three yards deep in the end zone, McElroy burst through a huge hole in the Texas coverage and was contested only by Longhorns kicker Scott Szeredy.

"That's like putting Carl Lewis in a 100-meter dash against Jerry Lewis," penned *Bryan-College Station Eagle* columnist Olin Buchanan.

And much as comedian Jerry Lewis used to thrill thousands of fans in France—for whatever reasons—the Aggies thrilled an overflow crowd of 74,748 that cold night at Kyle Field in the first UT-A&M game since 1987 to decide the Cotton Bowl entrant.

The Aggies also became the first team in Southwest Conference history (and, as it turns out, two years from the league's demise) to plow through three consecutive undefeated seasons in SWC play. And, of course, A&M snapped the league record of 21 consecutive conference victories (held by Texas)—essentially rubbing gas in the Longhorn's gashes following another loss to the Aggies.

And Mickens, the diminutive and fiery receiver from El Paso who'd go on to a successful NFL career, had a final word for Texas receivers Mike Adams and Lovell Pinkney.

"They didn't impress me," Mickens said, shaking his head. "I hope they come back stronger next year."

WHAT BECAME OF SAM ADAMS?

A few of those snot-nosed rich kids from *Beverly Hills 90210* might have learned a thing or two from unpretentious Aggies coach R.C. Slocum.

"I wouldn't be where I am today without R.C.," says Sam Adams, a two-time Pro Bowler who signed to play for the Buffalo Bills in 2003. "All of us owe him a lot. He taught me how to win, and he always preached for us to stay humble.

"Stay humble, and whip their butts, that's what he'd say."

Adams turned pro following his junior year in 1993 and joined Greg Hill and Aaron Glenn as first-round draft picks—the highest number of Aggies to ever be selected in the first round in the same year of the NFL draft.

"It was time for me to go," Adams says, "but the experience I had at A&M was wonderful."

These days Sam Adams coaches football as owner of the Eastside Hawks, a minor-league team out of Redmond, Wash. Adams serves as CEO, general manager, head coach, defensive coordinator and special teams coach for the Hawks during the NFL off season. Not bad for a Super Bowl champion, as he helped anchor a Baltimore Ravens defense in 2000 that became the first in history to hold opponents below 1,000 yards rushing (970) over 16 games.

"He's a key to taking the defense to another level," Ravens linebacker and Super Bowl MVP Ray Lewis said of Adams that season. "He tears stuff up in the backfield."

Back in College Station, Adams—nicknamed "Big Papa" by a couple of his Aggies teammates—used to regularly tear through the menus at the Wings 'N' More and Deluxe Diner restaurants—which was about as wild as he got in Aggieland.

Now, Adams is perfectly content to make his off-season home in Seattle—where he got his NFL start and more importantly where his wife, Erika, grew up. ("I keep the peace, brother, know what I mean?" Sam says.) He and his love have three children: Terin, Te-a and Sam Adams II.

"Marriage is a blessing," Adams says. "The best things that have happened to me in my life are meeting my wife and having children."

And Coach R.C. Slocum, too, considers Adams's three-year stint in Aggieland a blessing as well—considering A&M never lost a conference game in that span.

"Sam was as good as I've ever seen in terms of lining up on a down-by-down basis," Slocum says. "If he was really challenged, he could go one-on-one with anyone I've ever seen in college football."

Sam Adams Sr., an old NFL offensive lineman, once told a story when his oldest boy was still at A&M about how the two proud big men couldn't pass each other in a hallway at home without a little old-school shoving match goin' down.

"He makes his moves on me," Sam Adams Sr. said, laughing. "He spins, but his mom gets on him, because he knocks everything over."

The spin's sheer athleticism came from mama. The move? That's from daddy.

"I always wanted to be like my father," Adams says, softly. "I always wanted to be a football player."

CHAPTER 22

LEELAND
McELROY

Name: Leeland Anthony McElroy
Born: June 25, 1974
Hometown: Beaumont, Texas
Current Residence: Dallas, Texas
Occupation: Personal Financial Representative
Position: Tailback and Returner
Height: 5'11"
Playing Weight: 200 pounds
Years lettered: 1993-95
Accomplishments: All-American in 1995; three-time All-Conference (1993-95); tied for NCAA record for kicks returned for touchdowns in a game (two) and in a season (three); season kick return yards school leader (590 in 1993); Southwest Conference record holder for all-purpose yards in a game (359 against LSU in 1995).
Nickname: 'Lectric Leeland
The Game: LSU at Texas A&M, Sept. 2, 1995

Leeland McElroy. *Photo courtesy of Texas A&M Athletic Media Relations*

THE LIFE OF YOUNG LEELAND McELROY

Leeland McElroy, who'd grow into the most prolific kick return man in Texas A&M history, got caught from behind on his first elusive run. Two-year-old Leeland had darted across a busy street near the family home in Beaumont, Texas, sending his father, Lee McElroy, on a frantic chase.

Seventeen years later 11 Texas Longhorns special teams players experienced the same frenzied, gut-wrenching emotion as Lee McElroy at that frenetic moment—both thanks to Leeland McElroy.

"Oh, no! My baby's gonna get killed!" Leeland's mother, Maud McElroy, yelled as Lee gave chase to the li'l diapered dandy.

Lee finally caught the boy—and administered the only spanking the youngster ever received.

"I'm from the old school," Leeland's father once said in recounting that tale of whipping tail. "Up until my daddy died, I can only remember him giving me one spanking."

Leeland grew up the youngest of 12 kids, but the idea of a dozen McElroy kids gathered around the supper table every night, fighting for biscuits, isn't quite accurate.

"My parents had both been married before they were married to each other, so it was a combined family," McElroy says. "My oldest brother was 26 when my parents had me, so we were really spread out. Really, about the only time we all got together was on special occasions."

Leeland, too, truly came from a special family. Older brother Reggie played 14 years in the NFL as an offensive lineman. In 2003, oldest brother Lee served as the athletics director at the University at Albany in New York.

Leeland, too, created plenty of special occasions for the Aggies— although one wouldn't have guessed as much from his Pee-Wee football days, when coaches tried making a lineman out of the future burner. Leeland didn't play organized football again for another few years, until he was a freshman at Beaumont's Central High School.

"At that stage you just see your peers playing football, and you go out there so you can hang out with them," McElroy says. "That was reason enough to play. You didn't really think about going out and playing Division I football."

But by his senior year and at five foot 11 and 185 pounds, Leeland bench-pressed 315 pounds, squatted 500, and dashed 40 yards in 4.4 seconds. Thus he quickly became one of the most coveted tailbacks in the nation while earning the nickname "Mac Daddy" from his Central teammates.

"Some kids are speed guys—they have to get moving well in order to get the speed up—but he has that quick acceleration," McElroy's high school coach, Marvin Sedberry, said during McElroy's senior year at Central. "And he has the speed to top it off."

So much so that every prominent program in the nation beckoned, and McElroy will never forget his recruiting trip to UCLA—which convinced him more than ever to stay close to home. The journey among L.A.'s bright lights included a travel companion in Beaumont Westbrook offensive lineman Calvin Collins, a flashy UCLA Bruins senior running back named Kevin Williams from Spring, Texas, and, finally, a sweet Camaro that wound up on blocks.

"Calvin and I went out there thinking we'd go to school as far away from home as possible," McElroy says, grinning. "We came back thinking otherwise. Kevin Williams had taken us to a party near the Southern Cal campus on the other side of town from UCLA, and we all had a good time, but we'd only been there about an hour or so when we decided to leave the party.

"So we go outside to leave—and believe me, Kevin had a nice car—and it was up on blocks. The wheels were gone, the stereo was gone, the hood was open, and the lights were blinking but there was no sound coming from the alarm, because the thieves had disconnected it.

"That wasn't what deterred me from going to UCLA, but it didn't help."

McElroy and Collins both chose to attend Texas A&M, a place where their families would have a better chance to see them play—and where their wheels might rest a little more safely.

THE SCENE

Leeland McElroy 12, Rice 10.

Before Texas A&M's offense ever waded onto the field on a pleasant fall Saturday afternoon in 1993 in the Bayou City of Houston, the Aggies' soon-to-be prolific return man had already scored enough to clip the Owls over the span of three and a half more quarters.

The final team score on Oct. 23, 1993: Aggies 38, Owls 10. The more memorable tally: two swift, Evander Holyfield-like punches to the tender Rice gut courtesy of one Leeland McElroy, a serene and smooth runner who burst onto the college football scene that day.

Rice's 3-0, first-quarter lead against Texas A&M held up about as long as Arnold Schwarzenegger's floppy *Last Action Hero* at the box office that same season. In a word: Gone.

"Man, that was unique," McElroy says happily of returning Rice's first two kickoffs for touchdowns for a whopping 181 yards. "I'd grown up watching guys like Rocket Ismail at Notre Dame returns kicks, and just to return one was a thrill. But back to back? You just don't think something like that's going to happen."

Still, the Aggies' offense—which had yet to take the field—wasn't entirely thrilled with McElroy's stunning special teams display that sprang A&M to a 14-3 lead before the Owls caught their collective gasps.

"Can I please get on the field?" junior tailback Greg Hill half-jokingly told McElroy, a wide-eyed and winded freshman. "I do want a *little* rushing yardage."

McElroy, who's no relation to former A&M receiver Hugh McElroy, was too busy gulping in some of the humidity along the Southeast Texas coastline to bother with any playful repartee.

"After your first score you're still OK as far as your wind, but after that second one I was kind of pushing everybody away," McElroy says. "I needed to breathe."

The consecutive returns for touchdowns quickly pushed McElroy into Aggie lore, but the multipurpose threat more fondly recalls his kick return for a touchdown later that season against archrival Texas. The heavily favored Aggies trailed UT 6-0 early midway through the second quarter at Kyle Field in 1993, when the McElroy Magic again sprang to life.

"It was a cold, cold night, and Texas had just kicked a second field goal, and we needed to get back into the game emotionally," McElroy says. "I was amazed after receiving the ball how well the blockers did, because the hole was just huge. All I had to do was run through it and make the kicker miss, and if I couldn't do that, then they needed to put somebody else back there."

Funny thing, McElroy likely wouldn't have even attempted a return, had he realized where he fielded the kick against UT.

"I didn't know I was three yards deep in the end zone," he says, grinning. "I thought I was on the goal line. A lot of times when you catch the ball that deep in the end zone, it throws off the timing of the people blocking for you. And once I saw the replay and how deep I was, I thought, gosh, maybe I shouldn't have done that."

If he hadn't, McElroy wouldn't be tied for the NCAA record for most kicks returned for a touchdown in a season, with three. It was two seasons later, however, that McElroy, on a brutally hot day in College Station, captured the nation's attention with a record-setting, all-purpose effort against Louisiana State in the 1995 season opener.

Such an individual offensive exhibit by an Aggie in a win at Kyle Field wouldn't gain so much national celebrity for another three years, when freshman running back Ja'Mar Toombs rumbled for 110 yards on 10 carries in A&M's thrilling 28-21 win over No. 2 Nebraska.

Four years after that, sensational freshman quarterback Reggie McNeal sparked A&M to an upset of top-ranked Oklahoma on Nov. 9, 2002, in the three most striking individual offensive displays at Kyle Field since the mid-1990s.

THE SETTING

Leeland McElroy never asked for the nickname 'Lectric. Low-Key Leeland or Eclectic Leeland, after all, certainly seemed more apropos for the unassuming junior from Beaumont, an hour-and-a-half east of Houston. But the Aggies needed a super-charged handle for Heisman Trophy voters to take notice of McElroy's outstanding credentials springing into the 1995 season, one in which Texas A&M had chosen to orchestrate a campaign so unlike its usual conservative temperament: by hyping a player for the Heisman.

"They called me into the sports information director's office, sat me down and said this is what we're going to do, and this is how we're going to do it," McElroy says of the Heisman promotion that featured weekly postcards—"the most electric player in America"—for voters. "And this is the name we've chosen to go with it."

'Lectric Leeland.

"They asked how I liked it," McElroy says, smiling. "I said it was fine."

People expected electric things of the Aggies, as well, as A&M entered the 1995 season ranked third nationally, behind McElroy's all-purpose credentials and the physical play of senior linebacker Reggie Brown. The Aggies had finished the 1994 season 10-0-1, but hadn't played on TV or in a bowl game because of NCAA probation. In addition, the old Southwest Conference was closing shop following the 1995-96 school year—an item that Aggies coach R.C. Slocum reflected on as the season drew near.

"To win the national championship for the SWC would be one of the most ironic happenings we could have for a league that's folding, supposedly because it couldn't get recognition," Slocum said. "If it was A&M or anyone else in the league, it would certainly be a great tribute to 81 years of football, and some of the greatest players to ever play the game."

More ironically, future Big 12 Conference foe Colorado sidelined Texas A&M's national title hopes—along with McElroy's Heisman chances— three games into the 1995 season in Boulder, Colo, with a 29-21 win. But for one brutally hot Sept. 2 day in College Station in a 33-17 win over

Louisiana State University, and in a final nod to the league's fading glory, McElroy truly was one of the SWC's greats.

THE GAME OF MY LIFE
By Leeland McElroy

I was excited about all of the hype for the Heisman going into the season, but I also believed that hype should follow the performance, not precede it. I was a little bit nervous, honestly, after finally earning a starting spot at tailback, after redshirting and then playing behind (future NFLers) Greg Hill and Rodney Thomas.

I also appreciated the fact that Coach Slocum had enough confidence in me to feel like I was a legitimate Heisman candidate, and I didn't want to let him down.

I don't know that I've ever been hotter—literally—in a football game, because Kyle Field still had artificial turf at that point, and it was 120 degrees that day on the turf. Think what that must have felt like in helmets and pads.

Coach Slocum, too, proved he had confidence in me on that hot, hot day. When I looked back on my number of plays [43 touches, 229 rushing yards on 35 carries, five catches for 49 yards and three kick returns for 81 yards], even I'm surprised by the amount. It's not like you're actually counting when you're playing, but I knew going into the game that my durability was something people were concerned with, and I was determined to address that.

Midway through the fourth quarter and during a timeout, I took a knee at midfield and gulped some fluids. Good thing, because on that series I scored from 33 yards out on a simple draw. It was clear sailing as soon as I touched the ball, and that put away LSU by the final score. I know this sounds simple, but I really didn't have to do anything but find a hole and run through it.

Playing running back is so dependent on how the guys around you do, and they did a great job of blocking all afternoon. And on that day, everything clicked for the Aggies.

GAME RESULTS

In the final year of the Southwest Conference, Leeland McElroy's 359 all-purpose yards in a single game shattered the old league mark of 347 (set by TCU's Tony Jeffery and Andre Davis in 1986 and 1994,

Leeland McElroy, who was hyped for the Heisman Trophy (in 1995), once returned two kickoffs for touchdowns in the same game. *Photo courtesy of Texas A&M Athletic Media Relations*

respectively), and he bolted to the front of the oh-so-early Heisman race.

"He's a special kind of person," A&M offensive lineman and ol' Beaumont buddy Calvin Collins said after the LSU game, shaking his head in amazement. "In the fourth quarter, it didn't even look like he was breathing hard."

Wrote Mike Jensen of the *Philadelphia Inquirer:* "The Aggies just kept handing the ball to Leeland McElroy, who is going to be a Heisman Trophy candidate if it kills him. The Aggies' tailback had not started a college game before yesterday. Now, he is the Aggies' offense."

The third-ranked Aggies and McElroy continued their success a game later with a 52-9 victory over Tulsa and then stumbled on Sept. 23 at No. 7 Colorado. A game later, McElroy sprained his left ankle at Texas Tech in a 14-7 loss—which snapped A&M's record 29-game league unbeaten streak—and the injury hampered him the rest of the season. McElroy still wound up involved in one-third of all of A&M's offensive plays, in a 9-3 season and a final ranking of No. 15 for the Aggies.

And for a preseason and a couple of games in 1995, Aggieland hadn't experienced such national hype and attention for both a team and an individual combined in at least a decade. And the school hasn't since—as 'Lectric Leeland, on a hot and muggy yet extremely fulfilling day, lit up LSU like every Aggie hoped he'd do.

WHAT BECAME OF LEELAND McELROY?

Leeland McElroy's pro career started in a highly uncomfortable situation—at the 1996 NFL draft in New York. McElroy had elected to turn professional following his junior season at A&M, and most everyone had assured him he'd be a first-round pick. McElroy seemingly solidified that thought by running the 40-yard dash in a blazing 4.21 seconds at the NFL combine.

"Everyone had high expectations that I was going to be drafted fairly high, so they invited me to New York, and I had to sit through the entire first round before I was drafted two picks into the second," McElroy says. "And those cameras were constantly on me in the first round ... as far as an athlete and a person, sitting through that ordeal was hard for me to go through. Real hard."

The NFL's Cardinals, who've won one playoff game since 1947, drafted McElroy with the 32nd pick overall. Over his first two NFL seasons he played sparingly, rushing for 729 yards total. In 1997, McElroy—who returned four kicks for touchdowns in college—didn't even return a kickoff after averaging 21.3 yards per return as a rookie.

"I started asking myself whether I was good enough to play on that level," McElroy says. "Looking back, I really think it was the organization. I never said much at the time, because I didn't want to point fingers for it not having worked out.

"But in my heart and mind, I really think things would have been different in the NFL had I not started out there. We just weren't a very good club, and it was tough to climb out of that hole once I left."

McElroy spent 1998 in the Tampa Bay Bucs' camp and even registered a spectacular 25-yard run for a touchdown in the Hall of Fame game against the Steelers. He had led the Bucs in rushing after three preseason games when Tampa surprisingly released him, because of contractual reasons and its glut of running backs.

"Funny how that league works—money is such a big factor," McElroy says. "The Bucs had picked me up after the Cardinals had let me go, but they didn't want to pay on the contract, even though I'd played well in camp."

McElroy had two more shots in the league, with Denver (behind Terrell Davis) and the Colts (behind Edgerrin James) before his final release by Indianapolis in 2000.

"That's four different cities in three years, and my wife and I had a baby born right before I went to Indy," McElroy says. "I didn't want to be one of those guys who's 30 years old and still looking for a chance, playing in NFL Europe and Arena Football. I have nothing against those guys, if that's your passion and your desire, but I needed more stability for my family.

"And when I got a few calls from the XFL—I knew then that it was over."

That's when Leeland and his wife, Vinita, knelt and prayed about the situation—and not because the nutty (and quickly defunct) XFL (of World Wrestling Federation fame) had come calling.

"A lot of people wonder what happened, and to an extent, I do, too," McElroy says of his NFL career. "But if you asked me if I felt like I had the talent and the skills to play on that level—without a doubt, I know that I did."

And without a doubt, Leeland McElroy is happy these days as a personal financial representative for Washington Mutual in Dallas—as he put his A&M business degree (he finished up in 2000) to good use after retiring from the NFL. He and his college sweetheart married on July 5, 1996—they met in an A&M business law class—and the couple has two girls, Logan and Madeline.

   And Leeland McElroy, as fit as ever, still loves to lift weights and run. What he doesn't do is sit around and wonder "What if?" about his NFL career.

   "I'm content," McElroy says, smiling. "Everything's worked out."

   He smiles, too, about a harsh, early September day in 1995, when in the fourth quarter he knelt at midfield before an adoring Kyle Field crowd of 70,057, gasping a bit for some precious cool air and water, but yet soaking in the glory of a simmering, wonderful four quarters. The day that Leeland McElroy, in the Southwest Conference's final splash of a season after 81 memorable years, torched the turf like no other player in league history.

CHAPTER 23

DAT
NGUYEN

Name: Dat Tan Nguyen
Born: Sept. 25, 1975 in Fort Smith, Ark.
Hometown: Rockport, Texas
Current Residence: Dallas, Texas
Occupation: Retired NFL Player
Position: Linebacker
Height: 5'11"
Playing Weight: 230 pounds
Years lettered: 1995-98
Accomplishments: Lombardi Award winner and Chuck Bednarik College Defensive Player of the Year in 1998; All-American in '98; three-time All-Conference (1996-98); Texas A&M's all-time leader in tackles (517) and tackles per game (10.7); third-round pick of the Dallas Cowboys in 1999; recorded the second highest season tackles total (172) in Cowboys history in 2001.
The Game: Texas A&M vs. Kansas State, Big 12 Championship Game, Dec. 5, 1998

Dat Nguyen. *Photo courtesy of Texas A&M Athletic Media Relations*

THE LIFE OF YOUNG DAT NGUYEN

Penn State linebacker LaVar Arrington, barrel chest puffed and eyes wide in a menacing stare, couldn't believe Texas A&M's audacity as he prepared for the 1999 Alamo Bowl in San Antonio. Who, pray tell, had even played linebacker at Texas A&M, a school that also (and abhorrently, to Arrington) had dubbed itself Linebacker U.—the Nittany Lions' lofty designation?

One name turned Arrington from a man of indignation to one brimming with adoration.

"Oh, Dat Nguyen," Arrington said, gently. "Now, Dat Nguyen, he's a 'baller."

A 'baller, it seems, at the top of his game most against long odds—even before he was born. Tammy Nguyen was four months pregnant when she and her husband, Ho, and their five children fled South Vietnam in 1975 in a hail of gunfire from the invading Viet Cong.

After a harrowing 10-day boat trip in rough waters to Thailand, the family waited another three months on what to do next. Finally, they were sent to a refugee camp near Fort Smith, Ark., where Tammy gave birth to Dat. The family settled on the South Texas Gulf Coast in the shrimping community of Rockport, where the Nguyens have lived since.

"It's an amazing story," Dat says, smiling.

And one that became even better. In the seventh grade and before Dat became involved with organized football, he began running with a tough crowd of petty car thieves and burglars.

"Back then, everybody thought I'd be in jail by now," Nguyen says of a short span of trouble he caused in his youth.

But then Dat's mother threatened to send him to an all-boys school in Missouri, which straightened him out a bit. About the same time, as well, he discovered even more of a salvation from bad news than a caring mother's caveat: football.

"Football took up my time and kept me out of trouble," Nguyen says. "I couldn't do anything else but football and school. That was really a turning point in my life."

Nguyen excelled enough at Rockport-Fulton High—where he recorded 188 tackles his senior year—to earn a scholarship to Texas A&M, despite questions about his size and speed. Nguyen figures it'll be etched on his tombstone: "Too small, too slow to play linebacker." In fact, Nguyen's first starring role came as a shortstop, not a linebacker, in a forgettable Ed Harris movie called *Alamo Bay*, filmed in Rockport when he was in the second grade.

"I turned a double play," Nguyen says, laughing. "We were just out there running around, having fun, getting paid $50 a day to be in the movie. The show wasn't great and it talked bad about us—the Vietnamese people. But I think it got better at the end."

So, too, did Nguyen's sporting story, which eventually led to him making considerably more money than $50 a day—as a standout linebacker for the Dallas Cowboys—while running around, having incredible fun playing a game.

"We've had a long history of great linebackers at Texas A&M," Aggies coach R.C. Slocum said late in Nguyen's senior year at A&M. "And Dat has really outperformed all of them."

Enough, even, to cause the puffed-up, proud Arrington to nod respectfully about the Rockport 'baller, the best linebacker who ever played at Texas A&M.

THE SCENE

The unsung—and unshaven—martyr of Texas A&M's 1998 Big 12 Conference championship season, a li'l fellow named Oscar, showed up missing just before the Aggies' last-second loss in Austin that snapped a 10-game A&M winning streak.

"Oscar fell off of my face," 1998 Lombardi Award winner Dat Nguyen says with a hint of nostalgia.

So nicknamed by Nguyen teammates Rich Coady, Dan Campbell and Koby Hackradt, Oscar was a lone, long black hair sprouting from Nguyen's right cheek, that somehow (and somewhat strangely) morphed into one of A&M's good-luck charms that magical (and hair-raising) year.

"Oscar barely stuck out just after we'd lost a close game to Florida State in the Kickoff Classic," Nguyen says, shaking his head at the idea of even recounting the tale of a lone lock that affectionately became a team mascot. "Then we started winning games—10 straight, even—and with each week Oscar got a little longer. By midseason he had curled up, and that's when those guys named it.

"But just before the Texas game, Oscar was gone. Poof. I don't know what happened to him. And then, shoot, we lost in Austin."

Speaking of wild hair, it was dreadlocked Texas running back Ricky Williams, Heisman Trophy winner that year, who probably had more to do with Texas's 26-24 victory on a last-second field goal than the dearly departed Oscar.

But not even A&M's close loss in Austin could take the frizz out of the Aggies' best season in at least six years, and considering their stiff Big 12 competition as opposed to the old Southwest Conference, maybe their best season ever.

A thrilling 28-21 victory over No. 2 Nebraska at Kyle Field highlighted A&M's regular season, as Nguyen broke his right thumb early in the contest, but played through the pain to lead the Aggies past the Cornhuskers in one of the strongest wins in program history.

"For anyone who has ever worn an A&M jersey and for all of our fans, this is unbelievable," safety Rich Coady said afterward. "The fans were amazing. At times, it was so loud on the field we had trouble hearing ourselves think."

And before their oh-so-narrow loss in Austin on Nov. 27, the Aggies even had an outside shot at a national championship. But in the week after, they still found plenty of incentive in angling for their first Big 12 title, in a showdown against heavily favored Kansas State.

"We got beat the year before in the Big 12 title game 54-15 by Nebraska, and that game really opened our eyes to how much more physical we needed to be the following season," Nguyen says. "Nebraska had just dominated us, and we were bound and determined not to let that happen again."

*   *   *   *   *

Elsewhere around the nation in late 1998, Bill Clinton was in the midst of trying to save his presidency following allegations that he'd lied about an affair with a former White House intern, Monica Lewinsky. A Clinton impeachment trial loomed as Aggieland's love affair with the best-natured bunch to don the Maroon and White in years—a gang minus any true sex symbols—would climax on a brilliantly clear day on the banks of the Mississippi River.

(Dan Campbell may have been the closest thing to an A&M sex symbol that season. Teammate Rich Coady once said that the first time he met the six-foot-six tight end, Campbell was wearing a cowboy hat, a half-shirt, cutoff jeans, and cowboy boots all at the same time. It's a charge that Campbell vehemently denies.)

The event that transpired in St. Louis on Dec. 5, 1998, prompted Kansas State coach Bill Snyder to compare it to a death in the family—prompting widespread criticism for such a poor contrast to a mere football game. The Aggies, meanwhile, wisely kept Oscar's untimely passing (and ultimate reincarnation) to themselves en route to their highest ranking (11th) by season's end in four years—and their highest ranking since.

"Oscar," Nguyen says, laughing, "had started to grow back before the Big 12 championship game."

THE SETTING

Dan Campbell grew up on a lot of wide-open spaces in Glen Rose, Texas, a place he wouldn't have minded retreating to in the days after the 1998 Aggie Bonfire—which also turned out to be the last at A&M following the stack's awful collapse the next year.

Campbell, A&M's gregarious and ever-quotable tight end, stood before 50,000 delirious Texas A&M fans at the Aggie Bonfire and declared that he was proud to have attended a school where "men like women and women like men"—a not-so-subtle jab at the more liberal University of Texas.

Campbell's comment likely wouldn't have raised such a firestorm of protest in a more discriminate College Station setting—say, the Dixie Chicken—but the Bonfire often grabbed national attention as Texas A&M's most recognizable tradition. The university subsequently apologized for his remarks, as did a befuddled Campbell.

"I didn't mean to offend anybody by it," he said in the days afterward, adding that if he had the chance to do it over, he'd probably "just stay away from that whole subject."

Thus, Campbell's "heat of the moment" remark at Bonfire touched off a circus-like atmosphere at the Big 12 title game in St. Louis's Trans World Dome about two weeks later. Protesters, at the behest of a fire-and-brimstone preacher, showed up outside the dome complete with picket signs—all in *support* of Campbell's original remark and against the resulting apology.

Yes, sir, Glen Rose seemed a mighty fine escape for a perplexed country boy at that moment, but first, there was plenty of business for the Aggies to tend to, including a daunting task against the nation's top-ranked team. And the Aggies, behind the leadership of Dat Nguyen and Dan Campbell, had yet to back down from any obstacle that spectacular season.

"As seniors, we definitely didn't want to go out there and embarrass ourselves—or the university—against Kansas State," Nguyen says.

Based on each team's season leading up to that point, that wasn't out of the realm of possibility. While the Aggies had squeaked past some lesser opponents (24-21 and 17-14 against Kansas and Missouri, respectively), K-State had sprung to an 11-0 record behind quarterback Michael Bishop.

The Wildcats, angling for their first conference title since 1934, featured the nation's No. 1 scoring offense—which averaged a whopping seven touchdowns per game—and the country's second best defense.

Kansas State held the top slot in the *USA Today*/ESPN coaches' poll, but was only third in the all-important Bowl Championship Series rankings. Thus the Wildcats needed Miami to upset No. 2 UCLA on the same day in a make-up game in Florida (the threat of Hurricane Georges in September had delayed the contest). Or the Wildcats needed a big-time win over the Aggies in stating their case to play Tennessee in the title game.

"From my understanding, we need to blow A&M out to prove we're one of the top two teams," Wildcats receiver Darnell McDonald said, scratching his head and trying to make sense of it all a couple of days before the league title game. "But Texas A&M has a great team. They're in the Big 12 championship for a reason. Blowing them out is a very hard task, but I think it can be done."

Turns out that Miami did upset UCLA early that day, meaning all Kansas State needed was a mere victory over Texas A&M (a two-touchdown underdog). Turns out that couldn't be done, either.

THE GAME OF MY LIFE
By Dat Nguyen

Quarterback Michael Bishop was Kansas State's biggest offensive threat, for good reason. He could throw a dart, for sure, but he was more of a danger to tuck and run. He was fun to watch on tape, not so much fun to defense.

But we loved the challenge—and we liked the game plan devised by defensive coordinator Mike Hankwitz. The idea was to rush our outside linebackers upfield and then sink them down because we knew that Bishop liked to tuck the ball and that he didn't like to run up the middle, but to the side. Our outside 'backers, Warrick Holdman and Roylin Bradley, did a great job of speed-rushing and then getting underneath.

You figured Bishop would make a play here or there—because that was his style—but you couldn't worry too much about it; you just had to move on to the next one. When Kansas State was in a passing situation, we'd drop a nose guard to spy on Bishop, just in case he tried to run. By rushing the two defensive ends and keeping the nose guard as a spy, that gave us an extra player in space, so Bishop had less space to run.

Besides game planning against Kansas State, we also had plenty of incentive to try and slow down the Wildcats. In the week prior to the game, they'd talked a lot about needing to "blow us out" to ensure a spot in the national championship game.

During a timeout in the second quarter and with K-State up 17-3, the public address announcer in the dome excitedly told the crowd that Miami had defeated UCLA 49-45. The place went crazy, because most of the fans there were from K-State. That score meant the Wildcats only had to put us away to play in the national title game.

We were all on the field when Miami-UCLA score was announced, and you should have seen all of the K-State's players' faces. They were high-fiving each other and yelling, "We're going to the national championship game!" right in front of us. Amidst all of the hugs, our only thought was: "Man, it ain't over yet."

Honestly, it made us fight a little harder knowing they were already celebrating, thinking a victory was in the bag.

K-State had a 15-point lead against us in the fourth quarter, although I marveled at how strong we'd played to that point, without getting any breaks. And then the breaks started rolling in our favor—which is exactly why you play the entire 60 minutes. Kansas State played great that game —for three and a half quarters.

We won the game in double overtime on what I figured at the time to be a nutty call. Third and 17 from the K-State 32-yard line, and we're

Dat Nguyen, who played linebacker for the Dallas Cowboys, compiled a school-record 517 tackles from 1995-98. *Photo courtesy of Texas A&M Athletic Media Relations*

running a slant? I had my head lowered when Sirr Parker caught the ball, and the crowd started roaring. When he was running for the end zone, it was so dramatic it almost seemed to be in slow motion.

And then Sirr knocked over the pylon, and the referee was a little bit slow in signaling the touchdown. When he did, we went crazy. People had talked plenty about Sirr Parker's speed in his four years at Texas A&M, and that was a heck of a time to really showcase it.

As soon as the game was over their players didn't want to shake hands or anything—they were just so shocked. I looked up into the crowd, and just saw a sea of sad purple. We had a section of fans, right there behind the bench, about 5,000 people. Hardly anyone thought we were going to win that game—the players all knew that. But the Aggie fans who were there—we gave 'em something to remember, didn't we?

Winning that game is the biggest thrill in my athletics career. Against the No. 1 team in the nation, down by double digits in the fourth quarter, we push it into double overtime to finally win. I'll guarantee you that everybody on that team will tell you the same thing: It's their favorite all-time game. It was the best game we'd all been around and one of the best in the history of Texas A&M, and I'm thankful and blessed to have experienced it firsthand.

GAME RESULTS

Extra consonants their mamas gave 'em aren't the only things that Branndon Stewart and Sirr Parker shared as teammates on the 1998 Big 12 championship team—not after their performances in the league title game on Dec. 5, 1998.

Stewart, a sometime starting quarterback pressed into action after Randy McCown broke his collarbone a week earlier against Texas, threw for 324 yards against the vaunted Wildcats' defense. Parker, a versatile halfback, had a touchdown reception and a two-point conversion catch with 1:05 remaining in the game to tie it and force overtime.

The speedster from Los Angeles then blasted 32 yards on a slant on third and 17 and with the Aggies trailing by three in double overtime. When an outstretched Parker slammed into the pylon, A&M vaulted into a prestigious BCS bowl game for the first (and to date last) time in school history.

"You always see the people on TV making the big plays and you never know how it feels," a triumphant Parker said afterward. "Now, I know."

And while A&M lost to Ohio State 24-14 in the Sugar Bowl, Parker's score is by far the most indelible reminder of what many consider the Aggies' sweetest season under R.C. Slocum. A&M finished that year ranked 11th and never again reached the top 20 behind the venerable coach, whose last season was 2002.

But on that wild Saturday night in College Station following A&M's improbable burst to the Big 12 title, Aggieland's Northgate district partied like it was 1939—the year of A&M's lone national championship.

"To say this night is amazing," A&M senior Norma Fritsch said from the Dixie Chicken, as she enjoyed the Aggie ritual of dunking her class ring in a pitcher of beer, "would be an understatement."

WHAT BECAME OF DAT NGUYEN?

Former Dallas Cowboys great Roger Staubach offered a three-word announcement at a black-tie gathering at the Hyatt Regency in Houston to let the world know that Dat Nguyen had won the coveted Lombardi Award on Dec. 8, 1998: "Gig 'em, Aggies." The crowd erupted, and Tina Turner's rousing anthem "The Best" kicked in, as the humble Nguyen approached the podium.

"Gol-ly," Nguyen said, wincing a bit in the bright lights. "It's a shocker."

In the crowd, Nguyen's girlfriend of two years, Becky Foster, clapped enthusiastically.

"That's just awesome," Becky said, sporting a smile wider than Houston's Buffalo Bayou. "He's the most modest person, so I'm ecstatic because he really deserved this."

The encouraging words of Becky, who'd later become Nguyen's wife—and mother of the loving couple's three daughters—weren't just that of a happy, supportive girlfriend. They were grounded in fact, as Nguyen finished his Texas A&M career as the school's all-time leading tackler with 517—a whopping 62 more than two-time All-American Johnny Holland.

"I've always had a lot of respect for Dat," said the 1998 Heisman Trophy winner, Texas running back Ricky Williams, "because he plays the game the way it should be played."

And Nguyen, one of the game's most endearing and beloved figures, certainly appreciated and embraced his role as the first NFL player of Vietnamese descent.

"It's a huge honor," Nguyen says. "I don't know why God chose me for this role, but hopefully it can show kids that there are always opportunities out there, no matter your background.

"It doesn't matter where you come from or where you're at—it's where you want to be in life."

CHAPTER 24

SHANE LECHLER

Name: Edward Shane Lechler
Born: Aug. 7, 1976 in Wharton, Texas
Hometown: East Bernard, Texas
Current Residence: Katy, Texas
Occupation: NFL Player
Position: Punter
Height: 6'2"
Playing Weight: 220 pounds
Years lettered: 1996-99
Accomplishments: Two-time All-American (1998-99) and three-time All-Conference (1997-99); NCAA record holder for career punt average (44.7) and career games with a 40-yard plus average (37); fifth-round pick of the Oakland Raiders in 2000; Pro Bowler in only his second NFL season.
The Game: Texas at Texas A&M, Nov. 26, 1999

Shane Lechler. *Photo courtesy of Texas A&M Athletic Media Relations*

THE LIFE OF YOUNG SHANE LECHLER

The legendary tales of Shane Lechler's booming punts preceded his arrival at Texas A&M, beginning those many fall Friday nights on the prairies of Southeast Texas.

"One of my coaches went to see Shane play at one of those country stadiums, and he was kicking the ball out of the lights," Aggies coach R.C. Slocum said. "You couldn't even see it for a while, and then it would finally come back down."

Says a humble Lechler with a laugh: "Those lights were like parking lot lights."

It didn't take long for the legend to take hold in Aggieland, however, evidenced by a punt Lechler booted in practice early in his freshman year.

"We were practicing kickoffs after a safety, where you punt in that situation," A&M special teams coach Shawn Slocum said. "Shane punted from the 20-yard line, and the ball landed seven yards deep in the end zone. That was an 87-yard punt. In the air."

Shawn Slocum tried playing it casual with the youngster—"Keep kicking like that, son, and we may find a spot for you"—but it was hard to wipe the grin off the assistant's face. Lechler can't quite figure where he got all of that leg strength, although he's got his suspicions. The oldest of Dale and Javon Lechler's two boys, Lechler comes from a long line of athletes.

"Both my grandfathers played college football [at Baylor and Mississippi State], my dad played college football and my mom played college basketball [both at Baylor]," he says. "My dad was also the high school coach at East Bernard until I was in the eighth grade, and I'd go to two-a-days with him when I was little. My hands weren't big enough to throw around the football, so I kicked it everywhere."

Lechler played a little bit of everything back home in East Bernard, ranging from football to basketball to track to golf to baseball and then back to football—excelling at all.

"When he was about two years old somebody gave him a Nerf football set, with the football, goalposts and kicking tee and all," says Lechler's father, Dale Lechler, now the superintendent of the Sealy (Texas) school district. "So he started kicking field goals in the house and using perfect form.

"Then when he was in the fourth grade or so he'd come out to the practice field when I was coaching and he'd kick 30- and 40-yard field goals—and here I was with high school kids who couldn't even reach the goalposts. Shane never went to any kind of kicking camps or anything like that. He just had a gift, and he maximized it."

Lechler stayed modest through all of his honors—and all of his accomplishments since—and even refused to wear his heavily decorated letter jacket in high school.

"We spent all of that money to put all of those patches and accolades all over it," Dale Lechler says, "and he wouldn't wear it. Not once."

The Aggies recruited Lechler as a quarterback and punter, which made his collegiate decision all the easier, since Texas had other ideas. A UT assistant called Lechler and pitched this idea during the recruiting season: "Shane, we've got some good quarterbacks here. Would you mind playing fullback?"

"I went into my room where I had a list of teams," Lechler says of that moment, "and I scratched them right off."

Lechler redshirted his first year because A&M already possessed a strong-legged senior in Sean Terry, and in only Lechler's second game a year later he boomed a 73-yard punt at Southwestern Louisiana. Through his first two years at A&M, Lechler still practiced with the quarterbacks, but that all changed headed into his junior year, when he tore his quadriceps muscle at the beginning of two-a-days. R.C. Slocum then approached him about a possible shift in plans.

"Shane, you're going to be our punter here and you're going to punt for a long, long time," Slocum said.

"Coach," Lechler responded, "I've only got two more years."

Slocum smiled and shook his head.

"You're going to punt in the NFL, and you'll go on to some great things," the head coach said. "You need to concentrate on punting."

"From that day on I was able to save energy and the pounding your legs took as a quarterback," Lechler says. "Best advice I've ever received: Hey, stop playing quarterback. It's a lot easier to just punt."

Somewhat humorously, Lechler still had at least one pass in him—and very nearly a surprise appearance at QB before a national TV audience in A&M's biggest game of that era. Before that day, however, Lechler—the team's holder—had tossed a touchdown pass to tight end Dan Campbell on a fake field goal that helped beat Texas Tech 17-10 on Oct. 24, 1998.

A local columnist described the play thusly: "When the retread QB spun from the hold and rummaged for an open receiver, rust showered from his hips. ... [nevertheless] the quack-quack pass gave A&M the lead."

Afterward A&M offensive coordinator Steve Kragthorpe, who once described Lechler's build as comparable to that of fabled and frumpy ol'-time QB Sonny Jurgenson, tossed in his two cents about the play.

"Almost looked like a shotput," Kragthorpe said, "but it was effective."

And Dan Campbell, a jester who couldn't resist, piled on.

"It seemed like the ball was in the air for about 30 minutes," he said, smiling. "Just kind of floatin' and flutterin'. I'm just glad it cleared the defender."

At the time Lechler joked that he "knew his quarterbacking days were over" when he saw the slow rotation on the toss. Not so fast. The Aggies won the Big 12 South Division that season behind linebacker Dat Nguyen and Campbell and were set to play top-ranked Kansas State in the 1998 Big 12 title game in St. Louis at the Trans World Dome.

Starting quarterback Randy McCown had broken his left collarbone the week before, leaving the job to senior Branndon Stewart, who'd also started five games that season. No problem there—except for the lack of a capable backup to Stewart.

"That week in practice the coaches had told me they'd need me as a backup for the Big 12 championship game," Lechler says. "I figured they probably wouldn't really need me. I mean, what are the chances of another quarterback getting hurt? So I attended the quarterback meetings that week, but paid zero attention to anything about the running game.

"I like to throw the ball."

Sure enough, Stewart hyperextended his knee in the first quarter in the nationally televised game for all of the Big 12 marbles and with K-State angling to play in the national championship game, prompting Lechler to pop on a headset with Kragthorpe, who sat in the press box.

"Shane, ya ready?" Kragthorpe asked.

"Coach, I'll be honest with you," Lechler admitted, in a tardy moment of virtuousness. "I know zero part of the running game. But I know all of the pass plays."

"Awrighty," Kragthorpe said following a momentary pause. "Let's go throw it, then."

On the sidelines, a fervent Lechler airmailed pass after pass while warming up as worried A&M trainers even more fervently worked on Stewart's knee.

"I was just gonna be awful," says Lechler, who can now laugh about the whole situation. "I had kicking shoes on that were molded cleats, and I was gonna try and scamper on Astroturf in 'em. Let me tell you, it was setting up to be ugly. There'd have been plenty of jokes about me still today if I'd have played in that game. A minor miracle took place—for all of us—when Branndon returned and I didn't have to go in."

Certainly Lechler's diminished quarterbacking skills—nearly called into play in a game in which Stewart threw three touchdown passes in what turned out to be the biggest win of the Slocum era—brought about plenty of smiles. Meanwhile his right leg brought about plenty of NFL scouts to College Station—and he wound up only the second punter the Oakland Raiders ever drafted, following the legendary Ray Guy.

"There's a ton of baby pictures around my parents' house, and I'm kicking the ball in every one of 'em," Lechler says. "I'm not throwing in one. Maybe that was an early sign of what was to come."

THE SCENE

The Aggie Bonfire helped coax Shane Lechler, who would become the most prolific punter in NCAA history, to Texas A&M from his hometown of East Bernard an hour west of Houston.

"Growing up I was a huge University of Texas fan," Lechler says. "I didn't know much about Texas A&M or the Bonfire until my junior year of high school. That's when some friends and I came up for the '93 Bonfire and the Texas game the next night at Kyle Field—when Leeland McElroy returned a kick 100 yards for a touchdown.

"That whole experience, starting with Bonfire, completely changed my thoughts about where I wanted to go to school."

Five years later Lechler, well on his way to setting all sorts of NCAA punting records, stood on a platform with his A&M teammates before 50,000 thousand fans. The players soaked in the flames and festivities of what was to become the final official Aggie Bonfire to burn before the Texas game. Only no one knew.

"I wish I hadn't taken that one for granted," Lechler says of the 1998 Bonfire. "I thought I had a Bonfire coming up the next year, when I'd be a senior, and we'd be the leaders up front, talking. No one knew to 'watch this one, because it's going to be the last one.'"

About a year later the police knocked on the door of the home of A&M football players Randy McCown, Matt Bumgardner and Shea Holder. It was close to 3 a.m. on the morning of Nov. 18, 1999.

"We were having a party over there and we were still up, even though we probably shouldn't have been," Lechler says. "The College Station cops had come to tell us to keep it down—someone had complained about the noise. The cops were in the house, got a call, and they suddenly ran out.

"That's when it had happened."

The Bonfire stack of thousands of logs roughly 40 feet tall had collapsed, killing 12 Aggies at the home of the 12th Man and injuring another 27. In retrospect, Lechler finds many ironies in the entire, surreal and overwhelmingly sad setting of the following weeks in Aggieland.

"Texas A&M football players are taken care of pretty good," Lechler says. "It's not that we're given everything, but everything is made a little bit easier for us. The student body, on the other hand, those guys fight for everything they get.

"And they built that Bonfire every year as kind of what amounts to a big pep rally for us. To have people get killed doing something in support of us … at that point we needed to do whatever we could to help out."

The Texas A&M football team certainly did, by supporting the student body and the Aggie Spirit in a heartfelt gesture that occurred far outside the three decks of Kyle Field—in a genuine labor that truly helped the Bonfire recovery effort.

THE SETTING

As the police scrambled from the football players' party with nary a goodbye on the morning of Nov. 18, 1999, the players glanced at each other in relief—no ticket was written—and then in puzzlement. What had caused them to dash from the scene?

It didn't take long to find out. Within minutes of the Bonfire's collapse in the middle of the night, local TV station KBTX had flashed a crawl across the bottom of its screen, and soon the station reported live from the shocking and ghastly scene.

"The wires snapped and the lights started sparking and going on and off," said eyewitness Diana Estrada, who was working about 200 yards away from the stack. "We ran over there as fast as we could, and we could see legs sticking out and hear people screaming."

That clear morning on the opposite side of campus, stunned football players gathered in their locker room beneath the stands of Kyle Field, hollowly preparing for practice as the rest of the campus reeled from an awful tragedy still unfolding.

That's when several of the seniors—led by Shane Lechler, cornerback Jason Webster, running back D'Andre "Tiki" Hardeman and offensive linemen Andy Vincent and Semisi Heimuli—discussed how they might try and help in a seemingly helpless situation.

Webster then headed for R.C. Slocum's office with the gang's collective idea: Cancel practice and let the football players go help at the Bonfire site in any means possible.

"That was kind of a controversial deal with us going into a game with the University of Texas and us saying, 'Hey, Coach, we can't practice today. We're going to go help people at the Bonfire,'" Lechler says. "At first I think he figured we'd be more of a distraction over there—more in the way than anything.

"We knew we had a huge game coming up against our archrival and that we needed the preparation. On the other hand, we knew in our hearts that we needed to stick beside the student body, because they always stuck beside us. We could go play a game on the farthest reaches of the earth, and there'd be Texas A&M fans there, supporting us.

"Really, we just wondered, 'Is going to practice the right thing to be doing right now?' It was hard to reason going on with a normal schedule in the wake of what had happened. We needed to help out—and that was the time to do it."

So, upon telling Slocum it wasn't in their hearts to practice that day, a group of about six football players trekked across campus and into a tragic and surreal scene they'll never forget. There, amidst a horrific jumble of fallen logs, rescue workers gingerly removed one piece at a time, so as not to crush any possible remaining survivors trapped beneath.

The earnest gesture of the football players, who were quickly joined by all of their teammates at the Bonfire site, proved much more than just symbolic, as well. A worn rescue team welcomed the sight of all that beef and muscle in Texas A&M football practice shorts and shirts.

"Their effort came from the bottom of their hearts, and there was nothing ceremonial about it," says Bob Wiatt, Texas A&M's longtime police chief and a legendary Texas lawman. "Those boys were over there helping pull logs away from the collapsed stack and doing anything and everything they could to help out."

Says Lechler, "We didn't know they'd actually let us help. We thought we might just do a couple of little things, like give out water or food or something to that extent. We wound up picking a lot of the logs [that had already been shoved to the side of the fallen stack] and walking them away."

By day's end, torn, sweaty and filthy A&M practice shirts barely hung from the broad shoulders of the football players, who helped the best way they knew.

"These are our brothers and sisters," offensive lineman Semisi Heimuli said, wiping away tears between carrying logs. "We came to help our fellow Aggies."

The Aggies returned to practice the next day after the university had decided to continue with the contest and began to gear up for the biggest game of their lifetimes.

"If we wouldn't have gone out there and helped, it would have been much harder to get ready for the game," Lechler says. "You saw the looks on the faces of the people whose friends and family members had been killed, and you truly saw the emotions of the tragedy. When we were out there moving logs, we weren't just football players, separate from everyone else.

"We were a part of the student body."

So many students wish that they could be a part of a glorified crew like the Texas A&M football team. It's amazing that on Texas A&M's darkest yet most galvanizing day, the football players just yearned to be a part of the student body.

THE GAME OF MY LIFE
By Shane Lechler

Coach Slocum said he didn't want to burden us with trying to win our game against Texas for the Bonfire victims—only that we should honor their memory, win or lose. We understood that, and we appreciated it. We also understood that everyone in that stadium that day felt like we needed to win that football game.

We also appreciated the fact that the University of Texas had canceled its annual "hex rally" and replaced it with a candlelight vigil for both Longhorns and Aggies around the steps of the UT Tower. I respect them a lot for that.

The support UT provided us was tremendous. They really respected how much our traditions mean to us, and they realized the bind we were in because lives were lost because of one of them. You couldn't ask for anything more from a rivalry that's been that deep for so long. Our whole team respected it, and our entire university respected how Texas responded to our time of need.

We also had a football game to play on our home field against a team that was ranked seventh nationally. We'd certainly had our highs and lows that season, especially late in the year when we'd lost at Oklahoma 51-6 and at Nebraska 37-0. Fortunately, we'd whipped Missouri 51-14 just before the Texas game, to get back on track.

But against the Longhorns on a hugely emotional day after Thanksgiving at Kyle Field, we were trailing 16-6 at halftime, and things weren't looking good. For the first two or three minutes in the locker room at halftime, things seemed pretty dull.

Suddenly, we had a couple of guys stand up to speak, and that hadn't happened in a long time. Coach Slocum usually did all of the talking at halftime, and we did all of the listening. This time R.C. just said a few words, and a couple of the team leaders spoke from the heart.

"This university stuck together after the Bonfire fell," senior quarterback Randy McCown said. "And they're out there supporting us right now. Let's pull our heads out and go play some football."

The second half was a different story, as our "Wrecking Crew" defense held the Longhorns scoreless, and we rallied for a 20-16 win. The go-ahead touchdown pass came with about five minutes remaining, when McCown tossed a perfect pass to his roommate, Matt Bumgardner, in the back corner of the end zone. From the time those two had walked into Cain Hall together in 1995 as freshmen, they'd lived together.

And personally, I was really glad that "Bum" caught it. I was kicking field goals for us that week, and we were only down by two at the time. I

Shane Lechler, now an Oakland Raider, holds the NCAA career punting average at 44.7 yards. *Photo courtesy of Texas A&M Sports News*

really didn't want to try and kick a field goal in that situation. I always got a lot of leg into my kicks, but honestly, I didn't have a clue as to where they were going. Bum caught that ball and I was the happiest guy on the field.

We sealed the win with less than a minute left when cornerback Jay Brooks popped the ball loose from quarterback Major Applewhite, and linebacker Brian Gamble recovered.

The next day all of the pictures in the paper showed Gamble on his knees with his arms outstretched in celebration, and that's what people remember about that moment. No one should forget, though, that Jay created that fumble and gave a little extra effort in making that play.

When the game was finally over and we'd held on for the win, personally, that's the best feeling I've ever had after a football game, no matter the level I've played. I'll admit, there were a lot of tears flowing, and in the locker room afterward it was almost like you didn't even want to take the A&M uniform off, because you knew it'd be the last time you got to wear it at Kyle Field.

To have grown up with a group of guys over four and five years and to have pulled together in that situation to put a victory on the board in your last home game against the University of Texas—it's something I'll never forget.

GAME RESULTS

Texas A&M's 1999 season had plenty of disappointments, following its tumble from a Top 5 ranking early in the year. The Aggies were only 4-3 in Big 12 play (and 7-3 overall) going into their emotional game against their biggest rival on Nov. 26, but A&M prevailed 20-16 against the 9-3 Longhorns.

A stomach virus had forced UT starting quarterback Major Applewhite to the sidelines for most of the game, and freshman Chris Simms earned his first start. Applewhite, looking paler than usual, entered the game late in the second half, as the Longhorns failed to secure a 16-6 halftime lead.

And, in the end, Texas coach Mack Brown pointed to one player in particular as having affected the outcome—the Aggies' All-American punter.

"Shane Lechler was the difference in the ball game," Brown said. "He pinned us, and we couldn't get off the goal line."

Brown was referencing a couple of 50-plus yard punts by Lechler in the fourth quarter, including a 54-yarder with less than two minutes remaining, off of a bad snap, no less. Texas started its final, futile drive on its own 11-yard line because of the punt.

"The snap was low and to my right, but I just kind of hopped to it and luckily, when I grabbed the ball it was just one wrist turn away from having the laces up, and I was able to get it off," Lechler says. "Following that punt was a great way to walk off of Kyle Field for the last time."

Lechler finished the four-point A&M victory with eight punts that averaged 43.6 yards, ensuring him of the NCAA record for career punting average of 44.6 yards per punt.

At the same time McCown was appealing to the Aggies to get their act together at halftime, a moving tribute was under way on the field. As 86,128 fans—many with tears streaming down their cheeks—watched and listened in awe, the University of Texas band played "Amazing Grace" and Taps, as its members respectfully removed their white cowboy hats.

Following UT's stirring tribute, the famed Aggie Band silently and flawlessly formed a block "T" at the end of its performance, and slowly marched off the field in lieu of its typical sprint.

The Aggies accepted a bid to play Penn State in the Alamo Bowl following their upset of the Longhorns, and the Nittany Lions beat A&M 24-0 on Dec. 28 in San Antonio. But more than a month earlier on a solemn and overwhelmingly sad day in Aggieland, such on-field losses clearly had gained much perspective. And two rival schools had come together like never before.

"The tragedy touched everyone, but it was emotionally draining to Aggies, who have a common bond that God had in mind when he created man," wrote Robert Cessna of the *Bryan-College Station Eagle*. "Winning a football game … will hardly go down on history's timeline, but for the heavy hearts of so many Americans who poured out their love in the past week, a few million prayers were answered."

WHAT BECAME OF SHANE LECHLER?

The idea still makes Shane Lechler cringe a bit, although he won't refuse a compliment, of course. Still, even Lechler wonders why Coach R.C. Slocum insisted on labeling him—a punter—as the team's Most Valuable Player during the Aggies' 1998 run to the Big 12 Conference title.

"Especially with a team that had guys like Dat Nguyen and Dan Campbell," Lechler says. "It was kind of hard to believe that Coach really felt that way."

Slocum's reasoning seemed simple enough, citing Lechler's consistency in always giving the Aggies at least 40 yards of extra turf to defend every time he touched the ball behind the deep snapper. Lechler continued that success with the Oakland Raiders, and then signed with his hometown Houston Texans in 2013.

"He's very talented at whatever he does," then-Raiders coach Jon Gruden said during Lechler's rookie season of 2000. "At training camp, he won the long-driving contest [in golf], and if we had a contest with the quarterbacks throwing a football through a tire, he'd probably win that, too."

In one of Lechler's more persistent yet high-yielding plays at Texas A&M, he finally convinced Aggies freshman volleyball player Erin Gibson to date him late in his junior year—with the help of a little operation.

"I tried to go out with her for what seemed like about two years—really it was only a little over a semester—but she wouldn't," Lechler says, laughing. "During my junior year I had surgery on my left shoulder, and I came to in the hospital and she was one of the persons there. I asked her, 'What are you doing here? Do you feel sorry for me?'"

Apparently not—or possibly so. Shane and Erin married on July 7, 2001, and the two plan to begin having children soon. Lechler figures if he can play about 15 years in the league, he'll slide right into retirement like he used to slide into second base as East Bernard High's star shortstop.

"If my NFL career is any shorter than that, then I'm gonna have to go into coaching, because I won't be ready to give up football just yet," he says. "Otherwise, after 15 years, I'm done. From then on, it's relax, play golf and fish."

Not a bad life for one of the former ringleaders of a crew at A&M called the "Wednesday Night Riders." This was a group of six or so football players who, once a week, ate Mexican food together and then eased into an oversized booth at a Bryan watering hole called Carney's Pub.

"It was dollar beers there on Wednesday night, until 10 p.m.," Lechler says, grinning. "So somehow between the six of us—and I'm still not sure how because none of us had any money—we'd round up $100 and get 100 beers just before 10. We'd fill up that whole booth with beers, and we wouldn't leave until they were gone."

Which adds up to another legendary story, of course, for the easygoing punter who used to kick 'em out of the lights.

CHAPTER 25

VON MILLER

Name: Von Miller
Born: March 26, 1989, in Dallas, Texas
Hometown: DeSoto, Texas
Current Residence: Denver, Colorado
Occupation: NFL Player
Position: Linebacker
Height: 6'3"
Playing Weight: 240 pounds
Years lettered: 2007-10
Accomplishments: 2010 Butkus Award winner; two-time All-American; nation-leading 17 sacks as a junior; No. 2 overall selection of 2011 NFL draft (tying for highest ever for the program at that time); AFC Defensive Rookie of the Year in 2011; first Denver Bronco in history to make the Pro Bowl in each of his first two NFL seasons.
The Game: Texas A&M at Texas, November 25, 2010

THE LIFE OF YOUNG VON MILLER

W̲hen Von Miller blossomed into a football prospect at DeSoto High School near Dallas, the rangy, swift defensive lineman considered Southern Cal and Florida as ideal destinations to ply his considerable skills. Then he visited Texas A&M as a sophomore in high school, a journey that narrowed his vision to just a few hours south of DeSoto.

"I had never seen anything like it—all the fans standing up and yelling in unison," Miller recalled. "I was blown away."

So he locked away that memory as he continued developing at DeSoto, and then the letters began arriving from A&M. These weren't run-of-the-mill missives, mind you, and defensive line coach Stan Eggen's hard work paid off in the commitment of Miller to the Aggies on Halloween of 2006.

"The first letter I ever received came from Coach Eggen, and it really struck me because he took his time with it and handwrote everything," Miller said. "Outside of that visit to A&M when I was a sophomore, I hadn't really considered the Aggies. But he kept writing every week."

Head coach Dennis Franchione also sent handwritten letters to Miller, and their painstaking tasks paid huge dividends.

"The coaches taking their time to write their letters by hand? That really hit home with me," Miller said.

THE SCENE

D̲ennis Franchione first hinted to Texas A&M fans that his program was on to something with Von Miller on national signing day in 2007. Then, Franchione pointed to Miller's prowess not simply as a premier pass rusher, but as one of the state's top hurdlers in track and field."You don't put that in combinations with defensive ends a lot," said Franchione, A&M's head coach from 2003-07.

In retracing Miller's early years at A&M, one big thing emerged en route to the eventual Butkus Award winner's second overall selection in the NFL draft in 2011: While hurdles felled many around him, Miller was a survivor. He played defensive end under the Franchione regime as a true freshman, and then switched to linebacker under new coach Mike Sherman in 2008.

Early on, it wasn't easy. Miller missed the 2008 spring game with what Sherman simply dubbed "personal issues" at the time (the talented linebacker had earned a reputation as something of a hothead early in his college career). Miller set any "personal issues" aside, however, and came on strong under the stern guidance of Sherman and coordinators Joe

Von Miller in action against Mizzou. *Photo courtesy of Texas A&M Athletic Media Relations*

Kines and Tim DeRuyter. He led the nation with 17 sacks as a junior and notched another 10 1/2 as a senior even while fighting a bum ankle early in the season.

In January 2010, Miller announced his intent to return for his senior season, and Aggieland rejoiced. His motivation for returning included the opportunity for one more shot at rival Texas—and he'd get that shot on Thanksgiving night in Austin. No one knew it at the time, but the contest also marked the Aggies' final game in the state capital for the foreseeable future, after they moved to the Southeastern Conference in 2012, and left the Longhorns behind in the Big 12.

THE SETTING

Texas A&M receiver Ryan Swope offered a confession in the days leading up to Texas A&M's showdown at Texas on Thanksgiving of 2010.

"I grew up a Longhorn—my dad graduated from Texas," Swope said. "I grew up with a lot of burnt orange in the closet."

And when he signed with A&M in 2008 out of Austin's Westlake High School?

"I got rid of all of it," a smiling Swope said of his Longhorns loot. "We gave it to Goodwill."

So went what legendary A&M coach R.C. Slocum, who guided the Aggies from 1989-2002, annually dubbed tiny Texans' "predisposition" to either A&M or UT—you either grew up a little Aggie or a little Longhorn, there was no in-between.

"It's high school football players from Texas against high school players from Texas," A&M coach Mike Sherman said. "We also know each other so well, since we're only 90 miles apart. From the Aggies' standpoint, the rivalry is part of the school song. We're reminded constantly that this is a big game."

It was a big game in 2010 again, but for different reasons than in recent seasons. The Aggies had won five straight and were favored over the Longhorns for the first time in a dozen years. The struggling Longhorns were playing for a bowl berth—and of course both programs were playing for rivalry pride.

First-year A&M defensive coordinator Tim DeRuyter, who had revived the famed Wrecking Crew defense with the big-time aid of All-American linebacker Von Miller, had never attended a game at Kyle Field before that season. And that Thursday night in late November, he was also attending his first game at UT's Royal-Memorial Stadium.

"I always remember on Thanksgiving turning that game on and watching it," DeRuyter said of A&M-UT. "It's such a huge rivalry. To be a part of this is going to be special."

THE GAME OF MY LIFE
By Von Miller

When I decided to return for my senior season and put off the NFL for one more year, I never envisioned the injury bug would bite me really for the first time in my career. I suffered a concussion during spring drills, and played sparingly in the annual spring game. That was my first disappointment—I had really wanted to play in my final Maroon & White game. Then, following a decent training camp in August, I sprained my ankle in the season opener against Stephen F. Austin State.

It hurt so bad I thought I had broken it, and I really started to wonder why I had returned. This was my senior year, and everyone was expecting me to do all of these things after leading the nation in sacks with 17 the year before. That's where the guys in the locker room came in, and my teammates did a wonderful job of keeping my spirits up. I really leaned on them in that time.

I didn't even record my first sack until the fourth game, and meanwhile we had started the season 3-3 and Coach Sherman's job was in jeopardy. We knew we were better than that—we knew it. We finally started playing like it, too, in reeling off six consecutive victories to close out the regular season.

That November, we defeated powerhouse Oklahoma and a resurgent Nebraska squad in front of incredible crowds at Kyle Field, setting up a trip to Austin against the Longhorns, who'd defeated us the last two seasons. No one knew it at the time, but that Thanksgiving night would be the last time the Aggies played at Royal-Memorial Stadium for the foreseeable future. In the summer of 2012, A&M left the Big 12 for the Southeastern Conference, and while the Aggies said they'd love to keep playing the Longhorns as nonconference opponents, the Longhorns refused.

Texas had played in the national title game following the 2009 regular season in losing to Alabama, but had struggled under new quarterback Garrett Gilbert in 2010. Honestly, that Thanksgiving night it felt like we were whipping their butts throughout on national TV, but we glanced up at the scoreboard and it was 24-17. Texas was marching and on our 12-yard line with less than three minutes remaining, and suddenly something occurred that never had [happened before] in my college career.

An interception, one making that whole return for a senior season worth it by its lonesome. Defensive lineman Spencer Nealy got a hand on a Gilbert pass at the line, and I'd had my eyes on the ball even prior to the deflection. You know that old saying, "Keep your eye on the ball?" Oh, yeah. The ball just went all "cattywompus" but I stayed with it.

I caught the ball eight yards from the end zone and, I know it sounds crazy, suddenly had my eyes on the Longhorns' end zone. That would have been a heck of a way to go out, as well. Alas, I was tackled only three yards into my run, but that was just fine with me.

Von Miller awaits the snap. *Photo courtesy of Texas A&M Athletic Media Relations*

When I climbed to my feet, with the interception having preserved the win in my last regular season college football game, I remember really special teammates like Michael Hodges and Dustin Harris just surrounding me in joy. I cried in the locker room, about the fourth time that season I'd cried after a contest. But this time I had extra tears, because we would carry the previous three hours as a lifetime memory.

GAME RESULTS

Texas A&M had poked and prodded Texas for much of Thanksgiving night, and in the process exposed a fleshy weakness in the once-brawny Longhorns defense. It was a chubby underbelly, which A&M senior running back Cyrus Gray had exposed with touchdown runs of 84 and 48 yards right up the gut.

Gray—a DeSoto High graduate like Miller—finished with 223 rushing yards, the most ever by an Aggie against the Longhorns in the 24-17 A&M victory.

"Our players showed tremendous resiliency throughout the game," said A&M coach Mike Sherman, who earned what turned out to be his only victory over the rival Longhorns.

Afterward, the overjoyed Aggies gathered in the southeast corner of their rivals' stadium before their own fans and "sawed Varsity's horns off" as part of the Aggie War Hymn. Then, the team climbed on its buses and made the triumphant 90-mile trek back to Aggieland.

"And then we all went out to Northgate to celebrate," a smiling Miller said of College Station's famous entertainment district. "It was just an incredible night."

WHAT BECAME OF VON MILLER?

In April of 2011, the Denver Broncos selected Von Miller second overall of the NFL Draft. Later that year, he earned AFC Defensive Rookie of the Year honors, and by 2012 he was the first Bronco in history to earn Pro Bowl nods in each of his first two seasons. Along the way, Miller always proudly let the nation know from where he'd arrived: Texas A&M.

"The Aggies believed in me long before they knew I would become the No. 2 pick in the draft," Miller said of why he continually flashed A&M's famed "Gig 'Em" for pictures and interviews. "All I ever felt at Texas A&M was love—right from the beginning."

That's why he was adequately prepared when arriving at the NFL draft festivities in New York in 2011.

"I knew I had to make sure to have my Texas A&M hat on and certainly my Aggie Ring," a beaming Miller said of an A&M former student's most prized possession. "So when I was on TV everybody in the nation could see them—and know that I would always be an Aggie."

CHAPTER 26

JOHNNY MANZIEL

Name: Johnny Manziel
Born: December 6, 1992, in Tyler, Texas
Hometown: Kerrville, Texas
Current Residence: College Station, Texas
Occupation: College Student-Athlete
Position: Quarterback
Height: 6'1"
Playing Weight: 200 pounds
Years lettered: 2012—
Accomplishments: Heisman Trophy, Davey O'Brien Award winner in 2012; Associated Press national player of the year in 2012; Southeastern Conference single-season total yards record holder with 5,116 in 2012.
The Game: Texas A&M at Alabama, November 10, 2012

THE LIFE OF YOUNG JOHNNY MANZIEL

Johnny Manziel's football bravado earned him headlines in the Texas Hill Country as a teen, but Jerry Loggins first observed his grandson's incomparable competitiveness a decade earlier on fishing trips, when counting bass on a boat in the middle of an east Texas lake.

"If he caught more fish than I did, everything was rosy," Loggins said, chuckling at the memory of a pint-sized Johnny reveling in the conquering of his finned foe. "But, boy, he'd get mad if I caught more, and when we'd get back to the house, he'd shut the door to his room and you wouldn't see him the rest of the night."

Why? Apparently, the boy needed to ponder how to whip his grandpa in a competition—of course, others consider fishing a means of relaxation—requiring as much luck as skill.

"He's the most competitive kid … nah, I'm not even going to say 'kid'—he's the most competitive person I've ever met," said Loggins, whose Loggins Restaurant in Tyler, Texas, is adorned in Manziel memorabilia.

Manziel rose to prominence as a human highlight film at Kerrville's Tivy High to the northwest of San Antonio. But his unabashed competitiveness bloomed in Tyler, where he was born and raised and the Manziel name is prominent.

A great-grandfather, Bobby Joe Manziel, was a boxer known as "The Syrian Kid," and also a sparring partner with the legendary Jack Dempsey. Bobby Joe earned his own legendary status in East Texas as a prominent oil wildcatter.

Johnny was born in 1992 to two diehard golfers, Paul and Michelle Manziel, who were sweethearts at Tyler's Lee High and on the school's golf teams. Through his love of golf Paul later became friends with Jacky Lee, a former A&M golfer who also coached a powerhouse Pop Warner football team dubbed the Tyler Hurricanes.

Lee picked up on Johnny's extraordinary athleticism even when the boy was a skinny 8 year old, but Johnny's mother and grandmother, Lyana Loggins, insisted that the youngster not play football while in elementary school. Johnny finally joined the Hurricanes in the sixth grade—most of his peers had started with the team in the second grade—and was "immediately the best athlete on the field," Lee said.

So the young man now dubbed "Johnny Football" for his collegiate exploits earned his first of many monikers—"Johnny Hurricane"—on the Hubbard Middle School grounds.

Johnny Manziel in action against Arkansas. *Photo courtesy of Texas A&M Athletic Media Relations*

THE SCENE

John David Crow, larger than life in Aggieland, had a couple of poignant reminders in the month leading up to Texas A&M's ballyhooed game at Alabama in November 2012. In 1957, A&M's star back Crow won the Heisman Trophy over Iowa's defensive tackle and Outland Trophy winner Alex Karras. Weeks earlier, Crow's Aggies faced Darrell Royal in the budding legend's first game against A&M as Texas coach.

Karras died in October 2012 following kidney failure at the age of 77. Royal, 88, passed away three days before the Aggies-Crimson Tide collision on November 10, 2012, of complications stemming from cardiovascular disease.

"Alex and I played against each other in the NFL and he was a friend," a reflective Crow said. "Coach Royal was a good coach, good man and a great friend. He was tremendously loyal to his friends."

Crow, 77, said with a slight chuckle every morning he wakes up he's "glad to see the ceiling and not dirt."

"It's a good world we live in," added Crow, Paul "Bear" Bryant's lone

Heisman winner. It all tied together that week because the Aggies were making their first stop in history at Bryant's next (and final) stop from College Station: Alabama, where he won six national titles.

"This is the Saturday that you live to play for," vowed A&M center Patrick Lewis in the days before the game—one featuring Crow and plenty of other A&M football legends in attendance.

THE SETTING

The first time Texas A&M quarterback Johnny Manziel faced a defense nearly the caliber of Alabama, the former Kerrville Tivy High School star was almost two years removed from his last live action—in a high school playoff game.

Manziel didn't trust his arm in throwing the ball downfield with any regularity in the Aggies' 2012 opener against Florida, instead relying on the short passing game and his legs in a three-point loss to the Gators.

The next time he faced a first-rate defense, Manziel had gained more trust in his arm, but it still wasn't quite enough in a five-point loss to LSU on October 20. The Aggies were hoping the third time would be the charm, when Manziel faced the defense against which all others hope to compare: Alabama.

"We're a different team than we were in week one," A&M first-year coach Kevin Sumlin said in the days leading up to the Alabama game, of his offense's growth under Manziel. "Ten weeks later, we better be. And Johnny has a better understanding of what we do."

Manziel was also preparing to square off against an older quarterback he hoped to emulate—one who had already led his team to a national title (and would again following the 2012 regular season). While Manziel was drawing national attention for his sensational freshman campaign, Alabama junior A. J. McCarron had steadily led the Crimson Tide to a 9-0 record and a firm grip on the top ranking.

"It's keeping me up at night," A&M defensive coordinator Mark Snyder, bemoaning McCarron's flawless ability to execute the play-action game.

Meanwhile, the Aggies had crushed their previous two league opponents on the road, Auburn and Mississippi State, by a combined 67 points, thanks primarily to Manziel's amazing ability to escape tackles.

"He reminds me of Doug Flutie," Alabama coach Nick Saban said before the showdown. "He's not great big in stature or anything like that, [but] he's extremely quick and very instinctive, has a unique ability to extend plays, and seems to know when to take off and run with it."

THE GAME OF MY LIFE
By Johnny Manziel

In the week leading up to our game at Alabama, I was watching all of those sports shows on ESPN like "First Take," and I remember one segment in particular where a commentator gave us a zero percent chance to win in Tuscaloosa. Then another guy came on and gave us a five percent chance.

That was on a Monday, so throughout the week I told my fellow players on offense that, between those two so-called experts, they were giving us a 2.5 percent chance to win the game.

"Y'all realize they're not giving us any chance to go in there and beat these guys?" I told my teammates. "Look, let's just go out there at Bryant-Denny, not make a big deal out of it, not press or anything, and win this game."

It wasn't just all talk—I also had proof we were improving across the board. Our offense was finally getting into rhythm, where we were coming out early in games and putting points on the board. That was the big thing for us—put some points up early and put them in a hole. In our previous two games before going into Tuscaloosa, we had scored a combined 101 points at Auburn and Mississippi State, so we certainly weren't going into the game at the No. 1 team in the nation lacking confidence.

The atmosphere at Bryant-Denny before nearly 102,000 fans can best be described in one word: Crazy. It's almost like a dream looking back on that setting. Just how electric it was from the opening kickoff, to getting a three-and-out defensively on Alabama's opening drive, to going down and scoring three times in a row and really quieting the place.

I'll never forget coming out at halftime, when we led 20-14, and Alabama kind of got after us, and what I thought had been a "10" in terms of the noise level in the first half really ratcheted up to an entirely different intensity.

As for the fourth quarter? It was an absolute nail-biter. People will remember Malcome Kennedy's touchdown catch that proved the difference in the game, but don't forget Alabama's offensive possession just before.

Our senior safety, Steven Terrell, forced a fumble of Alabama's T.J. Yeldon, and Dustin Harris scooped up the ball.

We followed that up with a two-play drive, the first completion was to Ryan Swope along the sideline for 42 yards. I thought he'd gone out of bounds on the play, but he managed to squeeze it in and that was huge for what came next. Malcome beat his man on a corner route, but the ball came out of my hand really ugly. Fortunately, it found its mark and on that play, I remember flashing back to Ole Miss on October 6, when Swope won the game on a similar catch.

Kennedy's touchdown put us up 12 at 29-17 midway through the fourth quarter, but the game certainly wasn't over. Alabama countered with a long touchdown pass, and it took a goal-line stop finished off by an interception from defensive back Deshazor Everett to halt Alabama on its final offensive possession.

Even afterward, we needed a big special teams play, when we caused Alabama to jump off sides on our punt on fourth down and deep in our own territory. We took a knee—and that was the game.

I'll always remember what it was like when we arrived back in Aggieland that night, as well. The stadium lights were on, and it was just

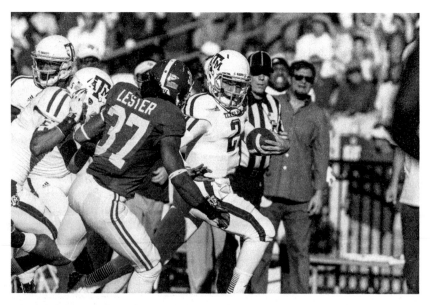

Manziel turns the corner against Alabama. *Photo courtesy of Texas A&M Media Relations*

absolutely crazy when we got off the bus and walked in before a whole parade of people. Incredible.

GAME RESULTS

The Aggies had spent three hours hustling all over Alabama's 100 yards of fabled field, but when time expired on their astonishing 29-24 victory over the top-ranked Crimson Tide, Texas A&M's exhausted players had one last mad dash to make: Straight toward the Aggie Band and A&M fans clustered in a corner of Bryant-Denny Stadium, for an emotional rendition of the Aggie War Hymn. There, Aggies offensive lineman Luke Joeckel glanced up at the A&M faithful and rubbed his eyes.

"I saw some tears up in the stands," Joeckel said. "That was special."

The architect of A&M's historic move to the Southeastern Conference also stood on that most hallowed of SEC grounds and grinned as wide as the Brazos River. A&M president R. Bowen Loftin, who spearheaded the university's conference switch that became official in the summer of 2012, summed up the Aggies' stunning upset of Alabama in one word as players, coaches and A&M fans hugged in joy near him, and as Alabama's players trudged off the field in disbelief.

"Whodathunkit?" Loftin wondered, later adding, "This team has improved every single game, and this win is a culmination of that improvement."

Loftin chuckled at the suggestion the surprising victory made the exit from the Big 12 after 16 years and the entrance to the SEC worth it for A&M by its lonesome.

"That was a 100-year decision, sir," a smiling Loftin said, shaking his head.

WHAT BECAME OF JOHNNY MANZIEL?

On December 8, 2012, Johnny Manziel became the first freshman in history to win the Heisman Trophy, after setting the SEC single-season total yardage record with 5,116.

"I never even thought about winning the Heisman," an aw-shucks Manziel said in New York City the night of his triumph. "I was more concerned about getting through a 12-game SEC schedule."

A month later, he was on hand for Alabama's whipping of Notre Dame in the national title game to wrap up the 2012 regular season.

"It was crazy to watch," said Manziel, who observed the Crimson

Tide's 42-14 triumph from the Sun Life Stadium sidelines.

He knew of only one view better for the title tilt: Through a facemask.

"All the tools are there," he vowed leading into the 2013 season, "for us to be one of the best teams in the country."

As of that summer, Manziel was preparing to lead the touted Aggies into their most anticipated season in program history. Asked if his goal was a second Heisman Trophy, Manziel shook his head, and offered a two-word response:

"National championship."

CHAPTER 27

THE 12th MAN

Yale Lary, the only Texas A&M football player in the NFL Hall of Fame, didn't see the Fightin' Texas Aggie Band perform at halftime on the revered grass of Kyle Field until five years after he'd left College Station.

What he'd missed while poring over Xs and Os in the Aggies locker room from 1948-51, serving in the U.S. Army from 1954-55 and then starring for the Detroit Lions for years thereafter, made Lary cry when he finally witnessed one of the true grand spectacles of college football.

"The first time I saw the Aggie Band, man ..." Lary says, pausing, "you talk about bringing tears to your eyes."

There's an old, dead-on saying in Aggieland about that hard-to-finger—and for many outsiders, hard-to-figure—desire called Aggie Spirit: "From the outside looking in you can't understand it; from the inside looking out you can't explain it."

And if Aggie Spirit is spread through the world by its former students, the force's generating plant is Kyle Field, the same plot of historic ground where Texas A&M has played its football since 1906 (the Aggies played on a campus drill field before then).

"Kyle Field is an extension of the mystique of Texas A&M," says Dave Elmendorf, an All-American for the Aggies in 1970 and an NFL All-Pro. "It's an extension of all of the A&M traditions—and there's a feeling there that we just can't explain."

Texas A&M stood united with its "Red, White and Blue Out" in the week after the tragedies of Sept. 11, 2001. *Photo courtesy of Texas A&M Athletic Media Relations*

Richmond Webb stoically faced down some of the best defensive ends to ever play NFL football as a seven-time Pro Bowl tackle, but that indefinable Aggie Spirit brings the six-foot-six, 330-pound giant of a man to tremble in describing its overwhelming allure.

"Hearing the 'Aggie War Hymn' at Kyle Field was a comfort," Webb says, softly. "An inspiration."

And there have been few things more inspiring at Kyle Field than what took place on Sept. 22, 2001—less than two weeks after one of America's darkest days.

On Sept. 11, 2001, terrorists killed thousands of innocent people by slamming hijacked jetliners into the World Trade Center in New York and the Pentagon in Washington, D.C. Another hijacked airplane crashed into a Pennsylvania cornfield following a heroic passenger uprising.

The events of that tragic day inspired a cluster of Texas A&M students—led by Eric Bethea, Nick Luton, Cole Robertson, Kourtney Rogers and Josh Rosinski—to begin a true grass-roots movement with precious little time.

Bethea originally concocted the idea to pass the word—as Aggies are so adept at doing—for fans to wear red, white and blue T-shirts to correlate with the Kyle Field deck in which they were to sit for the upcoming Oklahoma State game. Unbelievably, the fabulous five also spearheaded efforts to print 70,000 red, white and blue shirts that read in part, "Standing for America," to raise money for the 9-1-1 relief effort—in a task needing completion in about a week's time.

The plan—greatly aided by such Internet websites as texags.com—worked to perfection in the form of solid, majestic, red, white and blue sections (with a stark khaki portion courtesy of the 2,000-strong Corps of Cadets), an astounding nine stories tall. And even folks 90 miles across the prairie in Austin smiled in respectful admiration: Only in Aggieland could something so grand and consolidating be put together so fast, because of Texas A&M's unparalleled unity.

At halftime of the OSU-A&M game, the Aggie Band—the largest military marching band in the world—played "God Bless America" while in a "USA" formation on the field. The rapt and vigilant crowd of 82,601 stood and sang in unison, as tears flowed freely in one of the country's most trying yet unifying times.

"It's got to be heartwarming for the nation to see this type of response," Aggies linebacker Brian Gamble said, deferentially glancing into an amazing solid sea of red, white and blue, "from just a small town in Texas."

The Red, White and Blue Out "Fab Five" later hand-delivered two checks totaling an incredible $180,000 to the New York City firemen and police funds, based on the T-shirt sales. Indeed, only in Aggieland.

*   *   *   *   *

What causes one of the most intimidating linebackers in the history of college football—a chiseled hulk of a man who once broke an opposing receiver's jaw in three places with the flick of a forearm—to shake in recounting his beloved time spent between three decks of maroon passion? Simply, Kyle Field.

"I get chills just thinking about it," says Quentin Coryatt, the second overall pick of the 1992 NFL draft. "There's nothing like it anywhere else, on any level. When the Aggie Band starts playing that 'War Hymn', you just can't describe it ... and you knew an opponent was going to have to pay that day because of it. You knew that somebody was going to have to feel the wrath of the Wrecking Crew."

The late Dan Devine, who won the 1977 national championship as Notre Dame coach, once said he almost accepted a job at Texas A&M simply because of the inspiring and captivating strains of the "Aggie War Hymn."

"If you're coaching at Texas A&M," Devine said in admiration, "you should win one or two games a year because of that fight song alone."

E. King Gill, who dashed out of the stands to suit up for the Aggies in a 1922 game, serves as Texas A&M's original 12th man. *Photo courtesy of Texas A&M Athletic Media Relations*

Shane Lechler, an NFL Pro Bowl punter, enjoys sharing stories with his fellow pros who played on the opposing team at Kyle Field—men who often claim queasiness after staring too long into the crowd during the "War Hymn." Oklahoma linebacker Travian Smith was one such awed (and dizzied) adversary in 1996.

"When those people got together and swayed," an astonished Smith once told Lechler, "it looked like the whole stadium was *moving.*"

Actually, it was. When students, former students, and fans lock ankles and wrap their arms around each other and sway to the final verses of the "Aggie War Hymn" ("Saw Varsity's horns off . . .") the entire stadium moves as well. First-time visitors to the sky-high press box tend to pale when the building shifts a bit nine stories above the earth during the hymn.

"It moves, yes sir," says Billy Pickard, an A&M student trainer in the Bear Bryant days and the school's associate athletic director for facilities, explaining that expansion joints allow for the needed flexibility. "That's the design of the building."

The design of the fans is even more impressive. Aggie fans never boo their team or an opponent, and the students stand throughout, in honor of the school's 12th Man tradition. In the 1922 Dixie Classic in Dallas, Texas A&M student E. King Gill rushed from the press box—where he was working as a spotter—to help out his team if needed in a 22-14 win over Centre College.

"I put on the uniform of one of the injured players," Gill once remembered about the roots of A&M's most celebrated sporting legend. "We got under the stands and he put on my clothes and I put on his uniform. I was ready to play but was never sent into the game."

Sixty-four years later, powerful but wide-eyed freshman linebacker Aaron Wallace emerged from beneath the stands of Kyle Field in 1986 and sized up the enormity of the crowd that he was about to play before for the first time as a Fightin' Texas Aggie.

"I was awestruck by it all—even scared to death—but the atmosphere and the enthusiasm was just so contagious," Wallace says, finding words hard to come by in describing his great love for playing at Kyle Field. "All of that Aggie Spirit lifted you up, and left you no choice but to be ready."

The euphoria of each moment thereafter on Kyle Field endured for Wallace, just as it did for those who came before and after him. That's why on a crisp October 1989 afternoon against Houston, Wallace—by then a senior—practically shook in his shoulder pads as he fastened his chinstrap and glanced into the glorious gathering that stretched into the clear heavens above College Station, Texas.

Then, Wallace, heart to heart with the young men forever his teammates, sprinted onto that precious plot of God's earth to the roar of a reverent crowd, and headlong into the game of his life.

CREDITS

Bryan-College Station Eagle:
Ch. 2 quotes 3 (Nov. 29, 1951), 4 (Nov. 29, 1951); Ch. 3 quote 5 (Sept. 21, 1954); Ch. 4 quotes 1 (Nov. 24, 1956), 4 (Nov. 23, 1956), 6 (Nov. 30, 1951), 7 (Nov. 30, 1951); Ch. 5 quotes 2 (Oct. 31, 1957), 4 (Nov. 3, 1957); Ch. 6 quote 1 (Oct. 11, 1967); Ch. 8 quotes 2 (Sept. 17, 1970), 3 (Sept. 14, 1970), 4 (Sept. 16, 1970), 5 (Sept. 23, 1970); Ch. 9 quotes 3 (Oct. 11, 1975), 4 (Dec. 23, 1975); Ch. 10 quotes 2 (Nov. 27, 1975), 3 (Nov. 27, 1975), 4 (Nov. 29, 1975); Ch. 11 quotes 2 (Nov. 28, 1979), 3 (Nov. 28, 1979), 5 (Dec. 2, 1979), 6 (Dec. 2, 1979); Ch. 12 quotes 5 (Jan. 2, 1988), 6 (Jan. 2, 1988); Ch. 13 quotes 1 (Nov. 16, 1983), 2 (Nov. 21, 1984), 6 (Nov. 25, 1984), 7 (Nov. 25, 1984), 8 (Dec. 2, 1984), 9 (Dec. 2, 1984); Ch. 14 quotes 1 (Dec. 29, 1985), 2 (Nov. 24, 1985) 2 (Nov. 24, 1985), 3 (Nov. 28, 1985), 4 (Nov. 28, 1985), 6 (Nov. 29, 1985), 7 (Jan. 1, 1986); Ch. 15 quotes 1 (Jan. 3, 1986), 2 (Oct. 15, 1986), 3 (Oct. 18, 1986), 4 (Oct. 19, 1986), 5 (Oct. 19, 1986); Ch. 17 quotes 1 (Nov. 22, 1988), 2 (Nov. 22, 1988), 3 (Nov. 22, 1988) 4 (Nov. 25, 1988); Ch. 18 quotes 3 (Oct. 11, 1989), 5 (Oct. 14, 1989), 7 (Oct. 15, 1989); Ch. 19 quote 4 (Nov. 29, 1991); Ch. 20 quotes 2 (Nov. 24, 1992), 3 (Nov. 26, 1992), 4 (Nov. 26, 1992), 5 (Nov. 25, 1992), 6 (Nov. 26, 1992), 7 (Nov. 25, 1992); Ch. 21 quotes 3 (Nov. 25, 1993), 4 (Nov. 26, 1993), 5 (Nov. 23, 1993), 6 (Nov. 25, 1993), 7 (Nov. 24, 1993); Ch. 23 quote 2 (Dec. 6, 1998).

Associated Press:
Ch. 1 quotes 3 (Jan. 1, 1940), 7 (Jan. 2, 1940); Ch. 4 quotes 2 (Nov. 23, 1956), 3 (Nov. 29, 1956); Ch. 5 quote 1 (Dec. 7, 1957); Ch. 6 quote 3 (Nov. 22, 1967); Ch. 8 quote 1 (Sept. 17, 1970); Ch. 9 quote 2 (Oct. 8, 1975); Ch. 11 quote 1 (Nov. 30, 1979); Ch. 13 quote 5 (Nov. 21, 1984); Ch 14 quote 5 (Nov. 26, 1985); Ch. 17 quote 5 (Dec. 13, 1988); Ch. 18 quotes 6 (Oct. 12, 1989), 9 (Oct. 16, 1989); Ch. 19 quote 3 (Aug. 3, 1990); Ch. 23 quote 1 (Dec. 5, 1998); Ch. 24 quote 1 (Nov. 19, 1999).

San Antonio Express-News:
Ch. 1 quotes 1 (Jan. 1, 1940), 2 (Jan. 1, 1940), 4 (Jan. 1, 1940), 6 (Jan. 1, 1940); Ch. 2 quotes 1 (Nov. 30, 1951), 2 (Dec. 1, 1951), 5 (Nov. 30, 1951), 6 (Nov. 30, 1951), 7 (Nov. 30, 1951), 8 (Nov. 30, 1951); Ch. 4 quotes 5 (Nov. 30, 1956), 8 (Nov. 30, 1956); Ch. 10 quotes 1 (Nov. 28, 1975), 5 (Nov. 29, 1975); Ch. 11 quotes 4 (Dec. 2, 1979), 7 (Dec. 2, 1979); Ch. 16 quotes 4 (Nov. 26, 1987), 5 (Jan. 3, 1988).

Houston Chronicle:
Ch. 5 quote 3 (Aug. 3, 1995); Ch. 11 quote 8 (Nov. 25, 1999); Ch. 19 quote 5 (Jan. 2, 1992); Ch. 20 quotes 1 (Sept. 30, 1992), 8 (Jan. 2, 1993); Ch. 21 quotes 1 (Sept. 8, 1993), 9 (Sept. 8, 1993); Ch. 22 quote 1 (Oct. 17, 1991).

The Dallas Morning News:
Ch. 2 quote 8 (July 28, 1979); Ch. 3 quote 7 (Jan. 2, 1967); Ch. 6 quote 4 (Nov. 25, 2002); Ch. 17 quote 6 (June 26, 2001); Ch. 19 quotes 1 (Dec. 24, 2001), 2 (Dec. 24, 2001); Ch. 21 quote 2 (Dec. 31, 1993); Ch. 22 quote 2 (Aug. 19, 1995).

The New York Times:
Ch. 6 quote 2 (Oct. 11, 1967); Ch. 12 quotes 1 (Dec. 19, 1982), 2 (Sept. 2, 1983), 3 (Dec. 19, 1982); Ch. 13 quote 3 (Jan. 20, 1982).

Grand Prairie Daily News:
Ch. 3 quotes 1 (Feb. 4, 1971), 2 (Feb. 4, 1971), 3 (Feb. 4, 1971), 4 (Feb. 4, 1971), 6 (Feb. 4, 1971)

Fort Worth Star-Telegram:
Ch. 16 quotes 1 (Nov. 26, 1987), 2 (Nov. 26, 1987), 3 (Nov. 26, 1987).

New Orleans Times-Picuyne:
Ch. 1 quote 5 (Aug. 22, 1995); Ch. 12 quote 4 (Dec. 31, 1998).

The Kansas City Star:
Ch. 7 quotes 2 (Oct. 3, 1995), 3 (Oct. 3, 1995).

Newsday:
Ch. 18 quotes 1 (Aug. 27, 1988), 2 (Aug. 27, 1988)

Sporting News:
Ch. 3 quote 8 (Aug. 23, 1993)

Newsweek:
Ch. 4 quote 4 (Feb. 15, 1982)

Austin American-Statesman:
Ch. 9 quote 1 (Oct. 12, 2002)

Houston Post:
Ch. 7 quote 1 (Oct. 6, 1970)

Sports Illustrated:
Ch. 18 quote 4 (Oct. 23, 1989)

The Baltimore Sun:
Ch. 21 quote 8 (Dec. 14, 2000)

St. Louis Post Dispatch:
Ch. 25 quote 1 (Sept. 16, 1993)